The New Transnational Activism

The New Transnational Activism is a broad-ranging study that follows the paths of transnational activists through a variety of processes between the local and the global. From labor organizers to immigrant activists, from environmentalists to human rights campaigners, from global justice protesters to Islamist militants, it shows how ordinary people gain new perspectives, experiment with new forms of action, and sometimes emerge with new identities through their contacts across borders. The book asks how and to what extent transnational activism changes domestic actors, their forms of claims making, and their prevailing strategies. Does it simply project the conflicts and alignments familiar from domestic politics onto a broader stage, or does it create a new political arena in which domestic and international contentions fuse? And, if the latter, how will this development affect internationalization and the traditional division between domestic and international politics?

Sidney Tarrow is Maxwell M. Upson Professor of Government and Professor of Sociology at Cornell University. Tarrow's first book was *Peasant Communism in Southern Italy* (1967). In the 1980s, after a brief foray into comparative local politics, he returned to social movements with a collaborative volume with B. Klandermans and H. Kriesi, *Between Structure and Action* (1988); then to a reconstruction of the Italian protest cycle of the late 1960s and early 1970s, *Democracy and Disorder* (1989). His most recent books are *Power in Movement* (Cambridge, 1994, 1998); with Doug McAdam and Charles Tilly, *Dynamics of Contention* (Cambridge, 2001); with Doug Imig, *Contentious Europeans* (2001); and with Donatella della Porta, *Transnational Protest and Global Activism* (2005). Tarrow is a Fellow of the American Academy of Arts and Sciences.

Cambridge Studies in Contentious Politics

Editors

Jack A. Goldstone *George Mason University*
Doug McAdam *Stanford University and Center for Advanced Study in the Behavioral Sciences*
Sidney Tarrow *Cornell University*
Charles Tilly *Columbia University*
Elisabeth J. Wood *Yale University*

Ronald Aminzade et al., *Silence and Voice in the Study of Contentious Politics*
Clifford Bob, *The Marketing of Revolution*
Charles Brockett, *Political Movements and Violence in Central America*
Gerald F. Davis, Doug McAdam, W. Richard Scott, and Mayer N. Zald, editors, *Social Movements and Organization Theory*
Jack A. Goldstone, editor, *States, Parties, and Social Movements*
Doug McAdam, Sidney Tarrow, and Charles Tilly, *Dynamics of Contention*
Charles Tilly, *Contention and Democracy in Europe, 1650–2000*
Charles Tilly, *The Politics of Contentious Violence*
Deborah Yashar, *Contesting Citizenship in Latin America*

Advance Praise for *The New Transnational Activism*

"The global justice movement, anti-Iraq war protests, Al Qaeda, Eurostrikes, globalized ethnic diasporas, insider/outsider coalitions of local activists with international advocacy groups, transnational alliances and cross-border collaborations of the global human rights network, and the international diffusion of Truth and Reconciliation Commissions – throughout the social sciences, many are now studying the actors, relationships, forms, and strategies behind today's transnational activism.

"Tarrow takes aim at these now extensive literatures on globalization and on transnational protest – and he hits the bull's-eye. By offering the counterintuitive idea that transnational contentious politics still revolves around sovereign states – their domestic structures and the international institutions they have created – Tarrow makes a seminal contribution to this growing field. Deploying a rich matrix of case materials, conceptual distinctions, and theoretical arguments, he brings such unmatched conceptual and substantive richness to so diverse a theoretical and empirical literature that everyone else is disappointing. I am tempted to say that he is the only one here really worth reading – certainly the only one who will be read 20 years from now.

"Jewish sages emphasized that there are four types of students: the sponge absorbs everything, the funnel passes everything, the strainer retains the sediment and lets the fine wine pass, and the sifter retains the wheat and lets the chaff pass. Tarrow's strength is wisdom and judgment. He sifted through the growing literature on transnational activism, retained the important parts, and then erected a new political process theory of world politics. His approach to transnational contention represents the next major theoretical challenge to the fields of international relations and comparative politics."

– Mark Lichbach, University of Maryland

The New Transnational Activism

SIDNEY TARROW

Cornell University

CAMBRIDGE
UNIVERSITY PRESS

CAMBRIDGE UNIVERSITY PRESS
Cambridge, New York, Melbourne, Madrid, Cape Town, Singapore, São Paulo

Cambridge University Press
40 West 20th Street, New York, NY 10011-4211, USA

www.cambridge.org
Information on this title: www.cambridge.org/9780521851305

First published 2005

Printed in the United States of America

A catalog record for this publication is available from the British Library.

Library of Congress Cataloging in Publication Data

Tarrow, Sidney G.
The new transnational activism / Sidney Tarrow.
    p.   cm. – (Cambridge studies in contentious politics)
Includes bibliographical references and index.
ISBN-13: 978-0-521-85130-5 (hardback)
ISBN-13: 978-0-521-61677-5 (pbk.)
ISBN-10: 0-521-85130-0 (hardback)
ISBN-10: 0-521-61677-8 (pbk.)
1. Internationalism.   2. Coalition (Social sciences)   3. Political activists.
4. Transnationalism.   I. Title.   II. Series.
JZ1308.T377   2005
303.48′2 – dc22   2005000307

ISBN-13   978-0-521-85130-5 hardback
ISBN-10   0-521-85130-0 hardback

ISBN-13   978-0-521-61677-5 paperback
ISBN-10   0-521-61677-8 paperback

For Morris,
Quiet Activist

Contents

Tables

Figures

Preface and Acknowledgments

From the "battle of Seattle" to the movement against the Iraq war, the extraordinary international protests of the late 1990s and the early years of the new century suggest that something is new on this planet of ours. We are witnessing, if not a full-blown global civil society or an integrated transnational polity, at least a trend toward new forms and new levels of transnational contention. It was to reconcile my growing sense that new actors are appearing with my belief that states remain the fundamental framework for contentious politics that I decided to write this book. It is dedicated to the task of identifying those actors, trying to understand their relationships, and charting their impact on domestic and international politics.

Those who have followed my work in the past may wonder that someone who linked social movements so closely to the modern national state would now see them in transnational terms. If the world has changed, social scientists must be prepared to understand it. Besides, the forms of transnational activism that I examine in this book do not float above the earth but are shaped by states' domestic structures and by the international institutions that they have created. Although it has been made before, I hope to specify this argument through attention to the processes that link "the local with the global."

In my book I argue that the most effective transnational activists are "rooted cosmopolitans" – people who grow up in and remain closely linked to domestic networks and opportunities. The converse is also true: if there are structural effects of transnational activism, they are found primarily in the transformation of domestic politics and society. Whether these trends are producing a fusion of domestic and international politics is the big question that lies at the heart of these issues. I turn to it at the end of the book.

I did not come to these views all at once or all on my own. With Doug Imig I began to examine transnational contention in Western Europe. In our project on European contention, we found nonstate actors reaching beyond their borders but employing domestic resources, networks, and opportunities to do so. I thank him and the other authors of *Contentious Europeans* (Rowman and Littlefield, 2001) for helping me to see the interaction of the national and the transnational in the emerging European polity.

Two major grants took me from my home turf in Western Europe to the broader field of transnational contention: a grant from the National Science Foundation for research on transnational collective action,[1] and a grant from the Ford Foundation for research on grass-roots activists and international institutions. I thank Lisa Jordan of the Ford Foundation for her confidence that a social scientist whose roots were in Ithaca, New York, could understand the global problems she has dealt with as both an activist and foundation executive.

It was while I was a member of the "contentious gang" at the Center for Advanced Study in the Behavioral Sciences that the project advanced beyond its European origins. Shepherded by the gentle hand of Doug McAdam, watched over by the bemused eye of Bob Scott, and funded by the Mellon Foundation, Ron Aminzade, Jack Goldstone, McAdam, Elizabeth Perry, Charles Tilly, and I, along with a talented group of graduate fellows, explored new ways of examining contentious politics. Three collaborative books and the series Cambridge Studies in Contentious Politics emerged from that project. The center remains at the core of my intellectual debts, and my stints there are the source of my warmest memories of collegial collaboration.

If this book adds to our knowledge of transnational politics, it is in large part due to the help of colleagues whom I must thank as virtual collaborators. They are Donatella della Porta, Peter J. Katzenstein, Robert O. Keohane, Mark Lichbach, Doug McAdam, David S. Meyer, Kathryn Sikkink, Jackie Smith, and Charles Tilly. Lance Bennett, Valerie Bunce, Antonina Gentile, Mary Katzenstein, Margaret Levi, and Susan Tarrow also read every word – some of them twice – and I thank them for their collegial devotion. I also received advice on international relations – some of which I have even followed – from Matthew Evangelista, Peter Gourevitch,

[1] This material is based on work supported by the NSF under grant no. 0110788. Any opinions, findings, and conclusions or recommendations expressed in this material are those of the author and do not necessarily reflect the views of the National Science Foundation.

and Hans Peter Schmitz and help from my friends David Laitin and Nicolas Sambanis. I thank them all for their patience and their advice. Many other colleagues read and commented on parts of the manuscript and are owed sincere thanks.

At Cornell, a group of young scholars shared their expertise in the field of transnational contention. They are Mark Anner, Evelyn Bush, Kelly Dietz, Devashree Gupta, Jai Kwan Jung, Javier Lezaun, Eunyun Park, and Ion Bogdan Vasi. Jennifer Gomez, Sharon Sandlin, and Judy Virgilio helped make up for my slim organizational talents with their administrative abilities, while Melanie Acostavalle, Marwan Hanania, Angela Kim, Dana Perls, and especially Doug Hillebrandt worked progressively on bibliography, office administration, and making sure my books got back to the library. I especially want to thank the Russell Sage Foundation, its dedicated president and vice-president, Eric Wanner and Madge Spitaleri, and especially Kari Hodges and the rest of the hardworking staff there who provided me with a year in which I could work in contentment on this book.

Aurora, New York
December 2004

The New Transnational Activism

1

Introduction

It is 1920 in the port of Hamburg when a young man boards the steamer *Leviathan*, bound for New York. Moishke Tarabeur has left his *shtetl* in what was then Poland and is now Belarus. Kletsk has been caught in the war between Poland and the new Soviet state, settled when the border was established just east of town. In the 1920s it was one of hundreds of mostly Jewish towns in the Pale of Settlement between Warsaw and Moscow. It had a flourishing cattle trade but not yet the major shoe factory that would develop under Soviet rule. Its 3,000-odd Jews worshiped in seven synagogues, alongside Catholic and Orthodox churches and a mosque for the Tatar minority.

The Jews of Kletsk were mainly occupied in trade in the center of town, but there were few sources of employment for young people and virtually no public services. Through mutual aid and charity, the community provided itself with schools, but neither its residents nor their neighbors had a health service, and there was no hospital for miles. Like thousands of others, Moishke left home to escape poverty, disorder, and the anti-Semitism that invariably follows a popular uprising in this part of the world.

In 1928, by now naturalized with the "American" name of Morris, he traveled home to see his family and seek a bride. He carried with him remittances for family members and money from his New York fraternal organization to provide the town with a health clinic. Greeted like a prince by his Kletzker neighbors and friends, he stayed on for nine months. By the time he left Kletzk, the clinic was up and running, and he returned to New York with a sheaf of photos to show his landsmen the medical marvels that their hard-earned cash had brought their hometown.

Morris's activism didn't end with transferring remittances to Kletzk. In the 1930s he became an officer of the Kletzker Association in New York

1

City. Soon after, working as a candy salesman, he became active in his labor union, the Teamsters, and then in organizations working to get Jews out of Europe before Hitler's hordes descended. At war's end he worked with international aid agencies to locate Kletzker survivors in Europe's displaced persons camps. By the late 1940s, he was collecting money to help resettle displaced persons in Palestine and, by gradual extension, to fund the illegal arms purchases that helped the settlers establish the state of Israel. Morris never thought of himself as an activist, but as the global context changed from Jewish emigration to war and genocide to national renewal, he imperceptibly transformed into what I call, in Chapter 3, a "rooted cosmopolitan."

Transnational Activism

I begin this chapter with the story of my father's transformation from provider of private remittances to diaspora nationalist not only because I know it well but because it illustrates many of the facets of transnational activism we will encounter in this book.

First, it shows how even prosaic activities, like immigrants bringing remittances home to their families, take on broader meanings when ordinary people cross transnational space. Most studies of transnational politics focus on self-conscious internationalists; we will broaden that framework to include people like my father whose brand of unselfconscious transnationalism has become increasingly common in today's world.

Second, even as they make transnational claims, these activists draw on the resources, networks, and opportunities of the societies they live in. Their most interesting characteristic is how they connect the local and the global. In today's world, we can no more draw a sharp line between domestic and international politics than we can understand national politics in the United States apart from its local roots.

Finally, transnational activism is transformative: just as it turned my father from a provider of immigrant remittances into a diaspora nationalist, it may be turning thousands today from occasional participants in international protests into rooted cosmopolitans. That transformation could become the hinge between a world of states and one in which stateness is no more than one identity among many: local, national, and transnational.

My book argues that individuals who move into transnational activism are both constrained and supported by domestic networks; that in making this move they activate transitional processes between states and international politics; and that when they return home, they bring with them new forms of action, new ways of framing domestic issues, and perhaps new identities that may some day fuse domestic with international contention.

That raises the three main questions that the book addresses:

- To what extent and how does the expansion of transnational activism change the actors, the connections among them, the forms of claims making, and the prevailing strategies in contentious politics?
- Does the expansion of transnational activism and the links it establishes between nonstate actors, their states, and international politics create a new political arena that fuses domestic and international contention?
- If so, how does this affect our inherited understanding of the autonomy of national politics from international politics?

Identifying and tracing the processes that link the domestic to the international level of activism is the major methodological strategy of the book; placing these processes in a more general framework of internationalization is my major ambition; asking whether these processes and this framework are effecting a fusion between the local and the global is the major question it raises.

Here I limit myself to laying out three of the book's premises: that transnational activism has a history; that it is more than a reflex against globalization; and that it is shaped by changes in the opportunity structure of international politics. I argue that while globalization provides incentives and themes for transnational activism, it is internationalism that offers a framework, a set of focal points, and a structure of opportunities for transnational activists.

Historical Transnationalism

Even in the heyday of development of the consolidated national state, students of social movements have found abundant evidence of transnational activism (Keck and Sikkink 1998; J. Smith 2004a). It operated through two familiar mechanisms, diffusion and mobilization from above, and it revealed itself through the widespread adoption of similar forms of collective action.

The most familiar mechanism was the *diffusion of movements across borders.* From the Reformation, which swept across Europe through the missionary work of Protestant "saints" (Walzer 1971), to the antislavery movement that spread from England to France, the Netherlands, and the Americas

(Drescher 1987), to the diffusion of anarchism by missionaries like Enrico Malatesta (Joll 1964: 175), to the spread of nationalism through colonialism, print, and the railroad (Anderson 1991), the transnational diffusion of collective action is a familiar process. Recent episodes of ethnic conflict (Sambanis 2004: 270), the transmission of Ghandian nonviolence (Chabot 2002), and the spread of xenophobic nationalism (Rydgren 2004: 478–9) show that such diffusion has intensified in our era.

International mobilization is a second classical mechanism for transnational collective action. The campaign that made the First of May an international workers' holiday was transmitted to Europe from the American eight-hour-day campaign through the Socialist International. Esperanto, the movement to create an international language, was spread by the international Esperanto Society (Kim 1999). In the wake of the Italian war for independence, Henry Dunant founded the International Red Cross, which created chapters around the world (Finnemore 1999). And it was through Lenin's "Twenty-one Points" that the Comintern welded together an international movement from its center in Moscow. The process continues today in the spread of political Islam to Europe and Asia from the Middle East (Kepel 2002: chs. 4 and 8).

Both of these processes were observable through the *adaptation of the forms and the framing of collective action* – what I have elsewhere called "modularity" (Tarrow 1998). Looking west in the name of an imagined similarity between the Middle Kingdom and the French Old Regime, Chinese revolutionaries styled themselves Jacobins (Anderson 1991). Looking east, Italian Communist leader Antonio Gramsci saw parallels between southern Italian peasants and the rural masses who rallied to the Bolscheviks in 1917 (Tarrow 1967). Closing the circle, his successors in the 1960s extraparliamentary left saw themselves the urban heirs of Maoism, born in the rural vastness of China (Tarrow 1989). We will find new forms of modularity in the global justice and antiwar movements today.

So What's New?

If diffusion, international mobilization, and the modularity of protest are familiar from the history of transnational mobilization, skeptics may ask, What is new and different about the contemporary wave of transnational activism? We could answer simply that there is more of it, that it involves a broader spectrum of ordinary people and elites, and that it extends to a wider range of domestic and international concerns. All of this is true and will emerge from this book. But what is most striking about the new transnational activism is both its connection to the current wave of globalization and its relation to the changing structure of international politics. The former, I argue, provides incentives and causes of resistance for many (although not all) transnational activists; but the latter offers activists focal points for collective action, provides them with expanded resources and opportunities, and brings them together in transnational coalitions and campaigns.

Globalization and Contention

In recent decades, rapid electronic communication, cheaper international travel, diffusion of the English language, and the spread of the "script" of modernity (Meyer, Boli, and Thomas 1987) have facilitated transnational activism. Many observers add a fifth and more general claim: that globalization is responsible for the rise of transnational activism.

Although globalization is a powerful source of new actors, new relationships, and new inequalities, as an orienting concept for understanding transnational activism it leaves much to be desired. Philip McMichael (2005: 587) sees globalization as a process, an organizing principle, an outcome, a conjuncture, and a project. Peter Katzenstein sees "*globalization* as a process that transcends space and compresses time" and highlights the emergence of new actors and novel relations in the world system. He also sees it referring to "new 'transborder' spaces that are encroaching on traditional, territorial forms of social and political life" (Katzenstein 2005: 1.2). McMichael's and Katzenstein's concepts are rich and broad; I prefer a narrower concept of globalization, one that focuses on the *increasing volume and speed of flows of capital and goods, information and ideas, people and forces that connect actors between countries* (Keohane 2002b: 194). This definition has the virtue of parsimony and of allowing us to pose as a question globalization's impacts on transnational contention.

The equation between globalization and contention that we find in much of the literature on "global social movements" says both too much and too little: it says too little because it leaves out the intervening processes that lead people to engage in contentious politics; it says too much because a great deal of the transnational activism we find in the world today cannot be traced to globalization. The international structure of power is indeed changing in important ways that affect contentious politics but not in ways that reduce to the simple equation "globalization leads to resistance."

Let us begin with what we know about globalization's effects on transnational activism. Since the mid-1990s, a number of changes linked to global economic integration have combined to expand and extend its reach:

- The neoliberal economic orthodoxy summarized in the term "Washington Consensus" began to bear bitter fruit in the collapse of the Asian "tigers" and in the increasingly evident inequalities between North and South.
- The international institutions that enshrine neoliberalism – the International Monetary Fund, the World Bank, the World Trade Organization, and, with some countertendencies, the European Union – began to take on a more central role as targets of resistance.
- Transnational campaigns and movement organizations like People's Global Action and ATTAC (Association for the Taxation of Financial Transactions for the Aid of Citizens) have grown out of this dynamic.
- New electronic technologies and broader access to them have enhanced the capacity for movement campaigns to be organized rapidly and effectively in many venues at once.
- Countersummits and boycotts of big corporations have added to the repertoire of protest.

These are major changes. But students of domestic movements long ago determined that collective action cannot be traced directly to grievances or social cleavages (McCarthy and Zald 1977; McAdam 1999), even vast ones like those connected to globalization. Acting collectively requires activists to marshal resources, become aware of and seize opportunities, frame their demands in ways that enable them to join with others, and identify common targets. If these thresholds constitute barriers in domestic politics, they are even higher when people mobilize across borders. Globalization is not sufficient to explain when people will engage in contentious collective action and when they will not.

Moreover, while the most spectacular protest campaigns in recent years have targeted global economic injustice, many of the most successful campaigns have had more to do with struggles against dictatorship, hegemony, the abridgment of human rights, and demands for democracy. The links from globalization to contentious collective action are not as direct or as encompassing as many advocates and activists suppose.

Nor does combating globalization automatically give rise to "global social movements." For Charles Tilly (2004b: 3–4), a "social movement" is "a sustained, organized public effort making collective claims on target authorities" that uses a well-hewn contentious repertoire on the part of people who proclaim themselves to be worthy, unified, numerous, and committed. Other analysts would add the need for a durable network structure and at least the rudiments of a collective identity (della Porta and Diani 1999). Even if we do not accept all of these definitional requirements, the term "global social movements" cannot be used to describe every incident of transnational contention.

For one thing, forming transnational social movements is not easy. Sustaining collective action across borders on the part of people who seldom see one another and who lack embedded relations of trust is difficult. For another, repertoires of contention grow out of and are lodged in local and national contexts. Even more difficult is developing a common collective identity among people from different cultural backgrounds whose governments are not inclined to encourage them to do so. If this was true in the 1990s, the wave of national chauvinism and the reaction to it since September 11, 2001, has – if anything – led to a greater embrace of national identities.

Readers may wonder why I have gone to such lengths to underscore the difficulties of organizing sustained, durably networked, and self-identified global social movements around the countersymbol of globalization. There are two main reasons. First, I want to establish at the outset that social movements are only one form along a spectrum of types of contention that we examine in this book. Reducing them all to "global social movements" makes good grist for activists but not for serious analysis. Nongovernmental organizations (NGOs), labor movements, transnational coalitions, and elements of international institutions are important actors, even if their actions are not obviously "social movement" actions. Second, if globalization is not new, and if it has only a partial connection to contentious politics, we need to look elsewhere to explain the outpouring of contention across borders in the past decade. This takes us to the major orienting concept of this book – internationalism – and its relation to opportunities for collective action.

Internationalism as Opportunity Structure

Although globalization is a source of claims and a frame for mobilizations, it is internationalism – and particularly the *complex* form of internationalism that I describe in the next chapter – that channels resistance to globalization, offers a focal point for resistance to it, and provides opportunities for the formation of transnational coalitions and movements. If globalization consists of increased flows of trade, finance, and people across borders, internationalism provides an opportunity structure within which transnational activism can emerge. As internationalization increases, it can be expected to produce both new threats and new opportunities for activism.

Internationalization has sometimes been defined as deepening interstate relations and sometimes as international economic integration. Both are essentially horizontal relationships. For example, Peter Katzenstein (2005: 1.2) writes that "internationalization ... describes processes that reaffirm nation-states as the basic actors in the international system." As I do, he deliberately contrasts it with globalization, but by focusing on states, he limits himself to its horizontal dimension. My concept of internationalization includes three interrelated trends:

• An increasing horizontal density of relations across states, governmental officials, and nonstate actors
• Increasing vertical links among the subnational, national, and international levels
• An enhanced formal and informal structure that invites transnational activism and facilitates the formation of networks of nonstate, state, and international actors

We will find evidence of this internationalism and internationalization in institutions like the United Nations, the World Bank, and the World Trade Organization (WTO); in the growing tissue of intergovernmental relations that has grown up beneath the level of state-to-state negotiations (Slaughter 2004); in regional alliances and compacts like the European Union and NAFTA; in networks of informal ties among capitalists, nongovernmental organizations, and advocacy networks; and in transnational systems of migration, crime, contraband, religious activism, and political action. These venues both enable and constrain social and political activism.

Students of social movements will recognize in my concept of internationalism an extension of the theory of political opportunities that grew out of research on domestic social movements (Tilly 1978; McAdam, McCarthy, and Zald 1996; Tarrow 1998). That theory was specified in the framework of local and national politics and largely ignored contention that moves beyond borders. It was also static and focused excessively on contentious forms of collective action (McAdam, Tarrow, and Tilly 2001: ch. 1). I argue in Chapter 2 that internationalism both makes the threats of globalization more visible and offers resources, opportunities, and alternative targets for transnational activists and their allies to make claims against other domestic and external actors.

In other words, internationalism today is *complex*, horizontal and vertical, offering a wide range of venues for conflict and reconciliation and allowing activists to leapfrog over the simple dichotomy of "two-level games." In Chapter 2 I draw on both the social movement and international relations traditions to understand how domestic nonstate actors bring new issues to the international agenda and how these issues are processed and refract into domestic politics. I also argue for a more dynamic approach to transnational activism, one that identifies the major processes that it sets in motion and specifies them through their constituent mechanisms.

I am not the first to discern an increasingly complex structure of internationalism in today's world. In the 1950s Karl W. Deutsch and colleagues (1957) already looked at the North Atlantic area as a potential community. In the 1970s Robert Keohane and Joseph Nye (2001 [1979]) wrote of the "complex interdependence" they saw developing in world politics; in the mid-1990s Thomas Risse-Kappen and his collaborators (1995) described a new transnational politics that reaches deep into domestic structures; in the same decade, Jackie Smith, Charles Chatfield, and Ron Pagnucco (1997) developed a similar argument about the interrelations between global institutions and social movement actors. At the turn of the new century, Robert O'Brien and his collaborators (2000) wrote of the "complex multilateralism" that they saw emerging in relations among states and international institutions, James Rosenau (1997, 2003) insisted on the permeable walls between domestic and international politics, and Liesbet Hooghe and Gary Marks (2002) wrote of the "multilevel governance" in the European Union. If my book advances on these formulations, it will do so by examining the political processes that compose internationalism. My central argument is that there is no single core process leading to a global civil society or anything resembling one, but – as in politics in general – a set of identifiable processes and mechanisms that intersect with domestic politics to produce new and differentiated paths of political change.

Available Resources

These are no small tasks, but there are resources available on which to draw. In the social movement field, my book draws most centrally on recent work in the "political process" tradition (McAdam, Tarrow, and Tilly 2001), but it extends that tradition from its national moorings into international society. From the international relations field, it is in debt to work begun by Deutsch and colleagues (1957) on North Atlantic integration; to work on transnational politics by Keohane and Nye (1971); and to research on the links between domestic structures and transnational politics (Katzenstein 1976; Risse-Kappen 1995).

It also builds on more-recent work in transnational politics and international institutions:

- At the broadest level it draws on the work of political economists with a wide-ranging Marxist perspective, who emphasize global capitalism, countermovements, and the shift of conflict from the local to the global level; on students of international political economy who have tried to specify the links between domestic actors and international institutions; and on new institutional sociologists.[1]

- It draws on the work of anthropologists and students of public opinion who are beginning to track the impact of global trends on local actors.[2]

- It also draws on studies of international protest events, which offer extensive surveys of demonstrators, and on studies of social movement organizations that focus on the most dynamic actors in these events.[3]

- It builds on the work of scholars of international politics who have provided information on transnational advocacy networks and on that of students of international institutions who have provided data on how nonstate actors interact with international financial institutions like the World Bank, the International Monetary Fund (IMF), and the WTO.[4]

---

[1] For broadly Marxian and post-Marxian political economy perspectives, see Arrighi and Silver 1999; Evans 2005; McMichael 1996; Silver 2003; and Walton and Seddon 1994. For a synthesis of the best American work on international political economy, see Katzenstein, Keohane, and Krasner 1999. The work of new institutional sociologists is best reflected in the work by Meyer, Boli, and Thomas 1987; Boli and Thomas 1999; and Soysal 1994.

[2] For new anthropological perspectives, see Edelman 1999; Graeber 2002; Hannerz 1996; Kearney 1995; and Merry 2003a and b, 2004. For public opinion research on global attitudes, see Norris 2000 and Jung 2005. For evidence on elite responses to globalization, see Rosenau et al., forthcoming.

[3] For studies of international protest events, see della Porta and Mosca 2003; Levi and Murphy 2004; Lichbach 2003; J. Smith, Chatfield, and Pagnucco 1997; J. Smith 2002a and b; and Verhulst and Walgrave 2003. On transnational social movements, see della Porta, Kriesi, and Rucht 1999; Guidry, Kennedy, and Zald 2000; and della Porta and Tarrow 2005.

[4] A major statement from the international relations perspective was Keck and Sikkink 1998, followed closely by Risse, Ropp, and Sikkink 1999, and by Khagram, Riker, and Sikkink 2002. Major statements on international institutions is Cox and Jacobson 1973 and Martin and Simmons 1999. The interaction of activists with international institutions is examined by J. Fox and Brown 1998; O'Brien et al. 2000; Scholte and Schnabel 2002; and Stiles 2000. For a useful review of these sources, see Price 2003.

- Finally, it draws both on advocates of global civil society and on the work of critics of that concept who offer a more dispassionate and a sometimes pessimistic view of the possibility of effective transnational collective action.[5]

Disclaimers and Claims

These resources offer so extended an archipelago of approaches, subjects, and methods that it would be hopeless to attempt to synthesize them in a single volume. Three initial assumptions are designed to narrow the range of the study.

First, I do not attempt a deep causal analysis of the structural changes that are producing transnational activism. Others have done this better than I could and will no doubt continue to do so (Evans 2005; McMichael 2005). I focus instead on the political processes that activists trigger to connect their local claims to those of others across borders and to international institutions, regimes, and processes.

Second, although much material from Western Europe, Latin America, and other parts of the world appears in later chapters, the book is less contextualized than many area specialists might wish. A book that looks for robust mechanisms and processes rests on the assumption that they will operate identically across space and movement sectors (McAdam, Tarrow, and Tilly 2001). Readers and critics will want to ask if it applies to other regions of the world that they know better than I do.

Finally, I do not attempt to examine transnational activism in all its permutations. Because my goal is to look for robust processes, I draw on available literatures, which tend to favor some sectors of activism over others. The environment, human rights, immigration, labor, and opposition to neoliberalism are the sectors of activism most often mined in a study that looks primarily at processes, not at cases.

After outlining the theoretical perspective in the book in Chapter 2, I introduce and illustrate the core concept of "rooted cosmopolitans" in Chapter 3. (Readers without a taste for social science theory may wish to go directly to the narratives in Chapter 3.) The book proceeds by identifying

---

[5] The "civil society perspective" is developed in Edwards and Gaventa 2001; Clark 2003a, b; Florini 2000, 2003; Lindenberg and Bryant 2001. A related perspective has been developed by Rosenau 1997, 2003. Critiques and concerns about this perspective are elaborated by Bob 2005; Keane 2003; Olesen 2005; and Rabkin 2003.

and specifying three orders of processes that link domestic activists to the international system: two "local" processes, global framing and internalization; two transitional ones, diffusion and scale shift; and two "global" processes, externalization and international coalition formation.

Through concerted attention to these processes of transnational activism, the book goes beyond the equation of increased globalization with greater resistance; it specifies the institutional and political contexts in which a new stratum of transnational activists is developing; and it puts these activists in motion between their local roots and international politics, and then cycles them back into domestic politics. The most important question I hope to address is, Are we witnessing a short cycle of internationally oriented domestic contention or a fusion between international and domestic contentious politics?

PART ONE

Structure, Process, and Actors

2

Internationalism and Contention

On February 15, 2003, two and a half million Italians marched past the Coliseum protesting the impending war in Iraq. The banners they waved and the death masks some of them wore symbolized their outrage at American aggression and indifference to international law. But they were also protesting against their own government's support for the war and in favor of a host of domestic claims, ranging from pension reform to unemployment to the legal problems of Prime Minister Berlusconi (della Porta and Diani 2004).

Those Romans were not alone. On the same day in Paris, 250,000 people marched against the war; in Berlin, half a million walked past the Brandenburg gate; in Madrid, there were a million marchers, in Barcelona 1.3 million; in London, 1.75 million people – the largest demonstration in the city's history – spread out across Hyde Park to protest against the war and Prime Minister Blair's support for it. Even in New York, in the face of rough post-9/11 treatment from the NYPD, more than 500,000 people assembled on the east side of Manhattan.

On that day in February, starting from New Zealand and Australia and following the sun around the world, an estimated 16 million people marched, demonstrated, sang songs of peace, and occasionally – despite the strenuous efforts of organizers – clashed with police. This was probably the largest international demonstration in history.[1]

International relations specialists Fiona Adamson, Matt Evangelista, Peter Katzenstein, Bob Keohane, Hans Peter Schmitz, and Kathryn Sikkink worked hard to get me to understand the complexities of their field in drafting this chapter. I thank them for their patience and their openness to an outsider to their subfield.

[1] For data on many but by no means all of the demonstrations against the Iraq war, go to www.workers.org/ww/2003. The study by Verhulst and Walgrave (2003) provides

What Was Happening Here?

The demonstrations of February 15 provide us with an opening through which to examine the impact of internationalism on contentious politics. They illustrate many of the processes I examine in this book. February 15 also symbolizes some of the key problems in transnational contention: the wrenching shift of activists from global justice to international peace protest; the difficulties of maintaining transnational collective action once a temporary focal point has been left behind; and the complexities of forming sustained coalitions among people from different countries with different sets of interests and values.

In this chapter I first examine the relations between globalization and internationalization – two concepts that are often conflated – and put forward a framework based on the concept of international opportunity structure that provides a guide for this book. Next I lay out the rationale for the mechanism-and-process approach I take in the book and preview the six processes that are examined and illustrated in its central chapters. Finally, I signal the major problem the book is designed to address: whether we are witnessing a temporary spurt of transnational contention or, as many activists hope, are witnessing a progression from domestic contention to a fusion between local and global activism.

Globalization and Internationalization

In some ways, February 15, 2003, resembled the vast peace demonstrations that swept across Europe in the 1980s against the Reagan arms program (Rochon 1988). Those protests were also mounted in a number of capitals and attracted millions of people. Even in the United States, the source of the arms buildup, a simultaneous "nuclear freeze" movement was launched (D. Meyer 1990). But while that campaign was an isolated peak of protest during a period of relative calm, the antiwar campaign of 2003 was broader and deeper. First, it combined an internationalist message with domestic claims (Maney, Woehrle, and Coy 2003). Moreover, it involved an enormous range of participants, from grizzled veterans of the 1960s to religious groups and young people who had been inducted into political life during the global justice protests of the previous years. Indeed, in a classical

the most systematic evidence about these demonstrations from Europe and North America.

case of "social movement spillover," the protest of February 15 built on the momentum of the "global justice" protests of the late 1990s (Fisher 2004; Meyer and Whittier 1994).

But it would be mistaken to see the anti–Iraq war movement of 2003 as no more than a reflex of the movement against global neoliberalism. Although it drew on veterans of those protests, its target was not one of the great international governance institutions but the resurgent militarism of a hegemonic state. In its forms, it was closer to the large set-piece demonstrations of the 1960s and 1970s than to the ludic global justice presentations of the late 1990s. Nor was it composed primarily of activists with a global vocation: from the best evidence we have, most of the participants were deeply rooted in domestic civil society and many were protesting for the first time (della Porta and Diani 2004).

The fact that the campaign against the Iraq war had little to do with globalization suggests that we cannot be satisfied with reducing transnational activism to resistance to global governance. The main target was statist militarism, not global neoliberalism; it found objective allies in the form of several European governments; and both the European Union and the United Nations were international fulcrums of opposition to the war. The protests on February 15 also illustrate the forms of internationalism that structure the new transnational activism. To help us understand globalization's relationship to the structure of international politics and to transnational contention, we can begin with an analogy: the relationship between capitalism and state building in "the great transformation."

States and Markets in the Great Transformation

For Karl Polanyi (1957), the growth of market capitalism was driven by an ideology of liberalism that found expression in a legislative and regulatory program that allowed the first industrializers to release their economies from their mercantilist and corporatist strictures. This was the essence of Polanyi's "movement." Like today's international business class (Sklair 2001), Polanyi's early industrializers were empowered by a vision of how unfettered markets would release energies and increase wealth. Their vision was powerful, but it was not long before it engendered abuses and inequalities that led to a series of unplanned and unpatterned responses on the part of the state, eventually leading to the regulation of capitalism. This response was Polanyi's "countermovement." That countermovement was in part driven by the struggle of capitalism's victims to redress the balance of power, but it also involved the growth of institutions created to regulate capitalism and the abuses it fostered. Rulers most often took the side of well-heeled capitalists, but they also needed to keep public order, collect taxes, and regulate trade, and to do this they needed the support of their citizens to make war and legitimate their rule. Seeing the state's role as both the handmaiden and the regulator of capitalism was the core of Polanyi's vision.

Polanyi's theory was apt, but in focusing only on how the state responded to capitalist industrialization, he ignored autonomous sources of state building that were occurring both earlier and at the same time. Although parts of the state apparatus were indeed dedicated to the advance and regulation of capitalism, even in laissez-faire Britain, state builders had their own interests and motives. In the period following the Industrial Revolution, there were institutional changes independent of the need to regulate capitalism's abuses. Charles Tilly's model of state formation in his *Coercion, Capital, and European States* (1992: ch. 2) highlights a number of these processes: war making, state making, extraction of resources from the population to pay for them, protection of sectors of that population, production of goods and services to maintain the state and make war, and distribution and adjudication of conflicting interests.

These processes were cumulative, going well beyond the regulation of capitalism. Rulers who wanted to make war had to develop the means to extract resources and protect the population that paid the taxes; war making and protection led to a state role in production; by extension, states constructed mechanisms for reconciliation and eventually for participation. Under this umbrella, national social movements emerged around the fulcrum of the national state (Tarrow 1998; Tilly 1995b). Combining Polanyi's and Tilly's insights, the capitalist economy and the consolidated national state were interlocked institutional expressions of Polanyi's movement and countermovement.

Contemporary Conjunctions

In our era, globalization and internationalization parallel, at a higher scale, the relationship between capitalism and state building that Polanyi saw in the early industrial revolution. Just as they did, the two processes partially intersect and are partially independent. Following Polanyi's model, Philip McMichael (2005: 588–90) sees in the development of contemporary global neoliberalism an analogy of the development of liberal ideology in the early Industrial Revolution; also along Polanyian lines, he sees a contemporary countermovement against neoliberalism in the form of the global justice movement.

But just as we would misunderstand the development of the nineteenth-century political economy if we reduced it to capitalism and its institutional development, contemporary international politics would be seriously underspecified if we reduced it to neoliberal globalization. Like the movement that Polanyi identified in the Industrial Revolution, globalization creates new social victims and transforms the role of states; and like the expanding national state in the nineteenth century, internationalization constrains and creates opportunities for citizens to engage in collective action, both in resistance to globalization and around other issues. Globalization and internationalization are distinct processes that intersect but cannot be reduced to one another.

To be sure, the analogy to Polanyi's theory is imperfect because it ignores important overlaps, glaring differences, and significant new elements. The main overlap is that the nineteenth-century capitalist economies were never isolated from one another; their development, like today's, was marked by international domination, interchange, and diffusion. The chief difference is that there is no world government analogous to the role of the nationalizing state in the nineteenth century. The major new element is the extraordinary expansion of the capacity of nonstate actors to organize across borders and to interact with both states and international institutions (Boli and Thomas 1999: 23; Sikkink and Smith 2002).

Why is it so important to recognize this distinction between globalization and internationalization? Globalization, like early liberalism, is a source of interest, ideology, and grievances. It produces the flows and transactions of an interwoven international capitalist economy (Keohane 2002a). Internationalism is the institutional and informal framework within which transnational activism – some of it aimed at globalization but much of it independent of that process – takes shape. In the triangular relations among states, nonstate actors, and international organizations, regimes, and institutions, we find both resistance to globalization and activism of claimants whose claims have little or nothing to do with globalization. Internationalism provides a framework within which transnational activists respond to threats and seize opportunities that empower their activism. Developments in both international relations and social movement theory help us to see how this new reality has taken shape.

19

From International Relations Theory

Students of international relations have spent a great deal of time debating competing approaches to international politics. Until recently, three major approaches dominated debates: neorealism, constructivism, and liberal institutionalism. Although important insights emerge from the confrontation among paradigms, for our purposes it is more useful to draw insights from all of them. Like neorealists, I regard states as the enduringly major players in international politics, and the international system built on asymmetrical power relations among them. Like constructivists, I am interested how states' norms and identities affect their international behavior and how global – or at least transnational – norms are shaping international and domestic behavior. And like liberal institutionalists, I believe that states create international practices, regimes, and institutions to solve their collective action problems and monitor each others' behavior. But once formed, new norms, identities, and interests develop around these venues, attracting the attention of groups of states, nonstate actors, and other international actors. The creation of a distinct level of internationalism creates a triangular opportunity space in which nonstate actors can become active, form coalitions, and refract their activities back on their own societies.

This conception of transnational politics draws on three developments in international relations theory: transnational relations, the study of "domestic structures," and recent constructivist approaches.

Transnational Relations and "Complex Interdependence"

The work of Robert Keohane and Joseph Nye and their collaborators first drew the attention of international relations scholars to transnational relations. But it had two major limitations: first, Keohane and Nye (1971) saw transnational relations organized along an entirely *horizontal* axis (e.g., nonstate actors had relations with one another, in parallel to interstate relations); second, with few exceptions, they concentrated on the emerging phenomenon of the multinational corporation. The actors who would resist the power of those corporations and those who would form "principled-issue movements" in the 1990s were almost nowhere to be found.

In a second book, dedicated to what they called "complex interdependence," Keohane and Nye (2001 [1979]) moved beyond transnational relations. Although they did not challenge the realist conception of a state-centered international system, they argued that realism's reach is limited when three conditions obtain: when multiple channels connect societies; when there is no clear or consistent hierarchy of issues that relate states to one another; and when "military force is not used by governments towards other governments within the region" in which it obtains (pp. 24–5). In the post–Cold War world, this more pluralistic model appeared more realistic than the power-based model of the realists.

Although the logic of *Power and Interdependence* was pluralistic, Nye and Keohane focused almost exclusively on states as unitary actors; they were curiously silent on the topic of their first book – the role of domestic nonstate actors and their role in international politics. This was not because they assumed that international institutions had great authority or autonomy;[2] on the contrary, they thought of "international institutions less as institutions than as clusters of intergovernmental and transgovernmental networks associated with the formal institutions" (p. 240).[3] But taken together with *Transnational Relations in World Politics*, Nye and Keohane's work provided a foundation for later approaches that would posit a more pluralistic international politics, two of which contribute to the approach of this book.

International Political Economy and Constructivism

In the 1970s and 1980s a new group of authors was anxious to bring the study of "domestic structures" into the study of international political economy (for a review, see Katzenstein, Keohane, and Krasner 1999: 27ff.). In this tradition, domestic actors respond to the pressures of economic integration by working through national institutions. Spurred by these interests, states exposed to the international economy shape their domestic political institutions into different forms of "corporatism" to defend domestic interests (Katzenstein 1984, 1985). As in the case of Nye and Keohane's early work, the key actors in these models were the institutionalized domestic groups of labor and business; less institutionalized groups and transnational nonstate actors whose interests are more normative did not appear in their theories.

It was left to a third group of international relations scholars, the self-defined "constructivists," who partly overlapped with the second group, to

---

[2] In later work, Keohane (1984) saw institutions as a solution to market failures. But neither he nor Nye were microeconomists (cf. Ruggie 1998). Both saw institutions helping to set the international agenda, acting as catalysts for coalition formation, and serving as arenas for political initiatives and linkage by weak states (Keohane and Nye 2001[1979]: 35).

[3] These "intergovernmental" relations would become the subject of a new strand of literature that largely ignored the role of nonstate actors (Slaughter 2004).

draw attention to a broader range of nonstate actors and to their forays into the international arena. Building on the insights of Karl W. Deutsch and Ernst Haas (Deutsch et al. 1957; Haas 1958), constructivists concerned themselves first with how states acquire their identities and with the interests that flow from them (Ruggie 1998: 14). Identities, they argued, are neither fixed nor unique, and constructivists soon focused on how international events shape them and how a sense of collective identity can develop among groups of states. Following Deutsch's early example, the North Atlantic area served as a frequent example (Katzenstein 1996; Risse-Kappen 1996), but the European Union soon became a favored site for the examination of interstate identities.

From identifying norms and identities that cross state lines, it was a short step to a focus on the role of nonstate actors in transnational politics. Constructivists drew on the sociological institutionalism of John Meyer and his associates to argue that norms diffuse across state lines through institutional imitation (Thomas et al. 1987); they also applied constructivist thinking to nonstate actors, first in the form of epistemic communities of experts (P. Haas 1992) and then in the form of advocacy groups acting in the name of "principled issues" (Sikkink 1993; Keck and Sikkink 1998; Finnemore and Sikkink 1998). By specifying activism both vertically, toward international institutions, and horizontally, across borders, constructivists returned to the terrain of transnational relations that Keohane and Nye had scouted two decades before, but with a much richer conception of international advocacy.

Between these three strands of international relations theory, there were gaps and contradictions. But they converged to assign to nonstate actors a legitimate place in international relations theory and undermined the separateness of domestic and international politics. But the transnational-constructivist synthesis is weaker in specifying the kinds of groups and the range of collective actions that cross borders. This takes us to the contributions of social movement theory.

From Social Movement Theory

Like international relations theory, social movement studies enjoyed a revival in the 1970s – less in reaction to the ebbing of the Cold War than in relation to the movements of the previous decade. Movement scholars in both Europe and the United States rejected the "collective behavior" approach that had dominated their field in earlier decades, according to which social movements were products of abnormal politics, and turned their attention to the "normality" of protest, to its connection to resources and opportunities, and to its part in the political process. This "political process" approach narrowed into a "social movement paradigm."

The Social Movement Paradigm

During the 1960s and 1970s, much of North American and European research on contentious politics concentrated on social movements – mainly reformist movements in democratic states – and then assimilated other forms of contention to prevailing explanations of movements. Attention focused on four key concepts: *political opportunities*, sometimes crystallized as static opportunity structures, sometimes as changing political environments; *mobilizing structures*, both formal movement organizations and the social networks of everyday life; *collective action frames*, both the cultural constants that orient participants and those they themselves construct; and established *repertoires of contention*, particularly how these repertoires evolve in response to changes in capitalism, state building, and other, less monumental processes (Tilly 1978; McAdam, McCarthy, and Zald 1996; Tarrow 1998).[4]

Central to the social movement paradigm was the concept of "political opportunity structure." This referred to "consistent – but not necessarily formal, permanent or national – dimensions of the political environment that either encourage or discourage people from using collective action" (Tarrow 1998: 18). As summarized by Tilly (1978), McAdam (1996), and others, it was specified through a number of variables external to challengers' own resources and claims: the opening up of institutional access, shifts in political alignments, the presence or absence of influential allies, and the prospect of repression or facilitation. Later work specified the effects of threats more distinctly from opportunities (Goldstone and Tilly 2001), and expanded the concept of opportunity structure to include "discursive opportunities" (Ferree et al. 2002).

The social movement paradigm took scholars a long way toward "normalizing" contentious politics. But it had three major defects: first, a single-minded focus on single-actor movements and indifference to the broader field of contentious politics; second, a largely static framing of

---

[4] This paragraph and the ones that follow summarize passages from McAdam, Tarrow, and Tilly, *Dynamics of Contention* (2001: chs. 1 and 2).

its major constituting variables – opportunities, resources, framing, and repertoires of contention; and, third, the overwhelming tendency of its practitioners to study movements at the domestic level.

From Social Movements to Transnational Contention

Over the past decade scholars of social movements have expanded their interest from local and national to international forms of contention (della Porta, Kriesi, and Rucht 1999; Guidry, Kennedy, and Zald 2000; della Porta and Tarrow 2005). They also broadened their interest from social movements to encompass NGOs and international organizations (J. Smith, Chatfield, and Pagnucco 1997), activist networks (Keck and Sikkink 1998), and transnational labor activism (Waterman 2001; Anner 2004; Kay 2005). And while some authors sought to find equivalents at the international level for the stable opportunity structures that had been identified in domestic politics, others refashioned their theoretical approaches to a more dynamic mechanism-and-process-based approach.

In their book, *Dynamics of Contention* (2001), McAdam, Tarrow, and Tilly tried to address all three lacunae in the social movement paradigm by a more deliberately dynamic approach to contentious politics. Rather than focus exclusively on "social movements," they examined broader forms of contentious politics, which ranged from protest movements to strike waves, ethnic conflicts, nationalist episodes, and revolutions. Instead of limiting their range to contemporary Western liberal systems, they focused on a variety of episodes of contentious politics from the eighteenth to the twentieth century in North America, Europe, and the countries of the global South (see Table 3.1). And rather than positing opportunities and mobilizing structures, frames, and repertoires as additive but essentially static variables, they sought to put the standard model into motion by deducing key processes and mechanisms that constitute contentious politics.

This Book's Approach

This book builds on both international relations theory and on the social movement paradigm and follows in the tradition begun in *Dynamics of Contention* by dealing with a wide range of institutional and noninstitutional actors and focusing on processes and mechanisms that link "the local and the global." Like that book, it draws evidence from many parts of the world. *Dynamics* took the world of states as given and specified the processes examined on domestic soil alone. This book differs from it in three ways: first, by focusing on a variety of forms of *transnational* contention, which I define as *conflicts that link transnational activists to one another, to states, and to international institutions*; second, in posing as the ultimate question of the research whether there is a growing fusion between domestic and transnational contention; and, third, by asking if, as a result, the distinctive world of states that *Dynamics* took for granted is eroding. My starting point is the structure of internationalism. I then examine the unusual character of transnational activists, who mediate between domestic and international venues. I close by examining the processes through which these activists engage the local with the global.

Internationalism and Internationalization

Internationalism is a general phenomenon that has been specified by some authors as interstate relations and by others as economic integration. I use the term in a more complex way, to signify *a dense, triangular structure of relations among states, nonstate actors, and international institutions, and the opportunities this produces for actors to engage in collective action at different levels of this system.*

Although internationalism goes beyond concrete international institutions, regimes, and processes, these are at its core and provide a structure of both opportunities and threats to nonstate actors. The threats are very real – to sovereignty, to equality, to diversity – and have been well documented in the literature on globalization. But internationalism also offers an opportunity space into which domestic actors can move, encounter others like themselves, and form coalitions that transcend their borders, and this process has been less well understood. Although this book specifies internationalism in a variety of regimes, treaties, conventions, and informal networks, here I illustrate both its costs and the opportunities through international institutions.

Double-Edged Institutions

International institutions are carriers of threats to ordinary citizens around the world, which is a source of justified resentment and resistance. Some, like the World Bank and the IMF, control loans and grants to developing states. The damage they do to ordinary citizens through their policies of conditionality has led to waves of contention from the 1970s on

25

(Walton and Seddon 1994). Others, like NATO, are agents of collective security in which a thin patina of equality barely disguises the hegemonic power of the strongest partner. Others, like the European Union and, to a lesser extent, NAFTA, are frameworks for the development of common markets. Still others, like the International Labor Organization and the Landmines Convention, attempt to protect the interests of ordinary people.

International institutions are most often seen by students of globalization as agents of global capitalism, but that assertion is truer for some institutions than for others. It is most obviously true for the IMF and the WTO, with the World Bank divided into a market-oriented core and a more civil-society-oriented periphery (J. Fox and Brown 1998). NAFTA, which was created to open markets in Canada, Mexico, and the United States, has served to reinforce the interests of exporters from Canada and the United States and a small sector of *maquiladora* factories on the Mexican-American border. Even the European Union, which has the greatest claim to be a representative set of institutions, frequently acts as an agent for the interests of globalizing capitalists. Advocates of the global justice movement have plenty of evidence that international governance institutions are the agents of globalization.

But international institutions also offer an opportunity space within which opponents of global capitalism and other claimants can mobilize. Although these institutions are less susceptible to popular pressure than (democratic) national governments, in many ways domestic actors and institutions can shape and, to some extent, cushion the impacts of their policies (Keohane and Milner 1996).

International institutions are created by states to satisfy state interests but, once created, become focal points for contention (Martin and Simmons 1999: 106). For one thing, these institutions are sources of learning and information for both states and nonstate actors (pp. 95–100). For another, they serve as proxies for policies that member states support but do not want to carry out themselves (p. 107), thus transferring opposition to these policies from the national to the international level. Finally, they create complex rules, and from this complexity come unanticipated consequences that can provide openings that nonstate actors and member states can exploit.

Institutions need officials, and these officials have an interest in their stability and expansion. This can lead institutions to defend the interests of some member states, form alliances with groups of states and nonstate actors on behalf of policies that both benefit them and their supporters, and fashion international norms that eventually diffuse into member states. Finally, international institutions develop identities that they try to project in their relations with member states and client states. In doing so, they help to construct the global framing of domestic issues.

International institutions have emerged at the core of an increasingly complex international society around which NGOs, social movements, religious groups, trade unions, and business groups cluster (O'Brien et al. 2000). They both intrude on domestic politics through their policies and personnel and offer venues where nonstate actors and states can take their claims and build coalitions. Not all of these groups directly challenge or work within the ambit of these institutions; many protest against them and others respond only indirectly to their directives and policies. But as in domestic politics, in which states are both targets of resistance and fulcrums for social conflict and coalition building, international institutions, regimes, and practices are "coral reefs" in a broader sea of complex internationalism.

Of course, not all parts of the world are as internationalized as every other. Western Europe, with its dense tissue of horizontal and vertical ties, offers the most diverse and open opportunity structure for nonstate actors (Hooghe and Marks 2002). Asia, in which most interstate ties are bilateral, offers fewer such opportunities (Katzenstein 2005), although some experts see this situation undergoing change (Pempel 2005; Krauss and Pempel 2004). Latin America, with two functioning multilateral blocs and a number of bilateral ties, lies somewhere in between. Similarly, there is wide gap in opportunities for nonstate activism between the highly institutionalized climate change regime and the loose network of intergovernmental ties dealing with judicial cooperation (Slaughter 2004: ch. 2). Generalizing, we can hypothesize that the openness of the opportunity structure for nonstate actors is a function of the institutionalization of interstate ties and of the degree to which they have produced multilateral interaction.

Co-optation, Conflict, and Cooperation

Some advocates of internationalization see the process as a benevolent one that is pushing the world gently toward a global civil society, a world polity, or transnational citizenship (Florini 2003; J. Meyer, Boli, and Thomas 1987; Habermas 1992; Checkel 2001). Others see it as the handmaiden of globalization. The view taken in this book is less determinant. Internationalization is creating arenas for conflict and cooperation that will not necessarily lead either to the triumph of global capitalism or to democratic outcomes. It also reaches into domestic politics, bringing contenders into contact with one another at several levels.

Consider biotechnology, an arena in which both supporters and opponents oppose one another and cooperate both at home and in transnational space (Coleman and Wayland 2005). Now think of the efforts of the Vatican, the Christian right, and their orthodox Jewish and Islamic allies in the United Nations. They use that international focal point to undermine what they see as a radical-feminist-gay domination of global institutions and local cultures (Bush 2004; Buss and Herman 2003: 137–41). Finally, consider NAFTA, which has destroyed the livelihood of thousands of Mexican farmers and American workers; it has also provided mechanisms for transnational cooperation among workers affected by globalization with their transnational allies (Kay 2005). International institutions, regimes, and processes are not the expression of democracy, a global civil society, or a world polity: they are arenas in which conservative and progressive, global and antiglobal, religious and secular nonstate actors intersect. This takes us to the major actors in this study.

Rooted Cosmopolitans and Transnational Activists

Who are the activists we will find in this book? Some are dedicated internationalists seeking the development of a global civil society or a world polity; but many others are people who are simply following their domestically formed claims into international society when these claims can no longer be addressed domestically. Local activists do not migrate to the international level but utilize their domestic resources and opportunities to move in and out of international institutions, processes, and alliances.

Consider the recent port directives dispute in the EU with Peter Turnbull (2004). In the 1990s European freight rates were being driven down by port-to-port services, to the point at which the shipping lines needed to fill their vessels completely to turn a profit. Seeing the answer to their problem offering door-to-door service, they lobbied both national governments and the European Commission to oppose port agreements that protect the historical rights of port workers to unload cargo. It took a combined multilevel effort on the part of European port workers' unions, their international representatives, and their allies in the European Parliament and in several key governments to fend off this attack.

28

In the port directives conflict, globalization and internationalization converged, as they have in many arenas of conflict. In such conflicts, we see an expansion of the numbers of individuals and groups that operate within and outside their own societies, both in other countries and in the ambit of international regimes, institutions, and practices. I refer to this stratum as rooted cosmopolitans, whom I define as *individuals and groups who mobilize domestic and international resources and opportunities to advance claims on behalf of external actors, against external opponents, or in favor of goals they hold in common with transnational allies.*

It is important to underscore that this concept (which I explain in Chapter 3) includes not only transnational activists and advocates but also business executives, lawyers, and international civil servants and the national civil servants in regular contact with them. Transnational activists are a subgroup of rooted cosmopolitans, whom I define as *people and groups who are rooted in specific national contexts, but who engage in contentious political activities that involve them in transnational networks of contacts and conflicts.* What makes them different from their domestic counterparts is their ability to shift their activities among levels, taking advantage of the expanded nodes of opportunity of a complex international society.

Some transnational activists behave as "insiders," lobbying and collaborating with international elites to the point of co-optation, while others challenge international institutions' policies and, in some cases, contest their existence. But as in contentious politics in general, the line between NGO "insiders" and social movement "outsiders" is difficult to draw with precision, and coalitions between these two families of activists are increasingly common. Internationalization is producing mechanisms and processes that escape the narrow confines of international institutions and may be leading to an ultimate fusion between domestic and international activism. This takes me to the basic ontology and methodology of this book.

Mechanisms and Processes

In this book I undertake to identify the processes and their constituent mechanisms that are constituting transnational contention. Mechanisms are not variables; they either exist or do not exist. Nor are they ideal types that are more or less approximated in empirical reality. They are "a delimited class of events that alter relations among specified elements in identical or closely similar ways over a variety of situations" (McAdam, Tarrow, and Tilly 2001: 11). As in biology, the same mechanisms can appear in different processes.[5] Consider diffusion; we find it in the spread of "global framing" in Chapter 4, in "scale shift" in Chapter 7, and in the domestic absorbtion of new forms of transnational contention in Chapter 10. What differ are the circumstances in which they occur and their combination or sequence with other mechanisms. We will understand these processes better by disaggregating them into their component mechanisms and trying to understand their interaction with other mechanisms.

Processes are "recurring combinations of such mechanisms that can be observed in a variety of episodes of contentious politics" (McAdam, Tarrow, and Tilly 2001: 11). For example, the global framing of domestic issues that I study in Chapter 4 begins with domestic claims making, combines with international communication and the broader theorization of the claim, and hinges on the actions of movement brokers who work to transform the local framing of that claim. The logic of this book is that when mechanisms concatenate repeatedly in the same processes, we can say that those processes are robust; when such processes link domestic activists to international venues and to transnational networks and coalitions, they help to break down the walls between domestic and international activism.

Not all activism that is relevant to transnational politics takes place in the international arena. Relevant processes are found within domestic politics, in transitions from the domestic to the international level, and between states and within and around international institutions. A set of examples from France clarifies this threefold distinction and helps us to lay out the processes to be examined in this book.

Contentious (and Sometimes Transnational) French

France has always demonstrated an ambiguous mix of particularism and universalism. When the founders of what would become the United States of America met in Philadelphia in 1776, they were what Benedict Anderson (1991) would later call "creoles" who saw themselves as foreign-born citizens of the British Empire being denied the rights of Englishmen. But when the rump of the Etats-Généraux decamped from the Palace of Versailles in 1789, it claimed to act in the name of humanity (Aquarone 1959) and wrote

---

[5] For example, in biology the mechanism of muscle contraction contributes to respiration, locomotion, digestion, and even reproduction. Mitosis is a mechanism that prepares a cell for division but sometimes replaces healthy cells and produces cancer. If biologists are interested in any of these processes, they can ill afford to ignore their constituent mechanisms. The same is true in contentious politics.

a *universal* declaration of the rights of man. The Revolution (no adjective is ever thought necessary) was put forward as a model for mankind. And mankind – at least European men – responded as if the French Revolution was its own.

Nothing as portentous as the French Revolution has occurred in France in our time, but a series of episodes during the ten-year period, 1992–2002, will introduce the forms of contentious politics I examine in later chapters:

- In 1992 farmers and their allies blockaded Euro-Disney to dramatize their protest against pending EU agricultural reforms and, for good measure, against the "americanization" of Europe (Bush and Simi 2001: 97).
- In 1995 a wave of strikes began in the public services against the government's budget-tightening efforts to meet the EU's "growth and stability" pact (Béroud, Mouriaux, and Vakaloulis 1998).
- A few years later, farmer-activist Jose Bové gained worldwide attention by leading an attack on McDonald's and later appearing at the Seattle WTO protest lugging a wheel of Rocquefort cheese to demonstrate the importance of natural foods.
- In 1997 French Renault workers joined their Belgian and Spanish co-workers in a joint demonstration in Brussels following the closure of the firm's plant in Vilvorde, Belgium (Lefébure and Lagneau 2001).
- In 1998 the Association for the Taxation of Financial Transaction for the Aid of Citizens (ATTAC) was formed in France to spread the idea of taxing international financial transactions, the so-called Tobin Tax (Ancelovici 2002).
- In 2000 ATTAC was one of the organizers of the "World Social Forum," which grew into an annual countersummit contesting the World Economic Forum's neoliberal policies.
- Throughout the decade, French farmers protested against EU common agricultural policies, sometimes on domestic soil and often in Brussels (Bush and Simi 2001: 97).

Many observers saw these instances as part of resistance to globalization, and in a general sense, they were right. But the phenomenology, the dynamics, and the outcomes of the events were unequally connected to the international system. Although the 1995 strike wave closed down the French railway system and shook the foundations of the neo-Gaullist government, it had virtually no international resonance; in contrast, ATTAC-France was largely responsible for the international diffusion of the Tobin

31

Tax idea, leading to the creation of other ATTAC chapters and helping to found the World Social Forum (Evans 2005; Kolb 2005). And while the anti-Renault campaign failed to stop the closure of the Vilvorde plant, it provided a model for transnational labor organizing elsewhere in Europe (Lefébure and Lagneau 2001). All these French struggles could be labeled "global"; but some were more transnational than others.

Three Sets of Processes

We can use these events in France to introduce the three orders of political processes I examine in this book. Two of the events took place on purely domestic ground:

- In the Euro-Disney protest, we saw a process of *global framing* – the mobilization of international symbols to frame domestic conflicts.
- In the farmers' protests, we saw a process of *internalization*; a response to foreign or international pressures within domestic politics.

Two other processes connected French domestic contention to international conflicts and institutions:

- *Diffusion* is the transfer of claims or forms of contention from one site to the other, as when the ATTAC model created in France was adopted in Germany and elsewhere (Kolb 2005).
- *Scale shift* is the coordination of collective action at a different level than where it began, which we saw when ATTAC became, in effect, an international NGO that collaborated in the formation of the World Social Forum.

Two other processes took place at the international level and have the greatest potential to create transnational social movements:

- *Externalization* is the vertical projection of domestic claims onto international institutions or foreign actors, as when the Renault plant closure was brought to the attention of the European Union and European deputies voted a resolution to condemn the firm's action.
- *Transnational coalition formation* is the horizontal formation of common networks among actors from different countries with similar claims, which was evident when the World Social Forum brought together a wide coalition of NGOs and social movements from around the world.

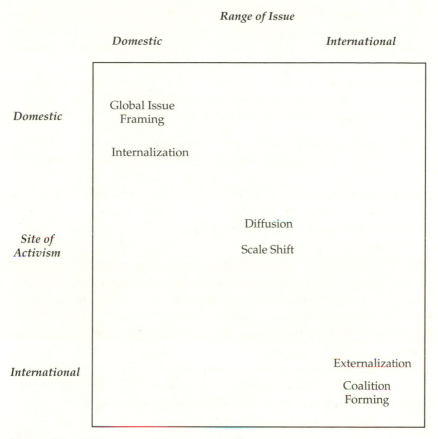

Range of Issue

Domestic International

Domestic

Global Issue
Framing

Internalization

Site of
Activism

Diffusion

Scale Shift

International

Externalization

Coalition
Forming

Figure 2.1 Six Processes of Transnational Contention

These six processes, which are examined and illustrated in a variety of venues and sectors of activism throughout the book, sometimes occur alone but often in combination. Figure 2.1 lays them out on a two-dimensional grid, which consists of the degree to which a particular issue is of primarily domestic or international importance and the extent to which it brings activists out of their domestic context into transnational space.

Three hypotheses can be proposed about the implications of these processes for fusing domestic and international activism:

- Although framing issues globally and mounting domestic contention against an international institution may lead to internationalization, they produce no permanent links across borders.

33

- Diffusion of particular forms of collective action and a shift in the scale of contention help to unify the repertoire of contention across borders, but both are temporary and can involve a decline in the domestic militancy on which true social movements must be built.
- Externalization of domestic contention and the formation of durable transnational coalitions are the strongest signs that a fusion of domestic and international contention is taking place.

Will the processes I have induced here turn out to be durable or only episodic? Will they be as sweeping as globalization or take different forms and combinations in different sites of contention? And will they concatenate into a master process that fuses domestic with international contention? These issues are considered in subsequent chapters. For now it is enough to pose three main questions, to which I return in the book's conclusion.

First, are we witnessing no more than a temporary spurt of transnational contention or is the world at the beginning of a progression from domestic forms of transnational politics, as described in Chapters 4 and 5, to an increase in diffusion and scale shift, and eventually to more-durable processes of externalization and transnational coalition formation?

Second, if transnational contention continues to increase, will it take the form of a cascade of dramatic but essentially episodic international protest events or a fusion of domestic and international contention?

Third, if transnational social movements are indeed taking shape both within and outside the state, what are the implications for the future relations between states and international politics?

The activists are necessarily our first subject. Within an increasingly internationalized world, a fluid, cosmopolitan, but rooted layer of activists and advocates is developing that uses domestic resources, expertise, and opportunities to advance the collective goals of the people it claims to represent. Some activists do so in the name of globalization, others against its ravages. Some are driven by more concrete and practical aims, others by ideological commitments. The next chapter examines the incidence and the relations of these "rooted cosmopolitans" and illustrates their presence in an important sector of transnational activity – immigrant activism and the diaspora movements that have emerged within it.

3

Rooted Cosmopolitans and Transnational Activists

The fundamental sociocultural change that has increased transnational activism is the growth of a stratum of individuals who travel regularly, read foreign books and journals, and become involved in networks of transactions abroad (Rosenau et al., forthcoming: ch. 1).[1] Underlying these activities are a number of mechanisms that link individuals into webs of interest, values, and technology. Through the use of both domestic and international resources and opportunities, domestic-based activists – citizens and others – move outward to form a spectrum of "rooted cosmopolitans" who engage in regular transnational practices.

This characteristic posture extends from the civil servants who spend a considerable part of their time in transgovernmental committees (Slaughter 2004; Wessels and Rometsch 1996) to the transnational business class examined by Sklair (2001), to the transnational advocates and activists who will be the main subject of this book. We find these activists engaged in a wide variety of transnational politics: from labor and global justice activists and immigrant transnationals to environmental and humanitarian aid workers, from peace activists to anti-landmine campaigners, from advocates for

So many people had the patience to sit through verbal presentations of this chapter or read and comment on various drafts that it is difficult to know whom to thank. I am especially in debt to Alejandro Portes and his research group for their work on transnational communities of immigrants (see note 12), and to Benedict Anderson for the inspiration for the section on "Birds of Passage."

[1] When Rosenau and his collaborators gathered information on a sample of American elites in 1999 and 2003, randomly chosen from leadership compendia, they identified 25 percent in the first year and 29 percent in the second who were highly involved in transnational activities. For details on their selection procedures, see chapter 3 and appendix A of their study. I am grateful to Professor Rosenau for permission to quote his and his collaborators' unpublished work.

transitional justice to religious advocates. They are a corollary, at the level of agency, of the internationalism that I posited as a structural condition of world politics in the preceding chapter.

In the first part of this chapter, I argue that cosmopolitanism is not new but has been accelerated by growing connections across borders and the increased capacities of citizens to mobilize both within and outside of their societies. In Part Two, I examine a recent debate on cosmopolitanism among philosophers and social scientists and then propose a more relational definition of the phenomenon. Part Three traces the outlines of the new transnational activism and its supports in new forms of communication, international networking, and institutions. In Parts Four and Five I use the sector with which I began this book – immigrant activism – to show how transnational activism has developed. In Part Six I explore its ambivalent nature between stable diasporas and birds of passage.

Historical Cosmopolitans

Transnational activism builds on resources and opportunities that are particular to our era: the availability of rapid forms of personal communication and cheap international air travel; greater access to higher education and widely diffused knowledge of the increasingly international language of English; expertise and mobilizing skills gleaned from domestic activism; and the visible evidence that decisions that affect peoples' lives are being made in international venues (Grenier 2004). But for all the recent flurry of interest in globalization, the consequences of foreign travel, knowledge of languages, and transnational networking go much further back than the end of the twentieth century. Here are three archetypical examples from three different centuries.

A Shipper from Bremen

When, in 1623, the shipper Christian Schröder died in the Hanseatic port of Bergen, his memorial portrait in the Maria Church at the edge of the German trading enclave described him as "a merchant of Bremen." The inscription is interesting, not only because it was written in the Low German dialect that was common to all the Hansa towns (Pichierri 1998: 44), but because it designated Schröder as "von Bremen," when the Bergen *Kontor* was actually controlled by Lübeck, Bremen's competitor. Perhaps it was

Lübeck's supremacy that led Schröder's colleagues to insist on his Bremenite origins, or perhaps the city council of that trader-dominated city paid for his portrait. But the inscription also reflected the unusual quality of the Hansa; although it was the earliest transnational capitalist trading system, locality mattered deeply to its members and was one of the reasons for its survival for almost five centuries.

The early Hansa took shape around the trade routes of the main European trading towns: Bergen in the north, London and Bruges in the west, south as far as Cologne and east as far as Novgorod (Dollinger 1970: 370–1). This "Hansa of the merchants" eventually gave way to the "Hansa of the towns," (p. 371); *only* towns, with the sole exception of the Teutonic knights, were its constituent units until its demise in the seventeenth century.[2] Their councils negotiated with other Hanseatic cities and foreign rulers, meeting from time to time in Hansetage and occasionally going to war together when their commercial interests were threatened (p. 268).

A town's membership in the Hansa enabled its merchants to trade in any of the *Kontore* in which the league had trading rights. Out of this network of mutual interest and obligation grew a transnational collective identity. "To the formal quality of Hanseatic merchant," writes Angelo Pichierri (1998: 42), "and to the opportunistic reasons for membership, a sense of common membership was progressively added." This translocal solidarity was a remarkable feature of a late medieval world in which cities were either beginning to be subjected to princes, as in France, or were warring with one another for supremacy, as in Italy. But as the inscription "von Bremen" under Schröder's portrait suggests, in the Hansa we find an early expression of "rooted cosmopolitanism."

A German Exile in Paris

By the 1800s national states had consolidated on most of the European continent and aroused opposition from people who either were forced or chose to leave their native societies. Lloyd S. Kramer (1988: 7) has given us vivid

---

[2] The actual number of Hanseatic towns is a matter of some controversy. Depending on how membership is measured, the Hansa at its height contained either 70-odd or 180 members. The league itself resisted providing a list of its members so as to avoid giving its trading partners the opportunity to divide and conquer. See Dollinger 1970 and Pichierri 1998 for details.

portraits of several of these exiles and of the role of Paris in receiving them. Paris in the 1840s gave them the experience of living in a cosmopolitan and relatively free environment and, ultimately, transformed their views of their own societies. One of them changed the history of the world with a theory blending his German philosophical training and his French political experience.

Karl Marx (1818–83) had spent only just over a year in Paris when the French government, under pressure from Prussia, expelled him in 1845 (Kramer 1988: 120). But although he spent most of the rest of his life in London, Paris had a profound effect on his thought. For not only did he interact with the cream of the Parisian exile community and meet his lifelong collaborator, Friedrich Engels, there; he also encountered the German artisans and the Parisian proletarians who were the vehicles guiding his transition from a left-wing Rhenish philosopher writing in the Hegelian tradition to the inventor of the Marxist revolutionary left. The concept of alienation that marked Marx's early work was the direct result of his encounter with the world of early capitalism in France.

But Paris's impact on Marx was more than biographical. While the French revolutionary tradition provided him with the raw material that transformed his German philosophical background, his Hegelian formation challenged the "merely" political radical tradition he found in France. It was through the criticism of both German Hegelianism and French radicalism that Marx forged the synthesis that would become the framework for his future work. The key passage in his "Critique of Hegel's Philosophy of Right" is worth quoting at length:

In France partial emancipation is the basis of universal emancipation. In Germany universal emancipation is the *conditio sine qua non* of any partial emancipation. In France it is the reality, in Germany the impossibility, of emancipation in stages that must give birth to complete freedom. In France each class of the people is a *political idealist* and experiences itself first and foremost not as a particular class but as the representative of social needs in general. The role of *emancipator* therefore passes in a dramatic fashion from one class of the French people to the next. (Marx 1967: 262)

"Paris, in short, offered a great deal of material to help a German philosopher become a European social theorist" (Kramer 1988: 175). The two influences merged in the Socialist International that was founded in his image.

A Nordic Cosmopolitan[3]

Growing internationalization extended transnational activism around insti-tutions like the League of Nations. Born in what is now Oslo in 1861, Fridtjof Nansen began his career as an explorer, making fundamental contributions to oceanography before taking an interest in politics. Interestingly, his first political foray was as a nationalist, in debates about Norway's independence from Sweden in 1905. He then represented Norway as a diplomat, first in London and then in Washington, before heading the Norwegian delega-tion to the League of Nations in 1920, where he negotiated the repatriation of prisoners of war from Russia.

In 1921 Nansen was appointed by the International Red Cross to bring relief to famine-stricken Russia. His crowning achievement was inventing an international agreement introducing identification cards for displaced persons that became known as the "Nansen passport." For this, he was awarded the Nobel Peace Prize in 1922. He then founded the Nansen Inter-national Office for Refugees, which won the same prize in 1938 (Ingebritsen 2005: 6–8). In parallel with the embodiment of Marx's cosmpolitanism in the Socialist International, international institutions were the fulcrum of Nansen's activism.

These vignettes not only tell us that cosmopolitanism is not new and has been associated with trade, exile, and humanitarianism in the past. They also suggest that the encounter between local socialization and a newer, different reality is interactive: it does not merely substitute the new reality for the old one, but transcends locality and, in some cases, produces a creative leap. If this was true in late medieval Bergen, in nineteenth-century Paris, and in early twentieth-century Norway, it should be even more true in our time, as lines of communication tighten, transportation expands, and globalization blurs the lines across borders. For example, the *négritude* movement in Africa and the Cuban mix of nationalism and socialism of Fidel Castro were both creative leaps that grew out of experiences in the metropole. But it was only in the 1990s, after the collapse of the Soviet bloc, that philosophers, social thinkers, and others launched a debate on cosmopolitanism. Although couched in the axiomatic language beloved of

[3] I am grateful to Christine Ingebritsen for calling my attention to Nansen's remarkable life and achievements. For a sketch of this representative of Norwegian internationalism, see her *Scandinavia in World Politics* (2005: ch. 4).

philosophers, it provides a window into the relational view of transnational activism I put forward in this book.

Rooted Cosmopolitanism

Cosmopolitan, *a*. 1. belonging to all parts of the world; not restricted to any one country or its inhabitants; 2. Having the characteristics which arise from, or are suited to, a range over many different countries; free from national limitations or attachments. (*Oxford English Dictionary* 1999)

Rootless, *a*. Without roots; destitute of roots. (*Oxford English Dictionary* 1999)

Rootless cosmopolitan ("bezrodny kosmopolit") was a Russian euphemism during Joseph Stalin's anti-Semitic campaign of 1948–1953, which culminated in the "exposure" of the "Doctors' plot."[4]

Stalin's and others' exploitation of the term "rootless cosmopolitans" to denigrate Jews and foreigners gave it a shady pedigree. But it was given a fresh look with philosopher Jeremy Waldron's 1992 article "Minority Cultures and the Cosmopolitan Alternative."[5] In this article, Waldron defined cosmopolitans cognitively, praising them as individuals whose cultural identities are not defined by any bounded subset of the cultural resources available in the world (p. 782). David Held vaunted cosmopolitan attitudes in his book, *Democracy and the Global Order* (1995). Sociologist Yasemin Soysal (1994) wrote in a similar vein in her book on "postnational citizenship," arguing that universal rules are emerging to govern the status of immigrants. Martha Nussbaum brought the discussion to the United States with her essay on "Patriotism and Cosmopolitanism" in 1996. Soon after, culture studies founder Stuart Hall (2002: 26) saw cosmopolitanism as "the ability to stand outside of having one's life written and scripted by any one community," while sociologist Craig Calhoun (2002: 90) saw it as part of the advance of global democracy.

But as the bloom went off the globalization rose in the late 1990s and soured in the new century, the cosmopolitan debate subsided. Europeans were becoming more concerned with plugging the holes in their borders against illegal immigration than claiming postnational citizenship, and Americans – especially after September 11, 2001 – became positively suspicious of foreigners. Among mass publics and elites, empirical studies

---

[4] From http://en.wikipedia.org/wik/Rootless_cosmopolitan.
[5] A good introduction to this debate will be found in Vertovec and Cohen 2002, and especially in Hollinger's chapter in that book.

in both Western Europe and the United States began to show a hardening of patriotic sentiments. We see this in extreme form in the xenophobic movements and parties that gained ground in Western Europe in the 1990s (Rydgren 2004, 2005) but also in a cooling of Europeans' ardor for European integration.

Cognitive and Relational Cosmopolitanism

In her 1996 article, Nussbaum took a largely cognitive view of cosmopolitanism, arguing that "the worthy moral ideals of justice and equality . . . would be better served by an *ideal* that is in any case more adequate to our situation in the contemporary world, namely the very old ideal of the cosmopolitan, the person whose *allegiance* is to the worldwide community of human beings" (p. 4, emphasis added). Most of the replies to her essay accepted her basically cognitive framework.

This cognitive view of cosmopolitanism extended to more-empirical observers. For example, from a story in the *International Herald Tribune*, anthropologist Ulf Hannerz told of market women from Nigeria who board London-bound planes wearing loose-fitting gowns under which they would hang dried fish to sell to their countrymen in Britain. "On the return trip," he pointed out, "they carry similarly concealed bundles of frozen fish sticks, dried milk, and baby clothes, all of which are in great demand in Lagos." "Is this cosmopolitanism?" asks Hannerz; he answers no, because these market women continue to *think of themselves* as locals (1990: 238; 1996: 102–3, emphasis added). But cosmopolitan identities, like other identities, are the product of social relations (March and Olson 1999: 319). Internationalism provides a wider and more complex set of relations in which cosmopolitanism can develop than were available to individuals in the more-restricted venues of the past.

This more relational concept of cosmopolitanism was actually present in the philosophers' debate. In a second article, Waldron shifted to a more relational view. He wrote, "we should not assume that *thoughts* about one's culture . . . loom very large in one's own involvement in the cultural life of one's community. What one does in a community is simply speak or marry or dance or worship. *One participates in a form of life*" (2000: 233–4, emphasis added).[6] It is through peoples' relations to significant others that

---

[6] Waldron's new view was closer to the view of cosmopolitanism put forward by Robert Merton decades earlier. In his classical essay on types of influentials, Merton (1957: 394–5) wrote of locals and cosmopolitans that "the difference in basic orientation [i.e., cognition]

41

cosmopolitan attitudes are shaped. What is new in our era is the increased number of people and groups whose relations place them beyond their local or national settings without detaching them from locality. This takes us to my concept of "rooted" cosmopolitanism.

Rooted Cosmopolitans

Mitchell Cohen, writing in *Dissent* in 1992, first used the term "rooted cosmopolitanism." Reacting against both Marxism's "abstract proletarian internationalism" and the parochialism of advocates of "difference," Cohen called for "the fashioning of a dialectical concept of *rooted* cosmopolitanism, which accepts a multiplicity of roots and branches and that rests on the legitimacy of plural loyalties, of standing in many circles, but with common ground" (pp. 480, 483). Legal scholar Bruce Ackerman (1994) followed with an article about American politics. Ghanaian philosopher Kwame Anthony Appiah (1996: 22) wrote of his father that "The favorite slander of the narrow nationalist against us cosmopolitans is that we are rootless. What my father believed in, however, was a rooted cosmopolitanism, or, if you like, a cosmopolitan patriotism."

What is "rooted" in this conception is that, as cosmopolitans move physically and cognitively outside their origins, they continue to be linked to place, to the social networks that inhabit that space, and to the resources, experiences, and opportunities that place provides them with. In the business world, in international organizations and institutions, in the "epistemic communities" that link professionals around the world, and in transnational and transgovernmental networks, we find more and more individuals whose primary ties are domestic but who are part of the complex international society that I sketched in Chapter 2. Some are normatively invested in international regimes and practices; others take advantage of them for primarily self-interested motives; but most are relational cosmopolitans, relying on a combination of domestic resources and opportunities to launch their transnational activities and return home afterward. This is the pattern we find among many of the transnational activists encountered in this study.

is bound up with a variety of other differences: (1) in the structures of social relations in which each type is implicated; (2) in the roads they have traveled to their present positions in the influence-structure; (3) in the utilization of their present status for the exercise of interpersonal influence; and (4) in their communications behavior."

Transnational Activists

Transnational activists are a subgroup of rooted cosmopolitans, whom I define as individuals and groups who mobilize domestic and international resources and opportunities to advance claims on behalf of external actors, against external opponents, or in favor of goals they hold in common with transnational allies.

The unusual character of the contemporary period is not that it has detached individuals from their societies or created transnational citizens but that it has produced a stratum of people who, in their lives and their activities, are able to combine the resources and opportunities of their own societies into transnational networks through what Margaret Keck and Kathryn Sikkink (1998) call "activism beyond borders." These include immigrants who are involved regularly in transnational political activities, but not all immigrants (Portes 2000: 265); labor activists from the South who forge ties with foreign unionists and NGOs, but not all workers (Anner 2004; Waterman 2001); ecologists who gravitate around international institutions and organizations, but not all ecologists (Dalton and Rohrschneider 2002); and members of transnational advocacy networks who link domestic activists to international institutions, but not all activists (Keck and Sikkink 1998). It has also produced "the dark side" of transnational relations: clandestine cells of militants, international drug rings, and traders in human beings.

In this context, only three additional comments are necessary. First, transnational activists do not usually begin their careers at the international level. As numerous studies show, they emerge from domestic political or social activities, and only a small percentage ever becomes full-time international advocates or activists (Grenier 2004). Second, most soon return to their domestic activities, perhaps transformed by their experiences, but perhaps not (we turn to this issue in Chapter 10). Third, they are better educated than most of their compatriots, better connected, speak more languages, and travel more often. What makes them different from their domestic counterparts is their ability to shift their activities among levels, taking advantage of the expanded nodes of opportunity of a complex international society.

A Growing Phenomenon

Although hard data are still scattered and fragmentary, there appears to have been a steady growth in the numbers of transnationally oriented activists over the past few decades. There are few statistics on the numbers of participants in internationally based protests. In the nature of protest campaigns, it is not even clear what these figures would tell us. Anecdotal evidence suggests that their numbers mushroomed in the late 1990s and in the early years of the new century. But the numbers may well decline as fear of terrorism and increased government surveillance bring exhaustion and changing life courses bring activists back to private life (Mittelman 2004a).

We possess better data on the number of transnationally organized advocacy groups. From the yearbooks of International Associations (YIA), Jackie Smith's studies have identified a subset that was founded to promote social or political change. The population of these transnational social movement organizations (TSMOs) "expanded at a tremendous rate over recent decades from fewer than 100 organizations in the 1950s to more than 1,000 today" (J. Smith and Wiest 2005: 2; also see J. Smith 2004b: 266).

This rise in transnational activism has been geographically unbalanced – as is internationalization – indicating the continued importance of domestic structures as a springboard for activism. Smith and Wiest found that through the turn of the new century, participation in TSMOs varied dramatically between its high levels in the industrial countries of the North and much lower levels in the less-developed countries of the South. Western Europeans were active in more than 80 percent of these groups, and citizens of the United States and Canada participated in nearly 70 percent of them. On the other hand, although participation from the global South grew during the 1980s and 1990s, the developing world is still less present in the transnational social movement sector (J. Smith and Wiest 2005: 3). In the new century, there is still a net advantage for the richer, better-connected citizens of the North, who have greater financial and organizational resources and who live close to the sites of major international institutions.

The sectors of activity in which transnational organizations are active have almost all expanded over the past half century but at an uneven rate. Smith's findings, reproduced in Table 3.1, provide a good summary. Human rights TSMOs increased in number from 41 in the 1973 YIA to 247 in 2000, environmental groups grew from 17 to 126 in the same period, and peace groups from 21 to 98, while groups dedicated to self-determination and ethnic unity grew much more slowly.

The biggest percentage increases were found in "development and empowerment" groups (which increased from 4 to 10 percent of the total over the three decades), and multi-issue groups, which increased from 7 to

Table 3.1. *Size and Geographic Dispersion of Transnational Social Movement Organizations*

Year	TSMOs		Countries in Memberships	
	Organizations	% Change	Mean (SD)	Median
1973	183	–	33.89 (23.17)	28
1983	348	90	31.02 (26.03)	23
1993	711	104	33.13 (29.55)	23
2000	959	35	34.39 (32.46)	23
2003 (estimate)	1,011	5		

Sources: J. Smith 2004b: 266; Sikkink and J. Smith 2002: 24–44.

15 percent over the same year period. A related trend was the rapid growth of groups organizing around a broad "global justice/peace and environmental" agenda, from 4 percent of the total in 1973 to 11 percent in 2000 (J. Smith 2004b: 268). The trend toward multi-issue activism is related to the increase in transnational coalition building, an important trend to which we return later.

The growing numbers of transnational advocates and activists are not homogeneous; some are "norms entrepreneurs," who attempt to diffuse deeply held beliefs to countries around the world (Finnemore and Sikkink 1998); others work at the international level on behalf of social categories like workers, women, indigenous peoples, or peasants. While some aim their activities at international institutions, others engage in service activities within the societies of the South on behalf of international NGOs, and still others mediate between these levels.

Crosscutting these many forms of activism are two main types: some are classical "insiders," gravitating to international institutions and taking part in highly institutionalized service and advocacy activities; others (and their numbers seem to be increasing) are activist "outsiders," who challenge these institutions and organizations. Two examples can help us both to get a better picture of who these "insiders" and "outsiders" are and to begin to understand their relationship to each other.

Working Transnationals

In his sweeping analysis of "counter-hegemonic globalization," Peter Evans (2005: 660) points out that organized labor has "not been seen as a promising candidate for becoming a transnational social movement." The pessimism he alludes to results from the fear that the "geography of jobs" constrains workers from international solidarity. Dubious of the traditional pessimism, Evans summarizes three important ways in which unionists participate in transnational politics: seeking basic rights, social contracts, and democratic governance (pp. 661–3). Some of these labor activists have become permanently active internationally, but others continue to operate on native ground on behalf of workers from elsewhere and in the name of global worker solidarity.

Working transnationalism reveals cosmopolitans without cosmopolitan ideology in the capacity of quite ordinary people, moving back and forth between the local and the translocal and among a variety of (not necessarily compatible) identities. Nathan Lillie found such a group when he studied the Flag of Convenience (FOC) campaign of the International Transport Workers' Federation (ITF).[7] FOCs are ships that sail under the registries of countries like Liberia that turn a blind eye to the labor conditions of their seamen. FOC practices are the most effective way of causing a "race to the bottom" in employment conditions. But "through coordinated bargaining and industrial action," Lillie (2003: 1) writes, "the ITF has stopped this race to the bottom, raising wages and improving conditions for a significant proportion of the seafaring workforce."

The ITF uses a variety of strategies in its campaign, but the most interesting here are the local unions who have "transnationalized" the FOC campaign network "by tying rank-and-file port workers and local union officials directly into a global strategy to enforce a uniform global minimum wage scale on FOC vessels." The network provides the ITF with the organizational capabilities needed to resolve the practical difficulties of enforcing a standard minimum wage on the global level, providing the federation with in-port resources on which many ITF affiliates now depend (Lillie 2003: 115). Although they work in the most institutionalized sector of national social movements – the trade-union movement – ITF port inspectors contribute to transnational goals.

Local "No-Globals"

What could be further in either spirit or tactics from the sturdy port inspectors of the ITF than the new generation of global justice activists whose

---

[7] I am grateful to Nathan Lillie for permission to quote from his 2003 Ph.D. thesis presented to the New York State School of Industrial and Labor Relations.

protests have been gathering force since the "Battle of Seattle" in 1999? Yet here, too, we find a deeply local rooting of transnational activism. Although Seattle was widely trumpeted as an incident in the struggle of the global "South" against the "North," in fact most of the protesters came from the American or Canadian Northwest and by far the largest proportion were unionists seeking protection for their jobs (Lichbach 2003). When Margaret Levi and Gillian Murphy (2004) traced the coalition that planned the Seattle protests, they found the core of the participants was drawn from among activists who had worked together in domestic protests in the United States.

Donatella della Porta and her collaborators found a similar domestic rooting among the activists they interviewed during three European protest events: the 2001 Genoa G-7 protest, the 2002 European Social Forum, and the February 15, 2003, anti-Iraq war protest. Summarizing this evidence, della Porta and Mario Diani found a widespread rooting of these participants in the traditional sectors of Italian activism. A trade-union background was reported by between 19 and 40 percent of them; a political party alignment was claimed by roughly one-third; religious activism by between 18 and 31 percent; volunteerism by between 30 and 41 percent; and student activism by between 40 and 52 percent.[8] These transnational activists came largely from familiar sectors of domestic politics and associations.

Both local port inspectors and "no-global" European activists are examples of the familiar finding from social movement research that the best predictor of activism is past activism. But they add a new dimension to their sequence of activities – involvement in transnational activism. Out of their local experiences came exposure to transnational activities, and from this experience, some will become participants in enduring transnational coalitions and movement organizations. For others, their "global identities" will be costumes put on during occasional external forays before returning to domestic activism or retreating into private life (della Porta 2005b). We are witnessing to an increasing degree the formation of a broad spectrum of activists who face both inward and outward and combine domestic and transnational activism and advocacy.

---

[8] These data were kindly provided by Donatella della Porta from her and Mario Diani's 2004 article, "Contro la guerra senza se ne ma: Le proteste contro la guerra in Irak." Other reports from della Porta's research program on the European global justice and peace movements can be found in della Porta and Mosca 2003 and della Porta 2005b.

Moreover, even a rapid look at these activists suggests that the distinction between "insiders" and "outsiders" may be blurring. For example, while I have described the ITF port inspectors as "insiders," other labor organizers are clearly challengers. Beginning with the Liverpool port lockout of 1995, British, American, Canadian, Japanese, and Australian dockers began to contact each other to prevent ships that had been loaded by "black" workers elsewhere from unloading in their ports. In ports as far apart as Liverpool, Oakland, Yokohama, and Sydney, international docker solidarity has resulted in slowing down – if not actually stopping – the strategy of shipowners to use nonunion casual labor to unload their ships (Gentile 2003; Turnbull 2004).

Insiders and outsiders increasingly cooperate around international institutions, conferences, and processes. Korzeniewicz and Smith (2001) found both conflict and cooperation in the opposition to the Free Trade Association of the Americas. Jeffrey Ayres (2002) found both sectors in the coalitions formed to oppose Canadian-U.S. trade cooperation and NAFTA. Participation in international protests may even resocialize insiders into outsiders: many of the protesters who went to Seattle, Genoa, or Quebec City as insiders became outsiders when they were attacked by the water cannon and stun grenades of the police. What insiders and outsiders have most in common is that they gravitate to and mobilize around international regimes, practices, and institutions.

Transnational Immigrant Communities

Both the labor and global justice examples are relatively recent forms of action; how has our more densely internationalized world affected the most familiar form of transnational activism – the activities of immigrants like the young man from Kletsk whose activities I described in Chapter 1? Like transnational activists in general, immigrant activists live in two worlds – in their case, the world of their adopted countries and the world of their homelands. In describing them, we can draw on a century of evidence about a truly global phenomenon. But we also see a dramatic expansion in immigrant transnationalism, ranging from the traditional practice of the sending of remittances to home countries to participation in home-country electoral politics to diasporic nationalism. And in the relationship of the latter to the more traditional forms of immigrant politics, we see the ambivalences and contradictions in transnational activism.

Back to History

In 1906, in language that was strikingly similar to what we hear from advocates of postnational citizenship today, an Italian official charged with the
protection of his country's immigrants abroad looked to the future. According to Gino Speranza ([1906] 1974: 310), "The old barriers are everywhere
breaking down. We may even bring ourselves to the point of recognizing
foreign 'colonies' in our midst, on our own soil, as entitled to partake in the
parliamentary life of their mother country."[9]

Speranza's hope for the recognition of foreign "colonies" in the United
States was dashed by the First World War and by the restrictive immigration
legislation that followed, but it reminds us that immigrant transnationalism
is not new. Like representatives of Mexican immigrants today, Speranza
wanted the Italo-American "colony" in America to be represented in their
home parliament; between Italian ports and New York and Buenos Aires
there was constant back-and-forth traffic, as there is today between North
American cities and the Caribbean; and immigrant remittances enriched
many southern Italian families and communities.

Contemporary Connections

Some would argue that all of the characteristics of todays immigrant
transnationalism existed a century ago. For example, the telegraph mim-
icked the same speed of light so admired in television and the internet
today (Wyman 1993). But if immigrant transnationalism is nothing new,
it has increased in magnitude, and a host of factors make the connections
among immigrants and their home countries more frequent and more integrated today. First of all, there was an epochal change in the state system
from the beginning of the First World War through the mid-1920s. Where
the bulk of pre–World War I immigrants came from the subject states of
the great European empires – Hapsburg, Prussian, Romanov – after that
war and the Treaty of Versailles, nearly everyone had at least a putative
nation-state. Hence, migration had a radically new color to it. The League
of Nations was a politically impoverished institution, but its title accu-
rately reflected this new reality. Henceforth, immigrants would think of

---

[9] I am grateful to Nancy Foner for calling this quotation to my attention and for her sensitive
reflections on the old and the new immigrant transnationalism in her "Transnationalism
Then and Now" (2001).

themselves in relation to states that reflected their national origins, and not in terms of empires to which they owed little allegiance.[10]

The post–World War II world added a host of new nation-states to those which were created after 1918 and did away with whatever vestiges of the imperial world had survived that war. In this process of state creation and state legitimation, the United Nations has played a key role. To citizens of the South whose national borders were often no more than lines on a map drawn by imperialists indifferent to tribe, ethnic group, or nation, UN certification gave national identity a real – as opposed to a purely imposed – meaning.

Cheap and rapid transportation and simplified electronic communication keep immigrants in contact with their families and hometowns. In Mexico, Mixtec villages that lack paved streets have modern phone lines and internet providers that allow people to make daily contact with their loved ones for a modest fee paid to neighbors who return from the North with computer equipment to create an internet café in their front rooms.[11] But these are no more than the surface manifestations of new forms of economic and political integration. These include segmented production networks, diasporic investment in home-country enterprises, an internationalization of mass consumption – if not of actual levels of consumption (Sklair 2001) – and, of course, mass migration.

Increasing immigration and the greater ease of travel have created occupational niches that require or invite people both to act as brokers with the local community and to maintain their transnational links. International trading in home-country products, investing back home, running travel agencies, and working in the "newcomer settlement industry" offer immigrants opportunities for making careers that link the immigrant community and the home community (Bloemraad 2005). Where Morris Tarrow returned once to his native *shtetl* and stayed there for nine months, his successors from Santo Domingo or Mumbai can hop on a plane to see to their business interests at home or monitor their childrens' upbringing by telephone from New York City (Foner 2001: 42–3).

David Kyle (1999) describes the effects of these structural changes on a traditional apparel-producing area in highland Ecuador. Since its

[10] I am grateful to Benedict Anderson for reminding me of this difference – obvious only after he pointed it out.
[11] I am grateful to Judy Hellman for this observation from her research in Puebla, New York, and Toronto on the transnational ties of Mexican immigrants.

occupation by Spain, the region of Otavalo has specialized in the production and marketing of clothing. Now increased international trade and cheaper and easier international mobility have transformed it. As Alejandro Portes (2000: 260) summarizes Kyle's thesis, "During the last quarter of a century or so, Otavalans have taken to traveling abroad to market their colorful wares in major cities of Europe and North America. By so doing, they have also brought home a wealth of novelties from the advanced countries, including newcomers to their town." But not all transnational activism is of a piece. Some activists settle into a regular routine of home-country visits, engaging in country charity work, ethnic festivals, and occasional intervention in the politics of their hometown; others become diaspora nationalists, religious revivalists, or clandestine organizers. I call the first type "nesting pigeons" and the second "birds of passage."

Nesting Pigeons

Transnational systems of exchange offer incentives and resources for immigrant transnationals to become politically active with their home countries as their targets. For example, in Los Angeles, Portes and his collaborators interviewed a Mr. Gonzalez, president of the local civic committee of a small town in El Salvador. When asked why he intended to stay in Los Angeles in the face of discrimination and nativism, Gonzalez replied: "I really live in El Salvador, not in LA. When we have the regular *fiestas* to collect funds for La Esperanza, I am the leader and I am treated with respect. When I go back home to inspect the works paid with our contributions I am as important as the mayor" (Portes 1999: 466).

How widespread is this pattern of transnational activism within immigrant communities, and what are its political implications? Because much of the evidence we have is ethnographic, it is difficult to generalize. But one source of systematic information does exist: a comparative study of the causes and consequences of the emergence of transnational communities among Colombian, Dominican, and Salvadoran immigrants in the United States.[12] Looking at "both electoral and nonelectoral activities aimed at influencing conditions in the home country...on a regular basis," Luis

---

[12] The three-country study was directed by Alejandro Portes and Luis Eduardo Guarnizo. Between 1996 and 2000, they and their collaborators carried out three phases of data collection in Colombia, the Dominican Republic, and El Salvador. For each of the three target populations, data collection was carried out in two North American settlement cities and in the country of origin, using the same set of survey instruments and sampling designs

Guarnizo and his collaborators (2003: 1225) report that one-sixth of the three immigrant groups they studied are "core" transnational activists, while another one-sixth engage in such activities on an occasional basis.

Are these proportions significant or trivial? Seen as a percentage of the enormous immigrant populations of New York, Los Angeles, Toronto, or London, they may seem derisory. But in the light of the shrinking proportion of civic involvement in these societies, they are impressive. The fact that one-sixth of struggling Colombians, Dominicans, and Salvadorans living in the United States, where participation in national elections has steadily shrunk, regularly engage in homeland-directed political activities, and an additional one-sixth do so from time to time, seems highly significant.

Not only the political context of their countries of origin but the opportunities, threats, and incentives of immigrants' places of arrival condition the nature and possibilities of transnational activism (Waldinger and Fitzgerald 2004). For example, New York's fragmented and ethnically organized local politics offers far more opportunities and fewer constraints to Dominican immigrants in that city than, say, Los Angeles' more concentrated system does for Mexicans.[13] The Netherlands' carefully constructed opportunities for Turkish activists to form local associations contrasts dramatically with the institutionalized reluctance of French officialdom to recognize the legitimacy of multiculturalism. Once "rooted" in a new and differentiated political environment, immigrant activists are conditioned by the domestic structures and political cultures of their environments.

The forms of exchange that immigrants are likely to engage in with their homelands are mainly traditional: sending remittances to families and for public works projects. But immigrants increasingly support candidates for local office, lobby local governments to allocate resources to their communities, try to retain home-country voting rights from their new homes, and engage in collective forms of politics in sending countries. For example, Mexican community organizations in the United States are beginning to unite at the (Mexican) state level (R. Smith 2003). This is producing powerful regional pressure groups, based on emigrants' resources north of the border, that are capable of negotiating with Mexican state

in both cases. For the products of the project to date, see the website of the Center for Migration and Development at Princeton at http://cmd.princeton.edu/papers.html.

[13] I am grateful to Roger Waldinger for reminding me of this point in a personal communication.

governments on behalf of their hometowns (J. Fox and Rivera-Salgado 2004).

Transnational activists engage in more-contentious forms of politics as well. When Mixtec leaders were arrested in Oaxaca, Radio Bilingue in Fresno, California, put pressure on the Mexican government. "If something happens in Oaxaca," declared a local organizer, "we can put protesters in front of the consulates in Fresno, Los Angeles, Madera" (Portes 1999: 474). Since the passage of NAFTA, solidarity groups in Texas and California work to help workers in Mexican factories fight exploitation, improve health conditions, and organize workers in the *maquiladora* factories (H. Williams 2003: 532–6). And in Western Europe there is growing evidence that immigrant groups are bringing their local resources to the politics of their home countries.[14]

Birds of Passage

There is a both a similarity and a radical difference between the ameliorative activities of "nesting pigeons" and the destructive potential of "birds of passage." The interaction between the two has produced a deep cleavage in immigrant communities, a xenophobic reaction among host populations, and deep resentment and a reservoir for recruitment into diaspora nationalism and religious extremism. In the 1990s Benedict Anderson (1998) wrote worriedly of "long-distance nationalism." By this term, Anderson referred to immigrant nationalists who mobilize resources from the diaspora to undermine their home governments. He observed that such activists – for example, Croatians in Canada, the Irish in Boston, Kurds in Germany – could cheaply, easily, and without major risk to themselves incite and support violence in their countries of origin. Anderson could not have predicted the horrors that would be inflicted upon the world by the Sikhs who blew up an Air India airliner or of the "birds of passage" who turned two airliners into flying bombs on September 11, 2001; but the phenomenon of long-distance religious militancy is similar to long-distance nationalism.

One source of long-distance nationalism is the odd dyslexia among many diaspora nationalists between how they remember the countries they have

---

[14] I make no effort here to survey the enormous literature on immigrant politics and communities in Europe. Perhaps the best-studied case is that of the Kurds. For good introductions to migrant transnationalism outside the United States, see Adamson 2002 and Ostergaard-Nielsen 2001, 2003, and the papers collected in Al-Ali and Koser 2002.

left and their current realities. Zlatko Skrbis's work on Croatian communities in Australia, for example, shows that the view of their homeland among Antipodian Croatians is at least fifty years out of date (Skrbis 1999). The same time warp, remarks Anderson, "is just as true of many American Irish, Armenians, Chinese, etc. To an amazing extent, they block out the real Ireland, Armenia and China of the present."[15]

Historical memories can distort identification with the homeland in a progressive as well as reactionary direction: liberal American Jews continue to support Israel unconditionally, both because they fear its increasingly unlikely destruction but also because they see the Israeli capitalist system of today through the lenses of the kibbutz society of fifty years ago, which has now disappeared. The source of much of diaspora nationalism is identification with societies that no longer exist.

Cosmopolitan Contradictions

In their radical goals and the outcomes of their actions, the religious zealots and diaspora nationalists who are responsible for many of the horrors of the new century are a world apart from the benign activism of immigrants who send remittances back to their families, invest in local enterprises, and attempt to influence elections in their hometowns. But they are connected to their home countries by many of the same mechanisms. As Anderson (1998: 68) writes,

The Moroccan construction worker in Amsterdam can every night listen to Rabat's broadcasting services and has no difficulty in buying pirated cassettes of his country's favourite singers. The illegal alien, *Yakuza*-sponsored, Thai bartender in a Tokyo suburb shows his Thai comrades Karaoke videotapes just made in Bangkok. The Filipina maid in Hong Kong phones her sister in Manila, and sends money in the twinkling of an electronic eye to her mother in Cebu. The successful Indian student in Vancouver can keep in daily e-mail touch with her former Delhi classmates.

These apolitical links are the basis of both nesting immigrant communities and militant birds of passage. Needless to say, it would be mistaken to assume either that all immigrant transnationals are potential long-distance nationalists or that all forms of long-distance nationalism are violent. But it is striking that just as immigrant nesting pigeons use their ties to their home communities to foster development and to keep family ties alive, birds of

---

[15] In a private communication commenting on an earlier version of this chapter.

54

director Theo Van Gogh began activism in a Muslim community center, which he deserted for more aggressive forms of activism. The Tamil Tigers were enabled to engage in protracted insurgency against the Sri Lankan government in part through the support of the Tamil diaspora (Wayland 2004). In the complex international environment of the early twenty-first century, nesting pigeons transmute easily into birds of passage.

This does not mean that the witch-hunt that was launched against the Muslim communities of the United States after September 11, 2001, is justified. But it does suggest that transnational immigrant activism is multifaceted; that it often involves people with little political intent as unconscious supporters; and that the internationalism of the world today no longer makes it possible to distinguish sharply between locals and cosmopolitans.

Conclusions

"Rooted cosmopolitans" are a broad stratum of individuals and groups that exist both in the past and among social activists today. Supported by technological change, economic integration, and cultural connections, the phenomenon expresses itself most dramatically in the ease with which young people participate in demonstrations outside their own borders. But when the demonstrations die down, more significant, though more difficult to measure, is the learning they bring back to their own societies and the ties they have developed across borders. While we lack good evidence of transnational activism's magnitude or its rate of growth, we see its importance in the growth of transnational NGOs and in the processes of transnational contention we will encounter in the next six chapters. Like many of the activists we encounter in this book, two of these processes, "global framing" and "internalization" of protest against external institutions and actors, are domestically rooted.

passage, "cheaply, safely, and in a self-satisfying way, can play national he
on the other side of the world" (p. 74).

The more-aggressive forms of immigrant activism have impacts on be
sending and receiving countries. On the one hand, the presence of lo
distance activists feeds the xenophobic nationalism of a Le Pen in Fra
or a Bossi in Italy. Resentful *Français de souche* who see young Arab wor
wearing the veil do not recognize it as a statement of female indep
dence but as an unwillingness to give up the link to an unknown "otl
across the Mediterranean. When middle-class *Milanesi* living in an imag
Northern League *Padania* see Albanians or Moroccans sweeping the str
or washing dishes in the neighborhood pizzeria, they may be reminde
their own unregretted past in the poverty of southern Italy. And v
well-established immigrant groups, like the American Jews or Italians
adapted eagerly to their receiving societies in earlier generations, ob
the self-conscious multiculturalism of recent immigrant groups, it can
a threat to their own assimilation.

Nativist xenophobia and diaspora extremism feed on one another. I
grant activists who sense their rejection by the indigenous population
back from hope of assimilation, thus fulfilling the prophecy of their
onists that they do not want to fit in. In turn, rejection feeds the divi
the immigrant community between those who feel themselves assin
and those who retreat into a long-distance identity. We are witnessi
phenomenon in France, Britain, and the Netherlands as a younger
ation of Islamic immigrants embraces a more radical form of Isla
their parents.

It is in the weak and unauthoritative states of the South that we see
visible effects of diasporic extremism. Some of the plans behind the
tling of the Babri mosque in Ayodhya, which triggered the greater
Indian bloodshed since partition, came from Indians settled overs
most fanatical adherents of an independent Khalistan live in Me
and Chicago; "Tamilnet" links Tamil communities in Toronto,
and elsewhere to the violent struggles of the Tigers of Sri La
Croats living abroad played "a malign role" in financing and armin
Tudjman's breakaway state and pushing Germany and Austria to r
it (Anderson 1998: 73–4; Wayland 2004).

Between nesting pigeons and birds of passage there are great di
but there are also similarities and connections. The killers of t
Trade Center lived unobserved in the midst of the Muslim com
Hamburg while awaiting the moment to fly. The accused murdere

PART TWO

The Global in the Local

4

Global Framing

During New York's great fiscal crisis, arson and abandonment left the cityscape scarred with crumbling buildings and rubble-strewn vacant lots. Rather than improve their properties, landlords would abandon them; thieves would move in to strip the copper plumbing from the walls and floors; pipes would overflow, and water would freeze and crack the floors; addicts and homeless people would take over the tattered hulks, and street crime would destroy the fabric of entire neighborhoods. The city's response was to bulldoze the worst of the abandoned buildings and put cyclone fences around the vacant lots. This was the decade in which the term "South Bronx" became a synonym for urban decay all over America.

A popular response was a movement to create "community gardens." Armed with bolt cutters and pickaxes, groups with names like "Green Oasis" and "Green Guerillas" colonized derelict lots with vest-pocket gardens. These activists offered free plants and trees to neighborhood volunteers and lobbed bags of peat moss and packs of wildflower seeds into fenced-off lots. "It was a form of civil disobedience," recalled an early Green Guerilla member. "We were saying to the government, if you won't do it, we will." By the late 1970s the community garden movement had won over important sectors of city government to its cause, enlisted the help of Cornell University's Cooperative Extension Service, and convinced the state and federal governments to provide financial support for new green spaces in the city. This was a successful local movement.[1]

Nearly thirty years later and a continent away, New York's community gardeners joined a human chain at the WTO Ministerial in Seattle to

---

[1] The information in this paragraph comes from www.interactivist.net/gardens/. For the flavor of the continued activist language of the Green Guerilla group, see www.greenguerillas.org.

59

prevent official representatives from entering the meeting place. "Why," ask Lesley Wood and Kelly Moore (2002: 21), alongside people demand-ing fairness to Third World farmers and relief from crippling IMF debts, "were the activists fighting to save community gardens at a meeting of an international trade organization?"

Why indeed? Surely they were not expecting representatives of the world's great financial institutions to roll up their sleeves and dig gardens in the seedier sections of Manhattan. They came to Seattle because they had come to see their local grievances in terms that connected them to economic globalization. This is part of the appeal of the global justice movement. But the incident also reveals a basic disjunction in that movement: the venue for action was spatially and politically distinct from the levers of possible response to their claims. Going to Seattle lent the numbers, the passion, and the sense of humor of the New York City community gardeners to a global event; but it was only by a broad reach of the imagination that Seattle could be connected to the substance of their claims.[2]

In recent years we have seen much of this kind of global framing, which I define as *the use of external symbols to orient local or national claims*. This is the most "domestic" of the political processes I describe in this book. When it works, it can dignify, generalize, and energize activists whose claims are predominantly local, linking them symbolically to people they have never met and to causes that are distantly related to their own. But most activists are embedded within the power structures of their own countries, where their fellow citizens need much persuasion to adopt such global thinking. Not only that: as returning transnationals proclaim the abstract themes of global justice, domestic activists who have been slugging it out against local power structures may ask in wonder: "What in the hell are you guys so excited about?" (Klein 2004: 227).

In this chapter, I give explicit attention to the framing of contentious pol-itics and, in particular, to how local activists cognitively connect to global symbols. I examine two main ways in which these symbols enter domestic political struggle: through *structural equivalence* and through *global thinking*. First, focusing on the wave of "riots" in the 1980s triggered by the IMF's policies of structural adjustment, I argue that, although opposition to IMF financial austerity triggered remarkably similar opposition in a number of countries, this was not a "global movement." Next I present evidence of

---

[2] David Meyer, as he often does, found this insight in a story I had originally recounted primarily for its human interest.

global thinking among elites and mass publics, which I find less widely diffused than many have claimed. Finally, I turn to the group of "rooted cosmopolitans" that has most effectively harnessed global thinking against international capital and institutions – the "global justice" movement. But before turning to the "global" in global framing, we need to have an understanding of the meaning of "framing."

Collective Action Frames

In the 1980s sociologist David Snow and his collaborators imported the concept of "framing" into the study of contentious politics.[3] Snow's basic argument was that although cognitive frames – which he called "schemata of interpretation" – are present in all societies to organize experience and guide action, a special type of frames, collective action frames, are constructed by movement organizers to attract supporters, signal their intentions, and gain media attention.[4]

Snow and his colleagues thought of collective action frames as the designs of movement organizers, but they were also aware that such designs are not cut from whole cloth. If activists want to puncture the crust of convention, they must relate their programs to the "common sense" of their target publics, to adopt Gramsci's familiar terminology. Activists are thus both consumers of existing cultural materials and producers of new ones. Proposing frames that are new and challenging but still resonate with existing cultural understandings is a delicate balancing act, especially since society's "common sense" buttresses the position of elites and defends inherited inequalities (Tarrow 1992). It is particularly problematic where activists attempt to import symbols and forms of action from abroad.

Frame Bridging and Frame Transformation

Under the broad umbrella of movement framing, Snow and his collaborators proposed a variety of mechanisms through which social movements

---

[3] Snow and his collaborators were not alone: about the same time as they wrote, Dutch social psychologist Bert Klandermans (1992) was observing that interpreting grievances and raising expectations of success are the core of the social construction of protest, Italian social theorist Alberto Melucci (1988) was proposing "collective identities" as a way of understanding social movements, and American sociologist William Gamson (1992) was arguing that collective action is structured by "ideological packages."

[4] I summarize this contribution from several sources: Snow et al. 1986; Snow and Benford 1988, 1992.

align their claims with those of relevant publics. The least ambitious mechanism they called "frame bridging," *the linkage of two or more ideologically congruent but structurally unconnected frames regarding a particular issue or problem* (Snow et al. 1986: 467); the most far-reaching they labeled "frame transformation," which involves *the planting and nurturing of new values, jettisoning old ones, and reframing erroneous beliefs and "misframings"* (Snow and Benford 1988: 188). In this chapter I argue that "global justice" passes the test of frame bridging but is much more difficult to employ for purposes of frame transformation.

For one thing, movements are never free to frame their campaigns as they wish, for they compete at a structural disadvantage with rulers and the media. Activists who import foreign symbols can throw authorities off balance, in which case the movement gains a temporary advantage; but states and elites are quick to attack the legitimacy of challenges in the name of defending domestic values. The media also act as representatives of the "common sense" of their societies, catering to the perceived tastes of their readers to preserve their share of the media market. On the other hand, if there is a "market" for dissent, the media can offer movement activists "standing," as the American media did in the case of abortion activists in the 1980s and 1990s (Ferree et al. 2002).

A Model of Global Framing

In their article on ACT UP, Wood and Moore (2002: 22) cite the broad process of internationalization and more-specific mechanisms that they see as relevant to the global framing of local issues:

- *Internationalization:* the growth of international government and private-public governance structures that lack institutionalized methods of citizen influence
- *Communication:* increased knowledge of targets and allies facilitated by increasing access to information
- *Convergence:* existing political streams that combine with long-standing bundles of ideologies, practices, values, and targets

Figure 4.1 plots a hypothetical trajectory of domestic global framing drawing on Wood and Moore's article in combination with Snow's categories of frame bridging and frame transformation.

Note that Figure 4.1 portrays only a descriptive trajectory. Later we will see that its conditions are not always met. Also note that I have not tried to

Figure 4.1 A Descriptive Model of Global Framing of Domestic Contention

63

specify the interactions between transnational activists and their domestic interlocutors, which would involve a whole new set of mechanisms. Global framing describes only the domestic diffusion of a message in global terms and ignores the contacts and conflicts between its receivers and their opponents. But even in the absence of such contacts, imported symbols can make a difference to both elite and popular response, as the wave of contention against international financial institutions in the 1980s and 1990s suggests.

Structural Equivalence: The IMF "Riots"

"On January 15, 1985," write John Walton and Jonathan Shefner (1994: 97), "hours after the Jamaican government announced an increase in the state-controlled price of petroleum products, protest demonstrations erupted across the Caribbean nation." Roads and train services were blocked, tires burned at intersections, schools closed, and government offices were paralyzed. After a crowd marched on the prime minister's residence, the protest spread from the capital to provincial cities. With ten people killed in skirmishes with police, snipers, and roving gangs, it was the worst violence the country had seen since the 1970s.

The cause of this spreading wave of contention was an increase in the price of fuel by a government trying to offset the savage devaluation of the currency that had been imposed by the International Monetary Fund as a condition for releasing new credits. Under continued pressure, the Seaga government added another price rise in June. This time the rioters were backed up by a three-day general strike called by the major trade unions. Failing to placate the populace with a wage increase, and with his support waning, Seaga tried to turn popular ire against the IMF, the external source of the country's misery. "I don't intend to let them [the IMF] add Jamaica to their tombstone of failures," he declared (Walton and Shefner 1994: 97–8).

Different national episodes of contention often arise through similar reactions to external threats, and this structural equivalence has grown with the increasing power of the great international financial institutions. In fact, one of the striking anomalies of the actions of these institutions is their "one model fits all" style of economic intervention. As Walton and Shefner (1994: 101) write, "Applied by the IMF with striking uniformity across debtor nations, structural adjustment required currency devaluation, increased interest rates, reduced imports, greater freedom for foreign capital, elimination of tariff protections, privatization of state-owned firms, and, above all, reduced public expenditures."

The IMF structural adjustment policy has had devastating economic effects around the world (Stiglitz 2002). But this structural equivalence does not in itself produce a unified transnational movement. In each country in which there were major anti-IMF "riots," there was a similar reaction; but there was no evident coordination across borders and, as domestic political forces entered the conflicts, there were very different outcomes. Internationalization was the source of structural equivalence and would produce similar forms of contention and framing but did not lead to a global movement, despite their similarities.

A Singularly Common Repertoire

Between 1976 and late 1992, according to John Walton and David Seddon's (1994: 39–40) calculations, 146 austerity protests broke out in thirty-nine of the world's most indebted countries, reaching a peak between 1983 and 1985. The epicenter was in Latin America and the Caribbean, where they count 14 major protests in Peru, 13 in Bolivia, 11 in Argentina and Brazil, 7 in Chile and Venezuela, and 6 in Haiti. But there were also austerity protests across Asia, the Middle East, and North Africa, and even in state-socialist Albania, Hungary, Romania, and Yugoslavia. As the IMF doggedly applied its recipe for market reform all over the world, it touched off an astonishingly similar repertoire of contention against the governments that implemented it.

Most of these protests were triggered by the cutting of subsidies and increases in public service fares (Walton and Seddon 1994: 40–3). In responding to these decisions, demonstrators typically targeted the domestic institutions perceived as responsible for their grievances, like treasuries and national banks. But in many cases they attacked international agents too, ranging from assaults on the local offices of international institutions to attacking "symbolic" targets like foreign cars, luxury hotels, and travel agencies. In the most recent cycle of protests at the end of the century, Argentine supermarkets became frequent targets of contention (Auyero and Moran 2004). Figure 4.2 traces the most visible of these protests over time from Walton and Seddon's work.

The term "riots" does little justice to the wave of contention that exploded across the world in those years. In Latin America, for example, "protests appeared in three distinct forms: strike, demonstration, and riot,"

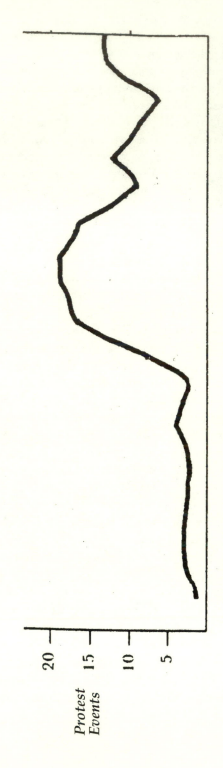

Figure 4.2 Austerity Protests by Year, 1976–91, $N = 122$. *Source:* Calculated from Walton and Seddon 1994.

66

yet seldom in their pure form: "Strikes often generated demonstrations and demonstrations encouraged looters" (Walton and Shefner 1994: 109). Where union traditions were strong, general strikes often followed. Violence was a frequent accompaniment of the protests, both between police and demonstrators and between sectors of the public, but nonviolent disruption was more widespread, as in the clattering of pots and pans, the so-called *cacerolazo*, in the recent wave of protests in Argentina (Auyero 2003). "From December 2001 to February 2003," writes Michael Cohen, "Argentines participated in more than 13,000 public demonstrations throughout the country, protesting the lack of jobs, food, and coherent public policy" (2003: 41–2; also see Cohen and Gutman 2003).

Participants were mainly drawn from among the urban poor, who were hardest hit by the removal of subsidies. But when their bank deposits were frozen, middle-class consumers, shopkeepers, students, and public employees were ready to join the poor in the streets (Walton and Shefner 1994: 111–12). Unions played an increasingly important role as the protests advanced, especially where, as in Latin America, there were strong traditions of union organization. Opposition parties added their voices to the clamor, even leading some of the food riots in Argentina (Auyero and Moran 2004: 18–22).

Three factors in particular emerge from Walton and Shefner's (1994: 99) analyses of the debt protests:

- IMF pressure and the level of debt to external lenders were joined by domestic conditions, especially urbanization, as predictors of the austerity protests (Walton and Ragin 1990: 884).
- Contrary to the then popular "dependency" model (Walton and Shefner 1994: 115),[5] the frequency of the protests in different countries could not be linked to their degree of integration into the world system.
- Domestic mobilizational capacity – and particularly the strength of the unions – had a positive but not always significant relationship to the severity of the protests (Walton and Seddon 1994: 44–5).

---

[5] In a separate analysis, Walton and Ragin specified world systems/dependency theory through overurbanization, the IMF pressure index, average debt service, inflation rate, state sanctions, and the percentage of the population employed in the tertiary sector. Apart from the fact that this specification included a number of factors that are only distantly related to the concept of "dependency," the results showed significant effects only for IMF pressure and overurbanization, a variable that has no theoretical connection that I can see to international dependency. See Walton and Ragin 1990: 885–6, for their specification and results.

No-Global Movement

Although activists today like to cite the anti-IMF protests as an early stage of the global justice movement, none of the evidence indicates the presence of transnational ties among activists or of a "scale shift" to a higher level of collective action (see Chapter 7). What was common to the wave of IMF riots was the framing of domestic contention by domestic activists against an intrusive international institution and its local clients.

To be sure, anti-IMF protesters were aware of protests in neighboring countries and used similar slogans. "Before long," conclude Walton and Shefner (1994: 107), "it was clear that the new phenomenon was an international protest wave." But in contrast to the processes of transnational contention we will see later, no transnational networks or solidarities appear in the accounts and no unified organization grew out of the protests to coordinate an international movement. In fact, the most striking aspect of the protests was their domestic resonance and their articulation with internal political alignments (Auyero 2001). Structural equivalence was the start of a funnel of causation that produced the IMF "riots"; domestic actors and domestic variables accounted for its processing and its outcomes.

Global Thinking

Have globalization and the campaigns against its neoliberal vision produced more-widespread global thinking since then? Judging from what we find in the media, it has. For example, when Hans Schattle (forthcoming) surveyed a sample of international news sources to find out how widely global thinking has been diffused, he found a dramatic increase in writers' use of the term over the last decade of the twentieth century.[6] "Global citizenship" registered an average yearly gain of 35 percent between 1991 and 2000 in Schattle's broad range of media sources. And although there was a sharp spike in the term's appearance during the excitement over the "Battle of Seattle" in 1999–2000, there was an even sharper increase at the beginning

[6] Schattle relied upon the *Westlaw All News Plus* archive from January 1, 1991, to December 31, 2000, a database that contains the complete contents of more than 6,000 newspapers, magazines, trade journals, newswires, press releases, and transcripts of broadcasts and speeches. He searched for references to world citizenship, global citizenship, international citizenship, earth citizenship, and planetary citizenship. He found more than 17,000 documents containing these terms, before settling on "global citizenship" as his key search term. For information on the methodology and the detailed findings, see Schattle, forthcoming. I am grateful to Hans Schattle for allowing me to consult and cite his as-yet unpublished book.

of the 1990s. Of course, what the media *say* about global thinking may be another matter: W. Lance Bennett and his collaborators found that even when journalists give adequate coverage to globalization protests, they appear to get most of their information from the movement's opponents (Bennett et al. 2004).

James Mittelman (2004b), who has done some of the most serious studies of globalization, tracked the term's use by intellectuals through a careful reading of scholarly books and articles. He argues that globalization has transformed the ways in which knowledge is produced and ideologies spawned. "Globalization is becoming a form of intellectual power embodied in a knowledge system, propagated by institutionalized authority, and manifested in neoliberal ideology" (2004b: xi). For those who hold power and possess wealth, writes Mittelman, globalization is an ideology of freedom; for those who do not, globalization is experienced as an ideology of domination.

Limited Elite Globality

But beyond the media and intellectuals, has global thinking produced global identities? Among elites, the data are less than convincing. Globalization is certainly a term that they recognize and, for the most part, find attractive. When James Rosenau and his collaborators interviewed a sample of American elites in 1999 and 2003, they found that proportions of more than 70 percent saw it enhancing the creation of jobs, of economic integration, and of capitalism in general (Rosenau and Earnest 2004: 4). And although roughly 30 percent saw it widening the gap between rich and poor (p. 7), virtually none saw it as a threat to their own well-being (p. 3).

But do elites think globally? That depends on what we believe "thinking globally" entails. The majority of the American elites interviewed by Rosenau and his colleagues think of themselves primarily as citizens of the United States (Rosenau et al., forthcoming: ch. 3). This was even true of those whom they categorized as being "on the cutting edge" of globalization through their international ties and activities.[7] These "cutting edgers did

---

[7] On the other hand, Rosenau and Earnest's (2004: 13) article shows that a high proportion of the respondents in both their surveys considered international institutions and organizations to be either very important or somewhat important in world affairs. This was even true after 9/11 and the approaching Iraq war had triggered an orgy of official unilateralism. Rosenau and Earnest report a small increase in the proportion who considered the UN to be "very important" between 1999 and 2003, and small declines in those who considered the World

not see the effects of globalization very differently than those who operate at home. When the elites were asked, "On balance, how would you assess the impact of the diverse processes of globalization" for a variety of problems and processes (e.g., its effects on local communities, human rights, political democracy, cultural diversity, the environment, and ethnic identities), there were few significant differences between the two groups (Rosenau and Earnest 2004: 17).[8] Overall, it does not appear that involvement in global processes induces elites to think more globally than others.

What about elites' working relationships? Surely, more and more business executives are engaged in international trade and finance (Ohmae 1995), and this could increase their involvement in transnational networks. But businessmen who are engaged in international markets are still tied into essentially national networks. William Carroll and Miendert Fennema (2002), who examined interlocking directorates among corporations and changes in these structures between 1976 and 1996, illustrate the difference. On the one hand, Carroll and Fennema found a moderate increase in the transnational integration of business directorates, offering support for the strong globalization thesis. But between 1976 and 1996 the actual density of the ties at the center of the network remained essentially constant (p. 410) and the increase in interlocking memberships was largely accounted for by an increase in the proportion of outside board members (pp. 411, 415). The book is still open on whether global macroprocesses are producing globalized elites or simply men and women who, through their work and travel abroad, have international contacts.

Unglobal Citizens

What of ordinary citizens? Have they begun to "think globally"? If there is anywhere in the world where we would expect to see such a shift it would be in Western Europe. But after fifty years of increasing integration, national attachments are still overwhelmingly dominant among Western European

Bank, the WTO, and the IMF "very important." Most of these changes were not statistically significant.

[8] Interestingly, those who were *not* involved in global processes became *more* concerned with the consequences of globalization after September 11, 2001, than the same group in 1999. The largest increases for these "non-cutting edgers" were found in assessing as negative the impact of globalization on local communities (+8 percent), on human rights (+6 percent), on political democracy (+8 percent), and on ecological sensitivities (+15 percent), the only change that was statistically significant at the .001 level.

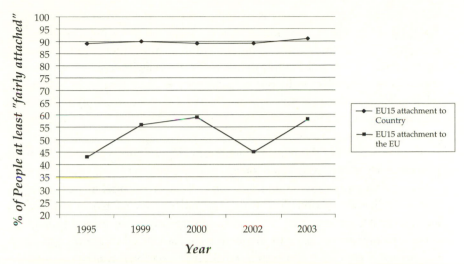

Figure 4.3 Supranational and National Attachments: Citizens of European Union Countries, 1995–2003. *Source: Eurobarometer* 44 (Autumn 1995); 51 (Spring 1999); 54 (Autumn 2000); 58 (Autumn 2002); and 60 (Autumn 2003).

citizens. Figure 4.3, based on Eurobarometer surveys between 1995 and 2003, compares the proportion of EU citizens who claim a national attachment with those who claim a European one. As the figure shows, as the European Union was creating a single market and instituting a common currency, the proportion of those whose primary attachments were local or national remained more than 80 percent and hardly budged over time. Nor is there is an overall trend toward greater European attachments, and these remain well below national or local identities. As Pippa Norris (2000: 157) concluded from her analysis of two World Values Survey polls in the 1990s, "there is little evidence that this process [i.e., globalization] has generated a growing sense of European identity and community among its citizens, even among the public in long-standing member states like Germany."[9]

Of course, Europeans' territorial identities are heavily colored by their attitudes toward the political implications of European integration. What of global thinking among the world's citizens more generally? Using World

---

[9] In their analysis of a 2001 Eurobarometer survey, Gary Marks and Liesbet Hooghe (2003: table 4) found a positive, significant, and largely robust correlation at the individual level between national attachments and support for European integration. They conclude: "The greater citizens' pride in and attachment to their nation, the greater is their support for European integration" (p. 19).

Values Survey studies of citizens in eighteen countries between 1981 and 2001, Jai Kwan Jung (2005) found slim evidence for the growth of global identities. He did find "continental" or "global" attachments more often among younger cohorts, but more than half the public interviewed in these surveys saw themselves as belonging primarily to their locality or region, while about one-third identified primarily with their nations. Only about 10 percent of the people interviewed were primarily attached to their continent or to the world as a whole.

In summary, from the bits and pieces of evidence surveyed have, it appears that while intellectuals and journalists have begun to propagate global thinking, among both elites and ordinary citizens territorial identities are narrowly diffused, nationally contingent, and remain rooted in national and regional contexts. If citizens' attitudes are becoming more "global," these attachments coexist with national identities. If elites are part of an international system, it is a system with strong national roots that more closely resembles a dispersed set of unequal spatial relations than an integrated global network. This takes us to the appeal of global thinking among transnational activists.

The Real Globalizers

During the 1990s protests against global neoliberalism and on behalf of global themes increased geometrically. When Bruce Podobnik (2004) carried out a content analysis of "globalization" protest events over the period 1990–2002,[10] his analyses showed that "the globalization protest movement has been a feature of the world-system throughout the 1990s," with an increase in the number of protest events in the second half of the decade and a sharp upward spike at the turn of the century (p. 8). While workers who were protesting plant closings, outsourcing, and exploitation by foreign corporations were the most consistently mentioned actors in the news reports throughout the period, protests against international institutions and the presence of "environmentalists, students/youth, and NGO/human rights advocates" mushroomed in the news reports after January 1999 (p. 12).

---

[10] Podobnik's (2004: 4) search was unusually thorough. In a model of effective event history analysis, he searched seventeen international press sources through Lexis-Nexus with the following combination of search terms: "(protest! And global!) or (protest! And (international ws/l monetary w/1 fund)) or (protests! And imf) or (protest! And (worldw/1 bank))or (protest! And gatt) or (protest!and (world w/1 trade w/1 organization)) or (protest! And wto) or (protest! And summit)."

What was the appeal? Although there are as many motives for protesting against globalization as there are aspects of the phenomenon itself, for activists the globalization theme has an extraordinary "frame-bridging" capacity, bringing together opponents of free trade, supporters of a cleaner environment, those who demand access for Third World farmers to Western markets, opponents of neoliberalism, and supporters of global democracy. As the final document of the second World Social Forum (WSF) in Porto Alegre proclaimed: "We are diverse – women and men, adults and youth, indigenous peoples, rural and urban, workers and the unemployed, homeless, the elderly, students, migrants, professionals, peoples of every creed, color and sexual orientation" (quoted in della Porta et al. 2006: ch. 3).[11]

The World Social Forum's stress on unity in diversity was not an isolated pronouncement. In recent years, growing numbers of NGOs around the world have adopted what Jackie Smith calls "multi-issue frames." According to Smith (2004a: 14), "the number of [transnational] groups adopting multi-issue organizing frames doubled between 1993 and 2000," especially in the countries of the global South.

Part of the explanation for this growth in global protests and multi-issue transnational groups is the availability of common targets. The WTO, which came into prominence in the mid-1990s, made a particularly attractive one. Although it made no pretense of representativeness, it appeared as a powerful force, holding its meetings to great public fanfare to decide the future of the global economy. Like any good "master frame," the WTO condensed in one simple image a wide range of prospective targets. At Seattle, writes Mark Lichbach (2003: 36–7), "Labor, anarchists, and other political groups used the idea that the WTO was a capitalist tool or an instrument for capitalist globalization to either mobilize constituents or cast doubts on the WTO's ability to reform itself."

The United States – often fused with the WTO in activists' framing of globalization – serves as a second condensing symbol. When an establishment figure such as Zbigniew Brzezinski (1997: 27) can describe the IMF and the World Bank as "part of the American system of the global web of specialized organizations," it is hardly surprising that protesters against neoliberalism make the same deduction. American militarism since 9/11 also builds up that country's image as a dominant economic actor. The fact that the hegemonic state in the world today is also the core of a global financial

---

[11] The translation is from Andretta 2005.

system governed by international institutions in which it holds predominant power facilitates the bridging of globalization, anti-imperialism, and internationalization into one unified supertarget.

Global frame bridging appears in many domestic protest campaigns too. Consider the protests against McDonald's that we saw in France and the antigenetic modification protests all over Europe in the late 1990s. In both cases, the protesters merged opposition to a foreign corporation with hostility to the policies of the United States, the European Union, and the national governments where they live (Kettnaker 2001). Global justice is an effective frame for domestic contention because it facilitates the condensation of many distinct targets in the same protest campaign.

From studies of transnational protest events in Europe, Donatella della Porta has investigated how participants in the European Social Forum of 2002 framed their participation in these activities. She emphasizes the shift from single-movement identities to "multiple, *tolerant* identities," which she sees helping the movement deal with its heterogeneous bases (2005b: 186). The activists stressed the diversity of the movement, its inclusiveness, their mistrust of institutions, and their insistence on their global identities. "If we look at the movement identities," she writes, "recent research indicates that a large majority of the activists taking part in recent demonstrations against international summits identify themselves with a movement critical of globalization" (p. 177). Global justice has proven an excellent frame-bridging symbol.

Frame Transformation

But does it have the same capacity for frame transformation? Here, the evidence is less convincing. This was already clear after the "Battle of Seattle," when observers wondered if such a movement could continue to unite "French farmers, Korean greens, Canadian wheat growers, Mexican environmentalists, Chinese dissidents, Ecuadorian anti-dam protesters, U'wa tribespeople from the Colombian rainforest and British campaigns against genetically modified foods" (Cockburn and St. Clair 2000: 28).

Gaps soon emerged in the global justice umbrella between material interests and global ideals; between global ideals and social identities; among northern and southern activists; between governments of the South and activists from their countries; and between reformers and radicals (Lichbach 2003: 54–8). In Chapter 9, I turn to the problem of building transnational coalitions against common targets among activists from different parts of the world. Here the issue is rather how activists construct a template that is both relevant to local issues and resonates with the broader theme of global justice.

The global justice frame lacks a clear directive toward a strategic repertoire of collective action. Consider how it relates to the more familiar theme of social justice. Massimiliano Andretta traced both concepts through a content analysis of five international meetings and countersummits (della Porta et al. 2006: ch. 5; Andretta 2005).[12] At the European Social Forum, he found that the salience of "social justice" varied from a quarter of the British activists to more than one-half of the Spanish ones (Andretta 2005: table 1). Even more uneven was the presence of the theme of "anticapitalism," which he found among half of the British activists but in just over 10 percent of the French ones. The "global justice" frame has not created a unified strategic repertoire.

Conclusions

In interpreting these findings, Andretta turned to the national social movement sector of each country as the source of these wide differences in framing global justice. And this is precisely the point: if national social movements vary in their "meaning work," this is because activists must work within the power structures and political cultures of their own countries. Resources, opportunities, and relative power positions differ; domestic allies are either available or absent; and few local citizens engage naturally in "global thinking"; the rest will need a great deal of persuasion to accept global interpretations of their local claims. At a rhetorical level, almost all such variations can be reconciled; but when it comes to organizing collective action, national political cultures are resilient obstacles.

This is a conclusion to which many international activists working in democratizing countries have reluctantly come. Consider the research that Sarah Mendelson and Ted Gerber report in the three regions of Russia where their group tried to encourage local activists to engage in "social marketing." With some differences from region to region, Mendelson and Gerber (2004: 2) found that the closed dissident culture of the Soviet period

---

[12] Andretta analyzed the documents of the Seattle protests in 1999, the first and second Porto Alegre meetings of the World Social Forum in 2001 and 2002, the Genoa protest against the G-8 in July 2001, and the meeting of the European Social Forum in Florence in November 2002. For his detailed analysis of the European Social Forum, see della Porta et al. 2005: ch. 3).

left local activists unprepared for the most elementary forms of strategic outreach. "Intelligentsia culture inhibits strategic action and engagement with the public on the part of organizations that Russians and outsiders might turn to for leadership on human rights. Rather than seek to influence public opinion via concerted campaigns, these organizations devote their energies to displaying the authenticity of their commitment to human rights norms."[13]

Transnational activists are often divided between the global framing of transnational movement campaigns and the local needs of those whose claims they want to represent. Consider the global campaign against the genetic modification (GM) of seeds. In wealthy Western Europe, this campaign produced a powerful grass-roots and lobbying movement against the importation of American genetic seeds (Kettnaker 2001). But in India, where many farmers are desperately poor and where the savings from genetic seeds may be substantial, ecological and development activists are divided between the "global" goals of anti-GM campaigners and the needs of the farmers they hope to represent (Herring 2005). For many Indians, the "local" has clear contradictions with the "global."

Global framing can dignify and generalize claims that might otherwise remain narrow and parochial. It signals to overworked and isolated activists that there are people beyond the horizon who share their grievances and support their causes. But by turning attention to distant targets, it holds the danger of detaching activism from the real-life needs of the people they want to represent. As Naomi Klein (2004: 227) writes,

We need to be able to show that globalization – this version of globalization – has been built on the back of local human welfare. . . . we sometimes seem to have *two activist solitudes*. On the one hand, there are the international anti-globalization activists who may be enjoying a triumphant mood, but seem to be fighting far-away issues, unconnected to people's day-to-day struggles. . . . On the other hand, there are community activists fighting daily struggles for survival, or for the preservation of the most elementary public services, who are often feeling burnt-out and demoralized.

---

[13] I am grateful to Sarah Mendelson and Ted Gerber for permission to quote this passage from their unpublished paper.

A Model of Internalization

I define internalization as *the migration of international pressures and conflicts into domestic politics and the triangular relationship that this creates among ordinary people, their governments, and international institutions.* The particular mechanisms we find within it are:

- *External pressure* to adopt the policies of international institutions, which can range from advice to incentives to the threat of financial sanctions and regulation
- *Implementation* of these policies by governments
- *protest* that results among citizen groups, whose object is the international policy but whose target is the government that implements it
- *Repression* by local governments against the protesting groups or *concessions* offered to them, as well as *brokerage* on the part of governments between the citizens and the international institution

Let me not claim too much. Figure 5.1 is intended as a scaffolding on which to develop evidence about the reciprocal interactions among international institutions, national governments, and their citizens. It offers no specific hypotheses about how different combinations of mechanisms intersect and makes no specific predictions about the outcomes of the process. But Figure 5.1 does make three important claims:

- International institutions that impinge on domestic politics trigger protests whose targets are mainly the governments that attempt to implement their policies.
- As a consequence, governments are forced into a two-level game between their citizens and these institutions.
- Governments are not helplessly caught in a no-win bind but can respond as brokers mediating between domestic claims and external pressures.

I illustrate these claims with evidence from protests against European Union policies in Western Europe, where two generations of political and economic integration have locked nonstate actors, national governments, and supranational institutions into a composite polity.

Protest in a Composite Polity

For several reasons, Western Europe during the past few decades is a good laboratory in which to study the process of internalization. First,

5

Internalizing Contention

In late August 2004, as American troops were pulverizing the holy city of Najaf to root out a group of Shi'ite insurgents from the holy mosque of Ali, two unfortunate French journalists were sequestered by a different group of militants. Like many other such kidnappings in Iraq, this one led to demands and to a threat of beheadings if the demands were not met. But there was a difference: rather than threaten the countries engaged in "Operation Iraqi Freedom," this kidnapping was aimed at a country – France – that had staunchly opposed the war and refused to join the occupation. If the French government did not revoke a recently passed law banning the wearing of Islamic head coverings in French public schools, the kidnappers threatened, the journalists would pay with their lives.[1]

This was a remarkable turn of events for several reasons. First, not for the first time, Islamist militants showed a total lack of understanding of who their friends were – or, at least, which countries they had a chance of exploiting in opposing their enemies. Second, as it turned out, the kidnapping had a perverse impact on Muslim opinion within France, turning many who had opposed the law banning the head scarf into supporters of the French republic's right to regulate its own mores. Third, and most broadly, the incident showed how deeply penetrated domestic and international contention had become by the beginning of the new century.

"Who would have thought a piece of cloth could threaten the stability of the French State?" journalist Elaine Sciolino wrote in the spring of 2004 in the *New York Times* (Feb. 8, 2004, 4). Who would not? In a country in which religious wars raged for over a century, where the Revolution savagely repressed holdout Catholic priests, the role of religious schools was settled

---

[1] http://www.cnn.com/2004/WORLD/meast/08/28/iraq.main/, visited November 23, 2004.

only in 1905, and the Vichy government sent more Jews to the death camps than its Nazi masters demanded, the relations between religion and politics have always been ambivalent.

But in the "affair of the head scarf," there was something new and more alarming to French secularists (Gaspard and Khosrokhavar 1995). Rather than reacting to an internal threat, or demonstrating a visceral xenophobia, the government's attempt to legislate head scarves out of the public schools reflected a deep fear of the intrusion of transnational Islam into French society, a fear that was reinforced when the journalists were kidnapped a few months later.

Was the government's fear of the head scarf exaggerated and no more than a reflection of domestic political conflict? In the background was the recent success of the right-wing leader of the Front national, Jean Marie Le Pen, who had forced the Socialist candidate, Lionel Jospin, out of the second round of the presidential elections in 2002. Many people thought that France's center-right government was aiming the head scarf law not at young female Muslims but at Le Pen's electoral threat. But at least one external source, Osama Bin Laden's lieutenant, Dr. Ayman al-Zawahiri, saw the conflict in more global terms. In a tape broadcast on the Dubai-based network Al Arabiya, he attacked the French government for banning the head scarf. "France," he declaimed, "the country of liberty, defends only the liberty of nudity, debauchery and decay, while fighting chastity and modesty" (*New York Times*, Feb. 25, 2004, A8).

Muslim immigration to France and the ensuing xenophobic reaction is nothing new. Immigration from North Africa began before World War II, mushroomed with the need for cheap labor in the 1950s and 1960s, and leveled off in the 1970s after the government passed restrictive immigration policies. As in many immigrant communities, the first arrivals were single men, often living in hostels and practicing their religion, if at all, in private. But as families began to follow and the second-generation population grew, Muslims became more numerous and more visible, often practicing their daily prayers in the fields or outside their workplaces.

This was not the only threat that French secularists feared from the expansion of Islamism. As Sciolino continued, "These days, a small but determined minority of France's Muslims has begun to make demands that clash vividly with [France's secular] ideal. They include calls for sex-segregated gym classes and swimming pools for girls and prayer breaks within the standard baccalaureat exams at the end of high school" (p. 4). These developments touched a deep nerve of French secularism, or *laicité*. But the

government's response was no mere problem *à la française*: the conflict over the wearing of the *foulard* in schools all over Europe was an internalization of the global Muslim revival of the past few decades.

That revival had begun with the emergence of small antisecular Islamist groups in South Asia and the Middle East after World War II (Kepel 2002); it crystallized around the creation of an Islamic republic in Iran in 1979, and the diffusion of its message to Lebanon and North Africa in the 1980s; and with its spread to Western Europe through immigration and diasporic links. It became more savage with the running sore of the Israeli-Palestinian conflict in the late 1990s, the anti-Semitic incidents that followed, and the American occupation of Afghanistan and Iraq. Political Islamism has become transnational in its constituencies, its organizations, and its targets.

Needless to say, not all countries are equally vulnerable to the intrusion of external forces. But in France, this transnational Islamist movement was quickly internalized, for it fed into both the residues of the domestic church-state cleavage and the threat from the National Front. The conflict over the wearing of the head scarf in French schools was a dramatic example of what, in this chapter, I call "internalization." By this term I do not mean internalization in a psychological sense, but the migration of international pressures and conflicts into domestic politics. When domestic groups employ contentious politics against international, state, or nonstate actors on domestic ground, we can say that their response is a case of internalization.

International pressures can take a variety of forms, from the kinds of threats reflected in the kidnapping of the French journalists in Iraq, to the use of foreign governments' power to influence domestic elections, to the imposition of common standards and rules of behavior by international institutions, as in the IMF's structural adjustment policies or the European Union's "growth and stabilization" pact in the 1990s. Narrowing the focus in this chapter to the impact of international institutions, I propose a simple descriptive model of internalization, specifying that process through a number of interacting mechanisms. I then return to Western Europe with an examination of protests touched off by European Union Policies in member states. My reasoning is this: if the process of internalization is general effect of internationalism, we should find it in particularly intense form in the domestic politics of "best case" scenarios like Western Europe, where a strong supranational authority provides a visible target for the claims of local citizens.

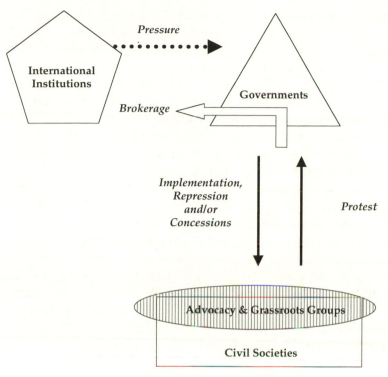

Figure 5.1 A Descriptive Model of Internalization

given its long history of integration and the extraordinary supranational powers it has developed, if the internalization of protest is occurring anywhere, it will be in the European Union. Second, the EU is built around both intergovernmental and supranational principles, its directives implemented by national courts and administrators, and its policies reaching deeply within the member states. Third, in Western Europe we have a body of fairly good empirical evidence about transnational politics.

In the long and many-sided debate about the nature and dynamics of the European Union three main models have emerged. For some observers the EU is a classical *intergovernmental* agreement, with the codicil that this agreement is ongoing and has produced powerful mechanisms for monitoring compliance (Moravcsik 1996; Hoffmann 1966). This approach has little to say about contentious politics but implies that it is the business of national governments.

For a second group of observers, the EU is a *supranational body* that has developed according to a functionalist logic in which the incentives for cooperation and compliance have produced deepening circuits of exchange and cooperation (Sandoltz and Stone Sweet 1998; Stone Sweet, Sandholtz, and Fligstein 2001). Unlike the intergovernmental approach, this one includes nonstate actors, most often in the form of elite interest groups interacting in institutionalized policy networks.

For a third group of scholars, the EU is a structure of *multilevel governance* in which subnational, national, and supranational agents continuously interact. Liesbet Hooghe and Gary Marks (2002) offer a down-to-earth focus on the transactions among public and private actors that reach deeply inside the member states. But their central concept of "governance" leads Hooghe and Marks to focus predominantly on elites – albeit at the subnational level – leaving citizens as objects of policy and offering no mechanisms of political change.

Drawing on the work of Hooghe and Marks but following historian Wayne te Brake (1998), I regard the European Union as a "composite polity," one in which different areas of policy produce a shifting set of alignments among nonstate actors, supranational authorities, and national states (Tarrow 2004). These alignments take four main forms:

- *National-supranational alignments* in which national states cooperate with supranational authorities in the implementation of common policies, sometimes against the wishes of their own citizens
- *Supranational-local alignments* in which EU officials form alliances with substate and nonstate actors, sometimes without the agreement of their own governments
- *Popular-national alignments* in which citizens and their governments combine against EU policies
- *Transnational coalitions* among governmental, nongovernmental, and supranational agents

What we see in the European Union is a variable geometry of internationalism in which alignments and conflicts shift according to the issue, the political and institutional context, and the stage of decision making. The alignment of nonstate actors with their national governments in response to an EU policy is the first form of internalization I examine. It can be seen in the following pungent example, one that also shows how domestic actors can externalize their claims (see Chapter 8).

Fish Wars[2]

The story begins with a bureaucratic regulation by a supranational agency, the European Commission, that involves the protests of Spanish fishermen (the domestic actors), their interest group, the Spanish government, and the governments and navies of other European states. Seeking to stem the decline of the ocean's fish stocks, the commission had passed new regulations in 1994 limiting the length of the nets that industrial trawlers could use. The big French and British trawlers were most affected by this regulation, while the much smaller Spanish vessels went after tuna with antiquated equipment and much smaller nets. The conflict pitted Spanish fishermen against their French and British competitors over fishing rights. As the *European* described it at the time: "Spanish tuna fishermen sailed home...after a two-day battle with their French counterparts some 700 km. off Spain's northwestern coast of Galicia. The Spanish brought back a captured boat [the *Gabrielle*] they claim will support allegations that the French violate fishing quotas and methods."[3]

In these days of depleted fish stocks, such conflicts were becoming common. But this one escalated. When the *Gabrielle* was seized on the high seas, the French replied that its nets were legal, demanded its immediate restitution, and reciprocated by capturing a Spanish ship and towing it into a French port.[4]

Whatever its legal basis, the French maneuver seemed to work. In Galicia, the *boniteros* who had made off with the *Gabrielle* were convinced by Spanish authorities to return the vessel. In Brussels, Spain's agriculture and fisheries minister met with his French counterpart, who agreed to cut the length of the French nets to the 2.5-kilometer limit and allow EU inspectors onto the French ships. The tuna war seemed to be over.[5] But in August, the *boniteros* were back on the high seas, this time hacking off the nets of two British fishing boats and an Irish one with their propellers, accusing them of using nets that were longer than the EU limit, and taking

[2] I draw here upon the narrative of this episode from my "Europeanisation of Conflict: Reflections from a Social Movement Perspective" (1995: 225–28).

[3] "Spanish Fishermen Seize French Boat in Tuna War," *European*, July 22–8, 1994, 6.

[4] See "La armada francesa captura un barco de España en repesalia por el conflicto pesquero," *El País*, July 25, 1994, 20, for the Spanish side of the story.

[5] See "Le conflit entre pêcheurs espagnols et français semble s'apaiser," *Le Monde*, July 22 1994, 13, "L'accord entre les professionnels de l'île d'Yeu et Jean Puech n'a pas calmé les courroux des pêcheurs espanols," *Le Monde*, July 28, 1994, 17, and "La 'guerre du thon' au large des Landes," *Le Monde*, August 20, 1994, 1.

endangered dolphins along with the tuna catch.[6] With typical British phlegm, Whitehall blithely claimed that *their* nets were environmentally friendly: though longer than the EU limit, they made up for their greater length with holes designed to let the apparently smarter dolphins through.[7]

Environmental activists sailed into the fray on the high seas as well, when Greenpeace sent a ship to inspect the British and French nets. The French – who have a long and violent relationship with this organization – attacked it with water cannon and a stun grenade, accusing its captain of attempting to cut the nets of French trawlers. Greenpeace denied it, claiming its ship was merely trying to record whether the French were taking endangered dolphins.[8]

A National-Local Alignment

Splashed across the headlines of four countries, the fish wars were redolent with folkloric images of sputtering French officials, archaic Spanish ships, tight-lipped British civil servants, and jeering fishermen. But beneath the surface, serious issues were at stake: the claims of a fishing industry that directly or indirectly employs over a million people, the ability of medium-sized states like Spain to protect their citizens' interests, and the power of international agencies to regulate a major global industry.

Nonstate actors, states, and international institutions interacted in a dynamic process of transnational contention that Figure 5.1 traces fairly well. Although there was no external pressure equivalent to IMF demands for stabilization and austerity (see Chapter 4), the EU fishing limits placed serious pressure on the capacity of the archaic Spanish fishing fleet to compete with larger French and British trawlers; although the object of the *boniteros'* protest was foreign trawlers, the aim was to embarrass their own

---

[6] See "Los boniteros espanoles rompen redes ilegales a barcos britànicos e irlandeses," *El País*, August 8, 1994, 21.

[7] See "Navy Moves in to Stop Tuna War 'Wolf Packs,'" *London Times*, August 5, 1994, 1.

[8] Six months after the episode in the Bay of Biscay, the fish wars were back in the news when Spanish fishermen were caught fishing for turbot in Canadian waters and the Canadian navy seized a Spanish ship, the *Estai*, that was violating Canada's self-declared 200-mile limit. When it was towed into the harbor of St. John's, its captain was spattered with rotten eggs as he walked a gauntlet of jeering fisherfolk. The Spanish responded by sending warships to the area, taking Canada to the International Court of Justice, and asking the European Union to impose sanctions on Canadian goods. In the end, Ottawa agreed to compensate Spain for the lost fish but, in return, gained a limitation on the size of the catch that European trawlers could take from the Grand Banks (Croci 1995).

government and force it to negotiate more vigorously on their behalf in Brussels. And that is exactly what happened: in meetings with the commission and the French and British ministers, the Spanish government brokered a deal whereby EU inspectors were placed on the suspected trawlers and the demands of the Spanish fishermen were partially met.

It would be hazardous to speculate about the long-term consequences of a single episode like the fish wars, either for Spanish politics or for the European Union. What we can induce from the story is that an external conflict was purposely triggered by a group of domestic actors (albeit on the high seas) to maneuver their government into defending their interests more effectively vis-à-vis other actors in the framework of an international institution. Is this a general pattern or only a fishy story? To gain confidence that the internalization of protest is a robust aspect of Europeanization, we need more systematic evidence.

The Changing World of European Contention

Has the shift of authority to the European level been matched by a secular shift in the targets of protest from the local and national levels to supranational authorities? Quantitative data will help us to see whether such a shift is occurring and if it is producing transnational alliances across boundaries, or merely the internalization of international pressures into domestic contention.

Mapping European Contention[9]

Using Reuters news wire reports, Imig and Tarrow tracked the patterns of European collective action over the recent history of European integration (Imig and Tarrow 2001: ch. 2).[10] They found a broad and evolving spectrum of routine forms of political engagement, including strikes, marches, and rallies, as well as more-violent forms, like rock throwing, hunger strikes,

---

[9] This part of the analysis draws on Doug Imig's and my chapter of the same title in Imig and Tarrow 2001. My thanks to Imig and to Rowman and Littlefield for permission to summarize our findings from *Contentious Europeans*.

[10] The data set covered the fourteen full years from January 1, 1984, through December 31, 1997, and was built from an analysis of every political report filed with Reuters for the twelve nations that were members of the EU for the majority of this time period. Within this record, there were accounts of some 9,872 discrete contentious political events, launched by a broad range of social actors. For more details, see the appendix in Imig and Tarrow 2001.

and soccer hooliganism. They also found a range of confrontational – but generally peaceful – forms of protest, including obstructions, blockades, and sit-ins.

Imig and Tarrow did not consider all protests that took place in the EU member states to be "European." On the contrary, the vast majority of the actions were carried out by domestic actors and aimed at domestic public or private targets.[11] Only those events that in some way involved the European Union fit the definition of European protests: that is, *incidents of contentious claims making in which the EU or one of its agencies was in some way either the source, the direct target, or an indirect target of protests.*

Within this broad category, there were two broad subtypes:

- *Internalized protests*:[12] contentious claims making in which the EU or one of its agencies was either the source or an indirect target of a protest by domestic actors, but the direct target of the action was either the state, its components, or other domestic actors present on its territory
- *Transnational protests*: instances of contentious claims making in which the EU was either the source, the direct target, or the indirect target, and actors from more than one EU member state took part

Working within this set of parameters, there were 490 contentious events during this fifteen-year period that fit the definition of European contentious events.[13] These events provide the foundation for the discussion of protests against the EU.

Euro-Protest

Figure 5.2 plots both the frequency and the percentage of Western European contentious events that were generated in response to EU policies

---

[11] This skewed distribution has since been confirmed in subsequent research based on different sources (Imig and Trif 2003; Rootes 2003).

[12] In their earlier analysis, Imig and Tarrow called these protests "domesticated," a locution I have since abandoned because it led some readers to assume that we were considering them to be pacific. The term "internalized" has no such implication.

[13] In order to be sure they were dealing with contentious events that were most clearly examples of Europeanization, Imig and Tarrow adopted a conservative operationalization of the concept of European contentious events. In the findings reported here, an institution or policy of the EU had to be linked to the protest action in the first sentence of a media report in order for that action to be included in our subset of Euro-protests.

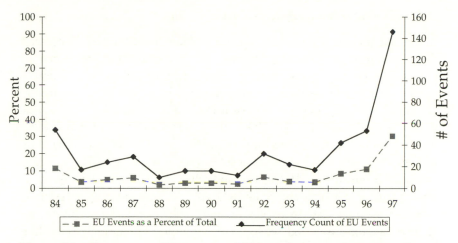

Figure 5.2 Frequency and Percentage of Western European Contentious Events Provoked by European Union Policies and Institutions, 1984–97. *Source:* Imig and Tarrow 2001: 35.

and institutions between 1983 and 1997. As the trend lines in the figure suggest, although EU-motivated protests account for only a small share of the total, they rose rapidly after the signature of the Maastricht Accords as a percentage of all reported contentious political activity. Europeans were moderately more likely to take to the streets in protest against the European Union, its agents, and its policies after 1992 – although still much less often than they protested against domestic grievances. We can infer that while Europeans continued to regard the nation-state as the source and the main target of their collective action in the 1980s and 1990s, there were hints of an increasing volume of protests against the EU or its policies.

Note that this trend was not observable in all sectors of EU activity. Christopher Rootes (2003: 383) reports from his research on the European environmental movements that, although "a few mostly small and symbolic transnational demonstrations have been staged in Brussels or Strasbourg," "collective action occurs overwhelmingly *within* nation states in the form of mobilizations confined to the local or national level." Dieter Rucht (2002) reports similar results for Germany. Later we will see that the social actors who make claims against the EU were very different than the "new" social movements that Rootes and Rucht studied.

Crucial Junctures and Long-Term Trends

In a recent analysis, Doug McAdam and William Sewell Jr. (2001) stressed the importance of "crucial junctures" in the timing and frequency of contentious politics. Were there specific events or phases in EU development that triggered peaks in European protest, or was there a more incremental and linear development of European contention? We have seen that, at least through the late 1990s, there was a long-term trend toward more Europe-directed collective action. But the more-erratic inflections in Figure 5.2 suggest that both processes were at work. A critical juncture marked the mid-to-late 1990s, a period when the EU was attempting to implement its "Growth and Stability Pact," an agreement that required each EU member state to reduce its budget deficits. Looking inside the Reuters data for this period, we see many attempts of domestic groups, like pensioners or public service workers, to demand exemptions from the deep budget cuts that their governments were threatening. The trend could be seen in many parts of the European Union, but it was particularly marked in Italy, where it coincided with a major change in political alignment.

Internalization in Italy

Since the initial expansion of its welfare system in the 1960s, Italy had accumulated a massive public debt, which could be met only through public borrowing. Successive governments met the crisis by allowing cycles of inflation, corrected by regular devaluations. That strategy could work as long as Italian finance was autonomous, but if the government did not curb its public spending in the years following the Maastricht Accords, it would suffer the humiliation of being excluded from the European Monetary Union. Two prime ministers, Carlo Azeglio Ciampi and Giuliano Amato – both, it should be noted, representing the Center-Left – used the menace of the growth and stabilization criteria to introduce cuts in the nation's spending that governments of the Center-Right had avoided. As a result of these budget cuts, by the late 1990s current spending was covered by revenues and Italy entered the Eurozone and adopted the Euro.

Italy's budget-cutting exercise was forced on the country by the Maastricht criteria, but it was fought out politically on domestic ground. In response to this external pressure, Italians engaged in their habitual protest behavior, especially pensioners who stood to lose the most, but also workers in nationalized industries, farmers and milk producers, and even shopkeepers who mainly supported the first Berlusconi government's effort to turn Italy toward a liberal market economy. But in the end, it was a Center-Left government, with support from internationally oriented business and neutrality from the reluctant trade unions, that used EU pressure as a lever to pry budget-cutting reductions out of many domestic actors (Sbragia 2001; Tarrow 2004).

Italians were not alone in responding to the Maastricht stabilization criteria with internal protests. As the deadline for meeting the Maastricht criteria approached, there was a sharp upturn in protests by various social actors all over the EU. Farmers, manufacturing workers, miners, pensioners, and public-welfare clients marched, demonstrated, blocked the entrances to offices and banks, and lobbied their governments to soften the blow. These subnational actors were protesting indirectly against European policies by demonstrating internally against their own governments. The same thing was happening in agricultural reform.

Opposing Agricultural Reform

When the Common Agricultural Policy (CAP) was reformed in the early 1990s, a wave of French farm protests followed (Bush and Simi 2001; Roederer 1999, 2000). As is well known, payments to farmers were then the largest item in the European Union's budget. These benefits helped large agricultural producers, like France, which had been careful to write aid to small farmers into the original European treaty and were resented by member states like the United Kingdom, which imports most of its food and was not present at the founding of the European project. This imbalance has led to continual pressure from nonbeneficiary countries to reform the CAP, and to resistance from farmers' groups and their governments to any reform that would reduce agricultural subsidies. In the early 1990s, proponents of CAP reform argued that the EU's generous farm subsidies distorted world trade and were the major stumbling block to a settlement in the five-year Uruguay round of international trade talks under the General Agreement on Tariffs and Trade (Bush and Simi 2001: 97).

As the negotiations on CAP reform got underway, farmers, especially French ones, took to the streets. Evelyn Bush and Pete Simi carried out a statistical analysis of some 184 protests in the member states of the EU that were mounted between 1992 and 1997. They found that the largest share of these events took place in the last quarter of 1992, during the debates on CAP reform (2001: 101). The only other significant peak of farm protest came during the British BSE crisis, when most of the protests came from Britain. Like Italian protesters against the growth and stability pact, farmers' protests against CAP reform took place mainly on domestic ground.

But although farmers saw the domestic level as their best terrain on which to exercise pressure, they sometimes protested directly against the EU. Farmers, like other Europeans, do not choose the targets of their protests at random: they protest against national ministries of agriculture when these are the immediate decision makers and against the EU when CAP reform moves to the European level (Roederer 2000). The European Union is a multilevel polity in the sense that it offers the possibilities for the *venue shopping* that is characteristic of all segmented or pluralistic political systems.

Europe's Rooted Cosmopolitans

In the 1980s many European scholars were struck by the differences between Europe's "old" social movements, mainly the labor movement, and the "new social movements" that emerged out of the 1960s, such as environmental, peace, women's, and alternative life-style movements (Kriesi et al. 1995). Two sets of hypotheses emerged about the transnational potential of Europe's "old" and "new" activists:

- With respect to the "old" movements, some observers were skeptical that, deeply rooted in their national political systems through their trade unions, workers would be able to mobilize at the European level (Marks and McAdam 1996, 1999).
- With respect to the so-called "new" social movements, drawn predominantly from the educated middle class, some argued that they may be more conscious of the global sources of the issues they care about and would be more likely to gravitate to the European level where these problems can be addressed (Yearley 1996).

Where does the truth lie? When we look at the Reuter's data, we find that occupational groups, especially workers and farmers, were much more likely than nonoccupational groups like environmentalists to protest against the EU.[14] Through the late 1990s, the former groups initiated a much larger

[14] Critics have voiced a concern that since Reuter's provides a service for international business, it may exaggerate – or at least give more prominence to – the protests of industrial

Table 5.1. *Occupational and Nonoccupational Protests against the European Union, 1984–97 (%)*

Period	Occupational Groups ($N = 402$)	Nonoccupational Groups ($N = 88$)	Total ($N = 490$)
1984–92	88.1	11.9	42.9 (210)
1993–7	77.8	21.2	57.1 (280)
TOTAL	82.1	17.9	100 (490)

Source: Imig and Tarrow 2001: 39.

share (82.1 percent) of the total EU-directed protests than the latter. It appears that the issues that affect the livelihood of farmers, workers, and other occupational groups are likely to encourage them to take contentious political action against the EU.

The greater presence of these occupational groups in European protests underscores the absence of the "new social movements" protesting against European policies and institutions. This was supported by Brussels NGO representatives in the environmental, migrant, and women's groups, who conceded that their national counterparts are largely indifferent to the importance of European decision making (see Guiraudon 2001; Helfferisch and Kolb 2001). These findings suggest either that the "new" social movements – now quite established in their own countries – are able to take advantage of political opportunities within domestic politics, or that they have found a comfortable niche within the EU's institutions and have no need to engage in contentious collective action.

This finding is particularly striking when we contrast it with data on who protests around *domestic* issues in Europe. Across the twelve nations that Imig and Tarrow studied between 1983 and 1997, they found nonoccupational groups accounting for more than twice as many protests against domestic grievances as occupationally based groups. Table 5.1 shows that occupational groups made up a much larger share of the protests triggered by the European Union in the 1990s than nonoccupational groups, who were much more domestically oriented.[15]

---

workers. I am, of course, aware of this danger, but nevertheless think it striking that so disproportionate a proportion of Euro-protests came from other occupational groups than workers.

[15] Note, however, that this imbalance declined slightly but significantly after the early 1990s.

Table 5.2. *Protests by Farmers and Other Occupational Groups against the European Union, 1984–97 (%)*

Period	Farmers (N = 200)	Other Occupational Groups (N = 202)	Total (N = 402)
1984–92	47.1	52.9	46.0 (185)
1993–7	52.1	47.9	54.0 (217)
TOTAL	49.7	50.3	100 (402)

Source: Imig and Tarrow 2001: 40.

Farmers and Other People

Which occupational groups were most active in protests against EU policies? Readers may conjecture that EU-oriented protests by occupational groups probably consist predominantly of farmers – and they would be right. Farmers' long involvement with the Common Agricultural Policy makes them more attuned to European policy than many other groups. Table 5.2 compares the distribution of EU protests by farmers with those of other occupational groups and verifies that farmers accounted for the largest share of protests against EU policies – accounting for roughly half of the protests launched by occupational groups across these fourteen years.

Alongside farmers, we find a wide range of contentious actions launched by other working people, including fishermen, construction workers, and miners, against EU policies. Not coincidentally, these groups confront the painful realities of economic integration at first hand – through reductions in agricultural subsidies and production quotas, shifting trade restrictions, limitations on net sizes and fishing territories, and layoffs and factory closures. Additionally, as West European plants relocate to newly acceding countries of East Central Europe and adopt forms of subcontracting and contracting out, Western European occupational groups have been hit by the costs of internationalism.

In summary, although there are dramatic cases of contentious politics on the part of the "new" social movements in Western Europe, the largest proportion of protests against the European Union continue to come from occupational groups fighting for their positions in Europe's economic order. Europe may be developing at the summit as the "Europe of the Bankers," but European contentious politics is emerging as the Europe of those who work. But are these protests internal or transnational? More-detailed analysis shows that an overwhelming proportion of the protests against European Union policies take place on domestic ground.

Internalization and Transnationalization

Although we find signs of both externalization and coalition building across Europe (see Chapters 8 and 9), Table 5.3 shows unequivocally that the largest number of protests against the EU in the years between 1983 and 1997 were internalized; they occurred within domestic, rather than in transnational political space and were mainly aimed at other domestic actors. Almost 83 percent of the EU-directed protests in Imig and Tarrow's events were examples of internalization, whereas only 17 percent were organized across borders. Table 5.3 also shows that the proportion of transnational and domesticated protests were more or less constant, with a slight but statistically insignificant increase in the transnational category after 1992.

Against whom were these European protests directed? Table 5.4 reports on the targets chosen when domestic contentious action was launched against European Union policies. By far the largest share of these events targeted national and subnational institutions. For example, when French farmers protested against threatened CAP reforms, most of their protests were aimed at the French state. These findings are supported by the work of Christilla Roederer (1999, 2000) on France and by Bush and Simi (2001) for three European countries. And as Bert Klandermans and his collaborators (2001) found in Spain, when Galician farmers rejected EU policies, they continued to hold their national government responsible.

Other domestic actors, foreign governments' outposts, and foreign citizens were also frequent targets of EU protests. Domestic nonstate actors

Table 5.3. *Internalized and Transnational Contentious Action against the European Union, 1984–97 (%)*

Period	Internalized Protest ($N = 406$)	Transnational Protest ($N = 84$)	Total ($N = 490$)
1984–92	84.2	15.7	42.8 (210)
1993–7	81.7	18.2	57.1 (280)
TOTAL	82.8	17.1	100 (490)

Source: Imig and Tarrow 2001: 36.

Table 5.4. *Targets of Internalized European Protests,*
1984–97 (%)

Domestic governments	56.6
Domestic private actors	17.5
Other governments and foreign nationals	17.1
Other targets	8.8

Source: Imig and Tarrow 2001: 36.

were targeted in almost one-fifth of these events. On a number of occasions, farmers angered by the imports of foreign foods responded by tipping over the produce carts of vendors who stocked the offending merchandise or by overturning the tank cars of companies importing foreign wine – a specialty of the French, in particular. Foreign nationals and foreign governments were targeted almost one-fifth of the time. These protests usually took the form of blockading foreign embassies or shutting the border to foreign imports. Finally, a smaller share of these events (just under a tenth) was aimed at a collection of objects that were tenuously linked to the EU.[16] If collective European protest is growing in relation to globalization, liberalization, and the Europeanization of policy making, it is doing so largely at home.

Conclusions

Given the goal of this chapter and the preceding one, explicating two of the "domestic" processes of transnational contention posited in Chapter 2, it will be useful to begin by stating what has *not* been claimed. First, I have not shown – nor do I believe such a trend exists – that there is a standard "resistance" to globalization around the world. We have seen in these two chapters similar protest forms independently developed against structurally equivalent situations in Latin America; global framing of what were essentially domestic claims; internalized protest by domestic actors targeting their own governments against external pressures in Europe; and a small amount of transnational protest using the resources of internationalism.

Second, by tracing the processes of global framing and internalization in Latin America and Western Europe in these two chapters, I do not claim

---

[16] This category also includes more generalized demonstrations where the direct targets of contention are difficult to identify, reflecting high levels of confusion when it comes to untangling both the "true" source of European grievances and the appropriate role for national governments to play in resolving European concerns.

that these two continents are the same or that their outcomes can be directly compared.[17] Third, I see no evidence that domestic conflict structures are giving way to the onslaught of globalization. On the contrary: most of the rooted cosmopolitans we have met continue to protest on domestic ground and frame their grievances in concrete terms against antagonists they can see, or at least reach through their own governments. And because the European Union is the archetypical international institution, what we found there is unlikely to be transcended in parts of the world in which internationalization has proceeded less far.

The claims I *do* make in this chapter and the last one can be rapidly summarized.

First, although globalization's economic impact has received the most attention in the literature, there are growing signs of political resistance as well (J. Smith and Johnston 2002). Through both conventional and unconventional forms of action, citizens are responding politically to the intrusion of external pressures and institutions on their lives. Their efforts may be less effective, as was the case in most of the IMF riots of the 1980s, or more effective, as in the well-organized protests of French farmers and Spanish fishermen. But internalized protest against external pressures seems to be a robust trend.

Second, contention does not always proceed *against* institutions, as we might be tempted to conclude from the dramatic farm protests in France or the Argentine *cacerolazos*. In domestic responses to external pressures, the institutional "moment" may be the most critical one – as it was in the illustrative "fish story." French farmers overturning tank cars carefully calibrated their protests with lobbying by their well-oiled associations in Paris and Brussels; the Spanish *boniteros* who kidnapped a French trawler lent leverage to their government in Brussels and to their representatives in Madrid. Even as they theatrically march on the highways or demonstrate in the streets of Europe, Europeans shop for the best institutional venue for their actions.

Third, when they face external pressure, governments are not as helpless as the Italian one pretended to be when it blamed the EU for the growth and

---

[17] Javier Auyero points out in a private communication to the author that when the World Bank and the IMF pressed Third World governments to decentralize health and educational services in the 1980s, there was a similar process of internalization of protest. The reforms established a triangular relationship among international institutions, states, and domestic protesters, as local governments implemented the reforms and became the targets of contention.

95

stabilization requirements. Governments' responses to external pressure vary from the enthusiastic embrace of globalization in the United States, to the populist response to IMF austerity by the Seaga government in Jamaica, to the opposition of the British government to EU pressures over the BSE crisis, to the resistance of the French government to reform of the CAP.

Caught between external pressure and internal constituencies, governments, it is true, are often highly vulnerable to the former. But they can use protest as a resource: when domestic groups take action against their implementation of international pressures, they offer governments leverage vis-à-vis international institutions. As Bush and Simi (2001: 118) concluded of the European farmers' protests they studied, "The extent to which government officials defend their citizens' interests in Brussels is a function of the level of domestic opposition at a given time."

This takes me to my final claim. Rather than seeing domestic resistance against international intrusion as either a pesky distraction from elite politics or, conversely, celebrating the resistance of struggling subaltern groups against the forces of globalization, we should see these efforts within the triangular structure of internationalism. Internationalism inserts international pressures and global frames into domestic politics, as we have seen in these two chapters; but it also provides channels for domestic contention to diffuse horizontally across boundaries and move vertically to higher levels. To these processes I turn in the next section of this book.

PART THREE

Transitional Processes

6

Diffusion and Modularity

The destruction of the World Trade Center by two suicide airplane-bombs on September 11, 2001, left most Americans dazed, humiliated, and enraged. Many would probably have been surprised to learn that the killings on September 11, 2001, compared in number – if not in spatial concentration – with the long record of suicide bombings since the early 1980s, in Beirut in the early 1980s, South Asia in the early 1990s, Israel/Palestine throughout that decade, and in Iraq against the American occupiers and their local allies in 2003–4.

In fact, when Eli Berman and David Laitin examined the number of victims of suicide bombers before and after September 11th, they found that 420 were killed in 1983, 400 in 1998, and more than 200 each in 1985, 1995, and 1996 (Berman and Laitin 2005: table A2), with probably much higher numbers after the Iraq war.[1] Figure 6.1, calculated from their careful reconstruction and tracing a three-year moving average of the number of suicide attacks around the world from 1983 to 2002, shows that suicide bombings grew steadily before September 11, 2001.

Before it became the privileged tool of Islamist martyrs, suicide bombing was part of a much broader range of actions. As the bloody 1980s gave way

This chapter and the next one both grow out of two earlier joint efforts with my collaborators, Doug McAdam and Charles Tilly. See McAdam, Tarrow, and Tilly 2001: ch. 11, and Tarrow and McAdam 2005. I thank them both for their help and their collaboration.

[1] I use the conditional "probably" because there are unsolved problems of coding actual – as opposed to media reports of – suicide bombings against the American occupation of Iraq. Both the occupying forces' and reporters' motives in reporting attacks as "suicide bombings" may be suspect. I am grateful for this observation to David Laitin as well as for permission to draw from his and Eli Berman's unpublished paper.

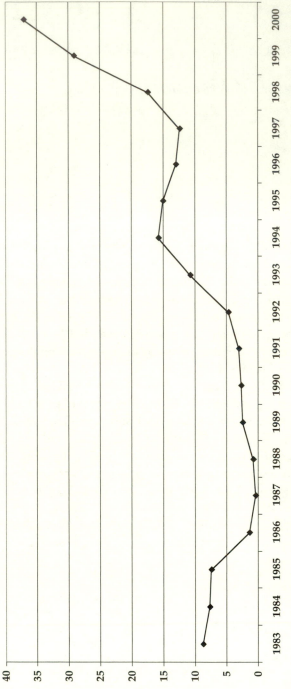

Figure 6.1 Three-Year Moving Average of Number of Suicide Bombing Attacks, 1983–2002. *Source:* Berman and Laitin 2005, table A2.

to the even bloodier 1990s, the tactic became "modular" – that is, like the demonstration and the strike in the past history of contentious politics, it was employed in a wide range of causes in a number of different places (Tarrow 1998: ch. 3). From the Lebanese Civil War in the early 1980s and Sri Lanka in the early 1990s, it spread to the "Second Intifada" in Palestine/Israel and then to the transnational Islamist movement. From a form that was employed only where more conventional forms of contention were too risky, suicide bombing became a routine part of the coordinated strategies of transnational political Islamism.

Much of the research on suicide bombers since September 11 has focused on the motives and the character of those who choose to end their lives in this way.[2] Less attention has been given to the processes that diffused this new and ruthless form of attack and made it part of the twenty-first century's repertoire of contention. There have been two unfortunate outcomes of this understandable focus on the actors: first, it distracted analysts from the varieties of its modes of diffusion (but see Sageman 2004); second, its almost unique horror diverted attention from comparing its diffusion with that of other, less lethal forms of contentious politics. When we do so, we will see that it has diffused across borders in ways that are remarkably similar to less lethal forms of contention.

In this chapter I focus both on the variety of processes of transnational diffusion and on diffusion among very different forms of collective action. As examples, I use evidence from two movements in different parts of the world: the diffusion of nonviolent resistance from India to the United States and then to former socialist countries; and the diffusion of the Zapatista solidarity network from Chiapas to North America. In both cases – as in the case of the suicide bombing – diffusion travels through well-connected trust networks ("relational diffusion"), through the media and the internet ("nonrelational diffusion"), and through movement brokers

---

[2] Interpretations of the motives of suicide bombers have ranged from journalists' images of crazed fanatics attempting to enter paradise, to more detached statistical analyses by economists (Krueger and Maleckova 2003), to realist and rational choice models of collective action by political scientists (Pape 2003; Berman and Laitin 2005). Microanalysis shows that the tactic cannot be reduced to a reflex of economic distress (Krueger and Maleckova 2003) and is most likely to be employed by members of one religious or ethnic group against another (Berman and Laitin 2005; Bloom 2004: 6). Geographic analysis shows that – with the exception of Sri Lanka, where seventy-five of these attacks took place– organizations that mounted suicide bombings mainly come from the Middle East (Berman and Laitin 2005: table 1). Leadership analysis points to a combination of psychological and relational factors (Sprinzak 2000; also see Bloom 2004).

("mediated diffusion"). Among them, these processes produce the emulation of local forms of collective action in other places and contribute to the spread of contentious politics across the globe.

Constraints and Inducements

How does a new form of collective action or a social movement spread? In his studies of what has come to be called "the repertoire of contention," Charles Tilly (1986: 10) writes that the existing repertoire grows out of three kinds of factors: a population's daily routines and internal organization, the prevailing standards of rights and justice, and the population's accumulated experience with collective action. But he also emphasizes learning: what people *know* about how to contend in various places and at different periods of history constrains change in the repertoire. If this is true, then there are both inducements and constraints on the spread of a new form of contention from one country to another.

Both the inducements and the constraints can be seen historically, as state building and capitalism triggered the invention of new forms of contention. As the early modern state consolidated, people resisted with tax revolts, conscription riots, and petitions; and as market capitalism took hold, grain seizures, strikes, and turnouts were used to resist its pressures. If there was no state trying to extract a surplus or build an army, there would be no tax revolts or conscription riots; and if there were no capitalists attempting to assemble workers in factories and exploit their labor, there would have been no strikes. Capitalism and state building were the major macroprocesses triggering the development of the modern repertoire of contention (Tilly 1995b).

But once invented in response to structural change, new forms of contention could be imitated and modified far beyond their origins and outside the structural relations that had produced them. For example, once its efficacy was demonstrated, the strike spread from industry to services; petitions that had proved useful against individual state officials could be employed as a political tactic against slavery; turnouts against local capitalists transformed into demonstrations against all manner of antagonists; protesters refusing to leave a particular official's office transmuted into the sit-in. Countering the specificity and locality of the repertoire of contention was its modularity and transferability across space and into different sectors of movement activity (Tarrow 1998: ch. 3). With globalization and internationalization, both the speed and the modularity of diffusion of forms of contention have increased.

This duality in the repertoire is the source of our central question for transnational contention: *How do forms of collective action that arise out of specific national configurations of conflict spread to other venues?* And, in particular, how do internationalization and globalization affect the speed and facility with which these forms diffuse? Determined activists have always been able to adapt new forms of contention across borders. But with the growth of internationalization and global communication, diffusion has both increased and accelerated. For example, while it took a half-century for antislavery agitation to spread from England to the European continent and across the Atlantic (Drescher 1987), suicide bombing diffused across Asia and the Middle East within a decade of its first use in Lebanon. What kinds of processes have speeded the diffusion of new forms of contention?

Pathways of Transnational Diffusion

Internationalization and communication are the large impersonal processes that lie in the background of all forms of transnational diffusion. Internationalization creates regular channels for communication and awareness of institutional similarities and differences among actors in different places. That information has to spread for diffusion to occur is true by definition, but what seems to be new in today's world is the rapidity and ease of information transfer. New forms of communication, such as text messaging and the internet, make it easier for activists to communicate with one another at great distances and even in the midst of an episode of contention (Danitz and Strobel 2001; Rheingold 2002; Tilly 2004b: ch. 5).

But *how* does a new form of contention spread, and what lessons does this have for transnational contention in general? From his study of the spread of the Salafist Jihad, Sageman allows us to identify three main pathways of diffusion: relational, nonrelational, and mediated diffusion.

As in any form of collective action, social bonds and personal networks were important in the spread of the Islamist network (Sageman 2004: ch. 5). Not only did Islam and Arabic provide a universal faith and a common language; interpersonal trust, family ties, and common local origins helped to create "small world networks" among people who identified with one another and were prepared to emulate one another's actions (p. 139). This

103

is what I call *relational diffusion*. It transfers information along established lines of interaction through the attribution of similarity and the networks of trust that it produces (Lee and Strang 2003).

The Islamist movement also spread through *nonrelational diffusion*. By this term I mean diffusion among people who have few or no social ties. Although this can occur by word of mouth, many of today's movements spread through the mass media and electronic communication. By historical accident, the Islamist movement's growth coincided with the coming of the internet, "making possible a new type of relationship between an individual and a virtual community" (Sageman 2004: 160–3). This not only sped the diffusion of the movement but favored its "theorization": a kind of "folk theory" that defines some thing or activity in abstract terms and locates it within a cause-effect or functional scheme.[3] Theorization can be highly abstract and complex, like the role of "class struggle" in the Marxist ontology, or it can be reduced to a few symbols and guides to action. The media and especially the Internet encouraged the diffusion of an extremely one-sided reading of Islam, reducing the level of discourse to the lowest common denominator and identifying the suicide bombing as a tool that would bring glory to the martyr and success to the cause (p. 162).

Third is what I call *mediated diffusion*. In the jihadi networks he studied, Sageman (2004: 169ff.) identified a number of movement "nodes" comprising individuals within a geographic cluster, with various clusters interrelated by a small number of weak links. What kept these weak links alive is brokerage, the connection of two unconnected sites by a third, which works through movement "halfway houses," immigrants, or institutions. Brokers may never participate in contentious politics, but their key position in between otherwise unconnected sites can influence the content of the information that is communicated.

The general tendency of students of social movements has been to focus on the first process, relational diffusion, in which innovations travel along established lines of interaction to be emulated and adopted elsewhere.[4] Like the spread of hybrid corn or the adoption of new medical practices, the adoption of new forms of collective action often

---

[3] I thank David Strang for offering this definition, drawn from his work with John Meyer. See Strang and Meyer 1993.

[4] See the discussions in Jackson et al. 1960; McAdam 1999; McAdam and Rucht 1993; Pinard 1971; Rogers 1983; Strang and Meyer 1993; and Soule 1997.

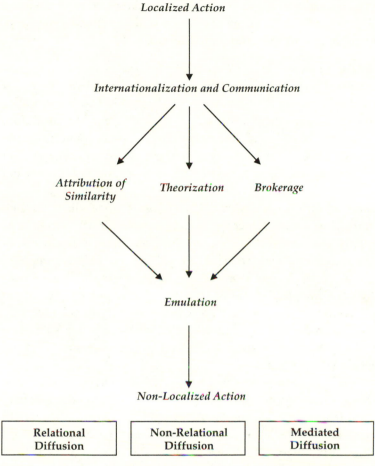

Figure 6.2 Alternative Pathways of Transnational Diffusion

follows the segmented lines of interpersonal interaction among people who know one another or are parts of networks of trust. But in an age of massive immigration and cheap and easy transportation, information about collective action can spread through third parties, or brokers, who connect people who would otherwise have no contact with one another.

Figure 6.2 offers a simple descriptive model of these three processes of transnational diffusion, with the key mechanism in the first path the attribution of similarity, in the second the theorization of political Islamism through impersonal media, and, in the third, brokerage. Each of the pathways in Figure 6.2 is familiar from the history of both cultural movements and contentious politics in Europe and America:

- *Relational diffusion in Norman England.* When the new style of Gothic cathedral building, which began in the Abbey of St. Denis outside of Paris in 1137, crossed the Channel to England, this was an example of relational diffusion – the Normans, after all, had invaded England from France in 1066. It was transferred by two contemporary connections: the numerous French clergy who served in England and the many English priests who had studied at the great cathedral schools of Chartres and Notre Dame (Scott 2003: 14).
- *Nonrelational diffusion in America.* The diffusion of rebellion through England's North American colonies had many relational sources (e.g., the famous Committees of Correspondence), but one of the most important was nonrelational: the availability of a plethora of printed pamphlets and books, of which Tom Paine's *Common Sense* was the most famous and the most durable. Bernard Bailyn (1967) points out that America in the 1770s was virtually flooded with newspapers and pamphlets. Paine's book, which "theorized" revolution for the American public, sold thousands of copies, many of them read aloud by purchasers to groups of listeners in village squares.
- *Mediated diffusion through movement missionaries.* Through individual missionaries and movement organizations, people who might otherwise have remained ignorant of one another's claims are brought together. Both the Protestant "saints" who smuggled Protestant tracts across Europe during the Reformation and the anarchists who brought their faith to southern Italy, Spain, and Latin America were "brokers" in the spread of revolutionary movements (Walzer 1971; Joll 1964).

Diffusing Nonviolence

Modern social movements have direct access to a variety of networked relational ties (Arquilla and Ronfeldt 2001; Keck and Sikkink 1998). In addition, autonomous channels of communication transmit information about new movements or forms of action. And various of institutions and "rooted cosmopolitans" are available to act as movement brokers. All three forms of diffusion combined in the transnational diffusion of one of the most successful innovations in contentious politics in the twentieth century: the strategy of nonviolent resistance.

The Gandhian Origins of Nonviolence[5]

"As the days unfolded," wrote Martin Luther King Jr. (1958: 84–5) of the early days of the American civil rights movement,

the inspiration of Mahatma Gandhi began to exert its influence. I had come to see early that the Christian doctrine of love operating through the Gandhian method of nonviolence was one of the most potent weapons available to the Negro in his struggle for freedom. . . . Nonviolent resistance had emerged as the technique of the movement, while love stood as the regulating ideal. In other words, Christ furnished the spirit and motivation, while Gandhi furnished the method.

Dr. King was not the first African American to try to bring the theory of nonviolence from India to the United States. Sean Chabot (2003: 3) writes: "King was certainly not the first – and arguably not even the most creative – actor involved in the Gandhian repertoire's transnational diffusion." From the 1930s onward, men like Howard Thurman, Benjamin Mays, James Farmer, and George Houser had visited India to meet with Gandhi and returned to the United States inspired by the doctrine of nonviolence. But King and others in the 1960s succeeded as domesticators of the practice of nonviolence in America.

The theory of nonviolence has sometimes been defined quite broadly as a moral preference for any form of contention that is not violent (Schell 2003) and sometimes very narrowly to refer to the specific forms of collective action that Mohandas Gandhi developed in South Africa and brought to preindependence India (Bondurant 1958). But at the heart of nonviolence is a strategic theory: "aggressive measures to constrain or punish opponents and to win concessions through disruptive but not violent means" (Ackerman and DuVall 2000: 2). It was the successful transference of this strategy by movement brokers – and not the specific forms that Gandhi developed – that would explain its success in places as far removed from India as the United States in the 1960s and Serbia and Georgia after the fall of communism.

---

[5] This section is much in debt to the original doctoral dissertation of Sean Chabot (2003). Also see Chabot 2002.

Of course, Gandhi developed the practice of nonviolence to resonate within the specific context of Indian civilization (Bondurant 1958: ch. 4). "The tendency of the Indian civilization," he wrote, "is to elevate the moral being" (quoted in Schell 2003: 123). This, in effect, *domesticated* the principle of nonviolence (p. 126). To this theoretical core, Gandhi added his own aesthetic and communitarian beliefs. Bondurant (1958: 105) writes: "Gandhi used the traditional to promote the novel; he reinterpreted tradition in such a way that revolutionary ideas, clothed in familiar expression, were readily adopted and employed towards revolutionary ends." The resulting amalgam was the doctrine and practice of *satyagraha* (ch. 3).

From India to America

To be successful in the United States, the strategy of nonviolence would need to be dislocated and relocated in very different conditions. True, both colonial India and the American South were repressive societies with a patina of Anglo-American rule of law. But the American South was a Christian, not a Hindu-Muslim society, and one in which a single racial divide replaced a society of many castes and where, in place of the naked domination of colonialism, a fiction of democracy overlay the reality of racial oppression.

All three of our pathways can be observed in the transfer of nonviolence from its Gandhian origins to the American civil rights movement:

- *Relational diffusion.* Indian exiles, religious pacifists, and African American theologians, and organizations like the Congress of Racial Equality (CORE) and the March on Washington Movement (MOWM) brought the movement directly to America.
- *Nonrelational diffusion.* The movement was promoted in the African American press and in writings of authors like Joan Bondurant (1958), who first went to India as an American intelligence agent during the war, became fascinated by Gandhi, and returned to study the movement and publicize it in the West. Through these impersonal agents, the movement was reduced in form and "relocated" in the United States (Chabot 2003: 7; R. Fox 1997: 75–80).
- *Mediated diffusion.* "Movement halfway houses," such as the Highlander Folk School, taught the methods of nonviolence to a range of future activists (Horton 1989).

The federal government served as a facilitator of nonviolence too. As beefy sheriff's deputies unleashed police dogs and aimed water cannon at peaceful demonstrators in the glare of national television, it was difficult for the federal government to avoid intervening on their behalf (Tarrow 1992). As the once-solid South shifted to the Republicans and African Americans began to appear as a significant electoral force, for the Democrats in power to acquiesce in the repression of civil rights demonstrators would have been political suicide (Piven and Cloward 1977: ch. 4; McAdam 1983). Washington's intervention was also fed by the country's foreign policy posture. It would have been hypocritical for a country that claimed to lead the free world to be seen to condone the brutalization of people demanding nothing more than the right to vote.

If relational, nonrelational, and mediated diffusion facilitated the diffusion of nonviolence to the United States, how would the strategy fare in settings in which communication is suppressed and political change is opposed by a brutal dictatorship? In this age of internationalization and electronic communication, and in the presence of transnational agents who assisted in its transfer, the constraints against diffusion of nonviolence are much weaker, and the strategy of nonviolence could travel quite far indeed, as the following examples show.

Postsocialist Nonviolence[6]

The brutal nationalist regime of Slobodan Milosevic would seem like the least likely venue to welcome the practices of Gandhi and King. A wily Leninist who was quick to scent the winds of change in the Balkans well before 1989, Milosevic undermined what was left of Yugoslav unity in the early 1990s by fomenting a war with Croatia and encouraging the Bosnian Serbs to attack Bosnia-Herzegovina. When the horrors of genocide in Bosnia led to a reaction from the West, Milosevic made a deal with the Americans and West Europeans that left his Bosnian henchmen adrift. When he invaded Kosovo, which the Serbs claimed as a Serbian province, NATO bombing forced him to withdraw.

---

[6] I am grateful to Jack DuVall for his advice in the preparation of this section. With Peter Ackerman, DuVall has followed closely and helped to advance the cause of nonviolence as producers of documentary films, one of which, *Bringing Down a Dictator*, had important effects in the diffusion of nonviolence to the Caucasus. For information on their International Center for Nonviolent Conflict, go to http://www.nonviolent-conflict.org/resources.shtml.

Politically unassailable as long as he controlled his army and police, Milosevic's position weakened in the mid-1990s as his regime's economic ineptitude and corruption and the costs of his wars began to sink in. As his country's isolation tightened, inflation raged, and unemployment grew, his popularity eroded. Ruthless cunning, control of the press, and support from the remnant of the Communist *apparat* helped Milosevic hold onto power until November 1996, when the formerly divided opposition parties mounted a coalition, Zajedno (Together), to challenge Milosevic in the local elections. When they won fourteen of the country's municipal governments, including Belgrade, the government blithely declared the results illegal.

Such a tactic could only work if three things were true: if the move was backed by a credible show of force, the media remained under state control, and no one from outside the country was watching. But by mid-1996 these conditions no longer held. Still smarting from the retreat from Kosovo, the army stayed on the sidelines, foreign media substituted for the repressed local press and television, and the Organization for Security and Cooperation in Europe (OSCE) investigated the electoral outcomes and validated Zajedno's success. That was the background for the wave of contention that began with the stolen elections of November 1996 and lasted until Milosevic was overthrown in 2000.

Would the Balkans once again explode into violence? When protesters pelted state media with eggs for refusing to cover their activities, the police responded with violence to drive them off the streets. But from the beginning of the campaign against the stolen elections, the centerpiece of the protests was a series of nightly marches through the center of Belgrade organized by an opposition using nonviolent sanctions. For nearly two months, demonstrators marched, sang, blew whistles, listened to speeches, alternately heckled and fraternized with the police, and went to court to keep the pressure on Milosevic. As one observer wrote, "The regime was fired at with eggs, blown at with whistles, banged with pots and pans, and ridiculed by clowns" (Vejvoda 1997: 2).

That was only the first stage of a widespread campaign of civil disobedience that culminated in 2000. Encouraged by the opposition's ability to turn around the stolen elections, a student movement called Otpor (Resistance) developed to challenge Milosevic's attempt to control the universities. From the beginning, Otpor's strategy was deliberately nonviolent. In the words of one activist, "We knew what had happened in Tiananmen, where the army plowed over students with tanks. So violence wouldn't work – and besides, it was the trademark of Milosevic, and Otpor had to stand for something different."[7] Otpor developed a sophisticated strategy of targeting Milosevic personally for all the country's ills, adopting slogans that implied the movement was spreading, and using antics and theatrical tactics instead of mass demonstrations that could be targeted by the police.

Brokerage in the Balkans

Otpor's understanding of how to use nonviolent sanctions was in part the result of diffusion from the United States. Miljenko Dereta, the director of a private group called Civic Initiatives, got funding from Freedom House to print and distribute five thousand copies of Gene Sharp's book on nonviolence, *From Dictatorship to Democracy* (1993). Otpor also translated sections of Sharp's three-volume work, *The Politics of Nonviolent Action* (1973), into a Serbian-language notebook they called the "Otpor User Manual." The activists also received advice from the Balkans' director of the U.S. Institute for Peace, from the National Endowment for Democracy, and from Colonal Robert Helvey, who had studied with Sharp and worked as an independent consultant organizing nonviolent trainings in Budapest for the International Republican Institute.[8]

Of course, the embrace of nonviolence was not the only reason for Otpor's success. The regime's failure to hold onto Kosovo, the bombings of Serbian cities, and the country's growing isolation and economic decline were important factors, too. So was the spreading belief among Serbs that the European Union and the United States had had enough of Milosevic. But the nonviolent protest campaign organized by Otpor and backed by its international allies was a major efficient cause of Milosevic's overthrow.

---

[7] Interview with Srdja Popovic, from a videotaped interview by Steve York, Belgrade, Yugoslavia, November 13, 2000, for the York-Zimmerman-directed PBS documentary, *Bringing Down a Dictator* at http://www.pbs.org/weta/dictator/otpor/nonviolence.html.

[8] In an interview for the PBS documentary, *Bringing Down a Dictator*, Helvey recalled, "You know, they [Otpor] had done very, very effective work in mobilizing individual groups. But there was something missing to take them beyond protest into actually mobilizing to overthrow the regime. I just felt that something was lacking. They were doing something very, very well, but there seemed to be an invisible wall here that they needed to get over. So we started with the basics of strategic nonviolent struggle theory. And I did it sort of as a review because apparently they were doing many things right so there must have been some basic understanding. But sometimes you miss some of the dynamics of it if you don't understand the theory." See the transcript of Helvey's interview for *Bringing Down a Dictator* at http://www.pbs.org/weta/dictator/otpor/ownwords/helvey.html.

From Belgrade to Tbilisi

Nonviolent sanctions played a crucial role in the diffusion of the Otpor model from the Balkans to the Caucasus. In November 2003 President Eduard Shevardnadze, one-time Soviet foreign minister turned Georgian patriot, rigged a parliamentary election to provide a sure victory to the parties that supported him. Since declaring independence from the Soviet Union, Georgia had drifted into a situation of corruption, economic decline, and ethnic separatism from three border areas, encouraged semicovertly by Russia. As the country sank into instability, its strategic importance grew because of the pipeline that American interests wanted to construct through its territory from recently opened oil fields in Azerbaijan. American political interests were also present in U.S. government support for political parties and civil society groups hoping to build democratic institutions (*Washington Post*, Nov. 25, 2003, A22).

Shevardnadze was no Milosevic. But as in Serbia, it was his attempt to foil the electoral process that brought down his government. Three weeks of peaceful street protests culminated in a "March of the Angry Voters," led by Mikheil Saakashvili, leader of the opposition coalition and the country's president after Shevardnadze was forced to step down. For months, activists led by the student group Kmara had engaged in graffiti, leaflet, and poster campaigns against corruption and police brutality, and for university re-form and media freedom. This was no spontaneous demonstration but "a coordinated plan . . . for tens of thousands of citizens to converge by buses, cars and trucks on the capital, Tbilisi."[9]

Where had the opposition learned these tactics? Although the deft hand of U.S. advisers could be read between the lines, this was no CIA-engineered plot. In the months before the election, Saakashvili had traveled to Serbia to contact the former organizers of the anti-Milosevic movement. He returned with a plan for nonviolent action modeled closely on the success of Otpor. This was followed by ex-Otpor activists traveling to Georgia to conduct trainings in strategic nonviolent struggle for Georgian reformists, civil society activists, students, and members of the political opposition, who, in turn, trained a cadre of grass-roots activists.

---

[9] The source of this report is a press release from the International Center on Nonviolent Conflict, "Georgia's Nonviolent Resistance: Briefing Sheet." I am grateful to Shaazka Beyerle, associate director of the center (sbeyerle@nonviolent-conflict.org), for help in preparing this narrative.

If electronic communication played an important role in Serbia, in Georgia it was crucial. An important tool in the campaign in Tbilisi, according to the *Washington Post* report, was the American-made documentary on the fall of Milosevic, *Bringing Down a Dictator*, supported by the Washington-based International Center for Nonviolent Conflict. The film was both used as a teaching tool at the Georgian trainings and shown on the independent national television station. "Most important was the film," said Ivane Merabishvili, general secretary of the National Movement party that led the revolt. "All the demonstrators knew the tactics of the revolution in Belgrade by heart because they showed . . . the film on their revolution. Everyone knew what to do. This was a copy of that revolution, only louder" (*Washington Post*, Nov. 25, 2003, A22).

The successful diffusion of nonviolence from India to the United States and then to the Balkans and the Caucasus does not mean that nonviolence is a panacea for defeating dictators or rolling back racism. After all, following Gandhi's death and the establishment of an Indian democracy, religious violence ran rampant across India. And following the successes of the civil rights movement, new forms of racial segregation developed in the American South (Andrews 2002, 2004). As for Serbia and Georgia, the future of those countries is still in doubt. But these examples show that innovations in the repertoire of contention can cross broad cultural and spatial divides even where established lines of interaction are weak. A second example – the diffusion of the Zapatista solidarity network – shows how important nonrelational and mediated diffusion have become in today's connected world.

Diffusion from Chiapas[10]

On January 1, 1994, a hitherto unknown guerrilla group in the southern Mexican state of Chiapas attacked police barracks in the city of San Cristóbal de las Casas and in surrounding towns. The rebellion broke out on the same day as the North American Free Trade Agreement treaty (NAFTA) came into effect among Canada, Mexico, and the United States. In committing Mexico to open its borders to trade with its more-powerful northern

---

[10] More than usual, this section is dependent on the observations of other scholars, graciously shared with me. In the case of the Zapatista movement, I was helped by the advice of Clifford Bob, Judy Hellman, Thomas Olesen, and Heather Williams.

neighbors, NAFTA promised a boon for commercial agriculture but threatened the survival of poor dirt farmers in the South.

The coincidence of the rebellion with the start of NAFTA gave the Zapatista movement an international allure from the start, although its "spokesperson," who called himself Subcomandante Marcos, was soon at pains to emphasize its roots in the historical oppression of Mexico's indigenous peoples. Although its guerrilla actions failed to spread to other regions of Mexico, the EZLN received instant support from both within and outside the country. In Mexico City, where hundreds of thousands of people demonstrated in favor of the insurgents, the progressive newspaper, *La Jornada*, emerged as an unofficial press agency for the rebels. In Rome, the left-wing newspaper, *Il Manifesto*, taking much of its coverage from *La Jornada*, spread word about the rebellion to an Italian public during a period in which the traditional left was in disarray. Soon, hundreds of activists from Europe and North America arrived in Chiapas to support the rebels and, by their presence, helped to hold off the threat of military repression (Bob 2005).

Meanwhile, in Austin, Texas, an important sympathizer, Harry Cleaver, began to filter e-mail messages about the insurgency to progressive groups around the United States, and soon a number of listservs and websites appeared that were dedicated to the insurgency.[11] The wave of solidarity produced what some excited spirits called a global "Netwar," the first cycle of protest to be fueled by the internet. That claim turned out to be exaggerated, but the diffusion of the movement's message from a backward state in southern Mexico to international public opinion was probably a factor in preventing the insurgents' repression. Ultimately, it created what Thomas Olesen (2005) has called an "international solidarity network."

As the movement developed and word about it spread, traditional borders of space and culture appeared to collapse. As Olesen (2005: 2) observes: "Notwithstanding the obvious distance in both physical, social, and cultural terms" between the core insurgents and their supporters, "the movement won a great deal of solidarity, mainly from Western Europe and North America." In fact, "the interest and attraction generated by the EZLN beyond its national borders is matched by no other movement in the post–Cold War period." All three of our processes of diffusion helped to spread word of the movement and create this movement of solidarity.

[11] Cleaver's role can be found at http://www.eco.utexas.edu/faculty/Cleaver.

Diffusion and Modularity

Relational and Nonrelational Diffusion

With a long *indigenista* tradition, Mexicans were prepared to interpret the insurrection in culturally resonant terms. In a country in which between 12 and 14 percent of the population are *indios*,[12] solidarity with the EZLN found its first basis among existing supporters of indigenous rights. Following the initial attacks in San Cristóbal, there were massive demonstrations of solidarity in Mexico City and elsewhere; in various parts of the country, representatives of other indigenous groups expressed solidarity with the EZLN. Recent events, like the repeal of Article 27 of the Mexican constitution, also made peasants fear that their land would be bought up by big agricultural interests.

But relational diffusion was not the only channel for the movement's diffusion; nonrelational diffusion played an important role too. Until the 1990s, press freedom in Mexico was extremely constrained by the government and the ruling party. Not only were newsprint and advertising revenue controlled by the government, but independent journalists would often fall prey to mysterious "accidents" and disappearances. Yet diffusion of news of the rebellion through the press was extremely important, both in spotlighting and limiting government repression in Chiapas and in the creation of the EZLN solidarity network.

There were several reasons for this. First, the EZLN emerged at a particularly conflictual period of Mexican politics, in which the press and the electronic media were beginning to escape the heavy hand of PRI control. Three major dailies signaled their independence from the government by publishing critical articles.[13] Second, information about the rebellion was transmitted to a specialized public of related groups and sympathizers through websites sponsored by the Zapatistas. It was also generated to a broader public through websites unrelated to the Zapatistas and through independent e-mail traffic and the press.

Taking control of San Cristóbal, and "distributing written statements, granting lengthy interviews, and posing for photographs by the city's gathered media" (Bob 2005: 128), the group developed a skillful media strategy from the beginning. Clifford Bob points out that gaining media coverage was one of the "primary objectives" of the movement, one that was

[12] Data from Wilkie 2001: table 532: 104. Also see Yashar 2005.
[13] Heather Williams, in a personal communication, points out that one of these three, *La Riforma*, was almost closed down for its independent views in the year before the rebellion and might not have survived without it.

actually facilitated by the government, which at first allowed news of the insurrection to get out, then banned reporters from the region, and finally relented from armed repression under broad international and domestic pressure.

As the mainstream press "corroborated Chiapas' long history of poverty and political repression" (Bob 2005: 165), reporting on the government's heavy-handed military reaction, it began to frame the movement as "an army of innocents" in danger of falling victim to vengeful forces, rather than as a guerrilla group that had taken over a major town (p. 145). Days after the cease-fire, Zapatista communiqués began reaching receptive journalists. Mainly the product of Marcos's "prolific, pointed and playful pen, these writings spanned hard-hitting communiqués and manifestoes, tendentious fables (told by a beetle), a fanciful children's story, and inexplicable, almost hallucinatory ravings" (p. 142).

Although it is never easy to measure the success of a media strategy, the press was important to the Zapatista rebellion in two important ways. First, it played a major role in framing the movement in a sympathetic light, thereby producing a positive reaction in Mexican public opinion. Polls showed a 61 percent approval rating for the zapatistas right after the uprising and 75 percent a month later (Bob 2005: 136). Second, the Mexican army was diverted from its original use of overwhelming force, in large part by the pressure of public opinion that was mobilized through the press (Arquilla and Ronfeldt 2001). Nonrelational diffusion was an important process in legitimating the rebels and preventing their immediate repression.

Mediated Diffusion

Much of the information that led to the formation of an international Zapatista solidarity network passed through a set of linked brokerage ties reaching into North American and Western European society. Olesen charts five different levels in what he calls transnational zapatismo's "information circuit": first there were the indigenous communities of Chiapas; then a range of Mexican and Chiapas-based organizations that functioned mainly as information gatherers and information condensers; next actors who passed the information beyond the borders of Chiapas and Mexico through the internet and other links; then a circle of "periphery actors" who were dependent on core actors for their information but still devoted a significant part of their time and resources to these issues; and, finally, people who had irregular and transitory ties to people closer to the core but devoted little time to the issue of Chiapas and the EZLN (summarized from Olesen 2005: 67–78).

The most central broker was, of course, the man who calls himself Sub-comandante Marcos. Coming from a traditional urban leftist intellectual background, Marcos was a classical rooted cosmopolitan, embedding himself deeply within the Lancandòn rain forest for a long period of time before the insurgency broke out. His words, according to Higgins, became "bridges between the Indian world of the southeast and the even-more-pervasive world of global politics" (2000: 360, quoted in Olesen 2005: 10). "With a well developed sense of public relations . . . he is a mediator," writes Olesen (p. 10), "translating the EZLN indigenous struggle into a language that is understandable to a non-Mexican audience."

The media image of Marcos carrying his laptop through the jungle and uploading communiqués via a cell phone assigned too much importance to this central node of the network. Much of the information about the insurgency came from second-level brokers, like *La Jornada*, which one Chiapenecan activist jokingly described as "*The Chiapas Gazette*" (quoted in Hellman 1999: 175). *La Jornada*, in turn, was the main source of information for sympathetic foreign journalists whose access to and information about Chiapas was rudimentary. Other second-level nodes were listservs like Chiapas 95 and Chiapas-L, and the *Ya Basta!* website established in March 1994 by Justin Paulson (Olesen 2005: ch. 3; Paulson 2000: 283). These sites were mainly responsible – far more than Marcos himself – for the construction of what Judy Hellman (1999) has called a "virtual Chiapas." In the process the complexity of the message was reduced, to the point at which many in the United States and Western Europe had only the vaguest idea of the ethnic heterogeneity and political cleavages within the region.

Conclusions

From this rapid survey of the diffusion of suicide bombing, nonviolent sanctions, and the spread of the Zapatista solidarity network, what can we infer for the broader question of when and how new forms of contention, new movements, and international solidarity will be diffused across borders?

First, a disclaimer. My account does not tell us why thousands of African American teenagers were willing to face the truncheons and police dogs of sheriff's deputies or why "thousands of people around the world would take notice of a group of less than one thousand mostly unarmed, bare-foot peasants carrying out brief takeovers of seven minor municipalities in a backwater state in Mexico."[14] Transnational diffusion does not guarantee either the success of a new form of contention or its popularity among people far from the field of struggle. Had the civil rights movement not coincided with the foreign policy and electoral incentives of the Kennedy administration, Jim Crow might have survived longer in the American South. Had nonviolence been employed in more efficiently authoritarian regimes than Serbia or Georgia, it might not have led to movement success. And had the Mexican government not already been under pressure to democratize, Marcos's amateur guerrillas might have been smashed. The mechanisms we have adduced produced three complementary processes of diffusion, but these processes did not guarantee success.

Three main conclusions do emerge from these analyses. First, as in Tilly's concept of the repertoire of contention, new forms of collective action emerge from the structural development of the societies in which they are invented and are sustained by people's understandings about how to contend, where to contend, and which forms of contention are legitimate. Islamist suicide bombers drew on the concept of jihad and on the image of the heavenly paradise they thought they would enter if they sacrificed their lives to the resurgence of Islam. *Satyagraha* and its associated cultural forms grew out of and were adapted to the Indian subcontinent and would have been exotic had they been transferred literally to the American South, Serbia, or Georgia. The EZLN drew on the heritage of Emiliano Zapata, and on the historical land hunger and ethnic identity of Chiapanecan Indians.

But, second, as we have seen, new forms of collective action diffuse to places in which they are not native. Facilitated by internationalization and global communication and through diffusion processes that detach it from its origins and domesticate it in new settings, direct ties between originators and adopters, nonrelational transmission through the media, and mediated diffusion through brokerage help to bridge cultural and geographic divides and diffuse new forms of collective action across borders.

Third, although we cannot predict outcomes from processes, we can hypothesize that these processes will vary in their effects according to their major driving mechanisms. In relational diffusion, the attribution of similarity facilitates trust, but its dependency on segmented networks limits its range. In nonrelational diffusion, "theorization" makes it possible to transport a message to a new venue, but the need to reduce it to a form of "folk wisdom" reduces its complexity and can produce a simplistic version

---

[14] Quoted from a personal communication to the author by Heather Williams.

that receivers can interpret as they like.[15] In the third process, brokerage through movement halfway houses and third parties speeds the transfer of information but gives intermediaries great importance in reshaping the message.

This takes us to the major question that emerges from these analyses: what are the global consequences of the three variants of diffusion? All three of the processes I have examined produced horizontal – and not vertical – patterns of diffusion. Although adherents of both jihadist Islamism and the faith of nonviolence see them as universally applicable, and many supporters of the Zapata rebellion saw it as the harbinger of a global movement, both universality and the formation of a global movement require a *vertical* shift in scale, and that cannot occur without the coordination of collective action at a higher level.

In earlier chapters, I argued that internationalism provides a setting in which, by using international regimes, institutions, and encounters as focal points, nonstate actors encounter one another in international venues. But meeting and recognizing others with similar claims is not sufficient to build a transnational movement. For that to happen requires sustained work at an international level, the formation of broader networks of trust, and the coordination of collective action beyond the national state. The next chapter examines this process in greater depth as I investigate the potential for "scale shift" of contentious politics.

---

[15] Judy Hellman reports that part of the appeal of Subcomandante Marcos's writings for European and North American Zapatistas was the possibility of interpreting his words to fit local realities. In interviews with Zapatista activists in Italy, one of them solemnly told her that "'The thought of Subcomandante Marcos teaches us that it is appropriate for us here in Padua to put forward a slate of candidates for the forthcoming municipal elections.' This at the very moment when Marcos was calling upon the Chiapanecan sympathizers to boycott the 2000 presidential elections in Chiapas." In a personal communication to the author.

7

Shifting the Scale of Contention

Hengyang County, in China's central agricultural belt, has a long tradition of resistance to local authority (O'Brien and Li 2004; also see Bernstein and Lü 2003). But constrained by the "cellularization" of rural China under Communist rule (Shue 1988), until recently farmers mainly limited their claims to complaint boards or poured them into frustrated rage against official wrongdoers. Their protests seldom rose to a higher level. But in the 1990s Kevin O'Brien and Lianjiang Li began to observe a shift in the scale of mobilization. "Activists," they observed, "increasingly speak of a common cause and identify themselves as members of a larger community of aggrieved local people. . . . As a result of trading stories and getting to know each other while lodging complaints at the municipal or provincial level, they have punctured the 'cellularization' . . . of rural society. In so doing, they have sometimes come to recognize that they must join forces and organize for self-protection" (2004: 16). "Local struggles," O'Brien (2002: 228) concludes, "begin in enclaves of tolerance, spread when conditions are auspicious, and evolve into inclusion in the broader polity." This is the process I call "scale shift."

As O'Brien and Li tell it, the shift of the scale of protest in Hengyang County was not limited to a change in the level of the targets of contention. Among activists who moved beyond the village level, it produced both "claim shift" and "object shift" – that is, a new language aimed at higher-level officials that went beyond their originally narrow claims. Activists started to say things like, "I will struggle on so long as the Communist Party is still in power and I am still alive" (2004: 16). Their move upward in the administrative hierarchy also seemed to produce "a growing sense of agency and self-worth," insofar as they began to feel that the center not only welcomed their assistance but required it. However modest its scope

120

and limited its impact, the shift in the scale of contention from the village to a higher level of the Chinese system occasionally seemed to produce changes in identity.

Scale shift is an essential element of all contentious politics, without which all contention that arises locally would remain at that level. We can define it as *a change in the number and level of coordinated contentious actions to a different focal point, involving a new range of actors, different objects, and broadened claims* (McAdam, Tarrow, and Tilly 2001: 331). It can also generate a change in the meaning and scope of the object of the claim. Think of the suicide tactic that we examined in Chapter 6. It did not simply expand from Lebanon and Sri Lanka to a world scale; the widening application of the tactic changed it in kind, becoming a shorthand for anti-Westernism and anti-Semitism, which transcended the particular claims and disputes to which it was locally linked.[1]

Scale shift can operate in two directions: *upward*, in which case local action spreads outward from its origins; or *downward*, when a generalized practice is adopted at a lower level. Today's international system offers a special challenge for activists because it both opens conduits for upward shift and can empower national, regional, and local contention with international models of collective action. But by the same token, as new forms of contention move downward, their original meanings may diffuse and the forms of organization they produce may domesticate.

In this chapter, I first offer a descriptive model of vertical scale shift. To illustrate that the process is a general one, I then apply it to two very different cases: the upward shift of Islamist radicalism from Pakistan, Iran, and Egypt to the global level; and the creation at the global level of the World Social Forum followed by its downward shift as a model of local and national fora in individual countries. I show that shifts in scale are not simply the reproduction, at a different level, of the claims, targets, and constituencies of the sites where contention begins; they produce new alliances, new targets, and changes in the foci of claims and perhaps even new identities.

A Descriptive Model of Upward Scale Shift

At the core of scale shift is the process of diffusion that we saw in Chapter 6; but where ordinary diffusion is horizontal and has an initiator and an

[1] I am grateful to Paul Ingram for this observation on an earlier version of this chapter.

adopter, scale shift involves the coordination of episodes of contention on the part of larger collectivities against broader targets, new actors, and institutions at new levels of interaction. In doing so, it can affect the character of contention and its claims as well as its geographic range. Scale shift involves five mechanisms in particular: the coordination of contention, brokerage, and theorization, as well as the shift of claims and objects. It may even lead to identity shift, as O'Brien and Li hint in their account.

By *coordination*, I mean the joint planning of collective action and the creation of instances for cross-spatial collaboration. But connecting activists from all over the world is not simply the result of coordination. Two by-now familiar mechanisms help organizers to do so: *brokerage* is the practical mechanism that constructs such bridges; *theorization* permits the generalization and abstraction of a core causal idea from a particular reality into a general frame that can be applied to other realities. Two additional mechanisms follow from the shift of contention to a new level of coordination: *target shift* and *claim shift* (Reitan 2003). Shifting claims from one level to another attaches them to new targets, leading to a subtle change in the nature of the claims and to the forms of collective action as well.

To this chain of mechanisms and processes, some would add a sixth, *identity shift*, which means an alteration in shared definitions of a boundary between two political actors and of relations across that boundary (della Porta 2005b). If this implies turning in one identity for another, it would be a difficult mechanism to demonstrate. More likely is the mobilization of new and "detached" elements of identity onto "embedded" ones, as activists who normally engage in collective action within their locality or country add transnational actions, targets, and alliances to their repertoire (Tilly 2004a: 59–60; Turnbull 2004: 19). This sequence of mechanisms is mapped schematically in Figure 7.1.

Scale shift within societies is a familiar domestic process, one that can be observed in cases as diverse as the American civil rights and nuclear freeze movements (McAdam, Tarrow, and Tilly 2001). It is helped by the spatial proximity, interpersonal networks, and institutional linkages within particular societies. But to come into effect internationally, scale shift must cross two distinct dimensions: the horizontal spatial divide between different political cultures and the vertical gaps between levels of the international system. That requires a shift in the focal point of contention, a move from familiar domestic structures of opportunity and constraint to new terrains, and the need to forge new alliances with different allies against different opponents. In economic language, the transaction costs of moving up the

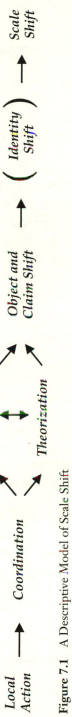

Figure 7.1 A Descriptive Model of Scale Shift

scale of contention are much higher than scale shift in familiar domestic settings.

There are supports for transnational scale shift. As in the cases of diffusion examined in Chapter 6, it is helped by the general processes of internationalization and communication at work in our era. But structural change will not on its own move a new form of contention from initiators to adopters; it requires hard work among people who may know each other only slightly and who may have very different expectations and claims. Two paradigmatic cases – political Islam and the global justice movement – can help us to identify how transnational scale shift works. The first shows how domestic repression and the claims of a universalistic religion led Islamist activists from the national to the global level; the second shows how an innovation – the World Social Forum – that was a result of upward scale shift was refracted downward as a model for regional, national, and local instances of coordination.

Political Islamism Shifts Upward

Modern social movements often have a variety of sources. In his definitive study of political Islam, Gilles Kepel (2002: ch. 1) traces the origins of the modern political Islamist movement to three main sources: Egypt, Iran, and Pakistan. In Egypt, Sayyid Qutb made a signal contribution to transnational Islamism, according to Kepel, along with Ruholla Khomenei of Iran and Mawlana Mawdudi of Pakistan. Despite their differences, and the differences in their three countries, "All three men shared a vision of Islam as a political movement, and they all called for the establishment of an Islamic state" (p. 23).

Qutb, who was hanged in 1966, attracted a cross-section of Muslim youth to a movement against the secular nationalist regime of Gamal Nasser. He stigmatized secular nationalism with an Arab word from the Koran, *jahiliyya*, "which describes the state of ignorance or barbarism in which the Arabs are supposed to have lived before the revelation of Islam to the Prophet Mohammed" (p. 25). The Muslim Brotherhood, which predated Qutb by several decades but which he helped to revive, spread his ideas to Saudi Arabia and Jordan. But it was in Egypt, with the resounding defeat of Arab nationalism in the Six Day War, that the movement was able to gain a hearing (p. 32).

Political Islamism has its core in the Arab world, but Arabs are less than a fifth of the world's Muslims, and modern Islamism also took root in

without exception, their targets were the secular nationalist regimes of their own countries. But determined repression in some countries and calculated co-optation in others led these national movements to pose broader claims against more distant targets like Israeli occupation of Jerusalem, American troop presence in Saudi Arabia, and the secular regime in Algeria. Ultimately, they shifted the scale of their claims from the implementation of the law of the Koran in the Muslim world to defeating "the conspiracy of the Jews, the Americans, and their Muslim puppets" wherever they could be found.

Down the Up Scale

Upward scale shift was eventually followed by its opposite. When the United States government, seeking retribution for the mass murders of September 11, 2001, and a new foothold in the Middle East, invaded secular Iraq in 2003, there was no more than a shadow of an Islamist presence in that country. In reaction to what could be painted as a new Western "crusade," Islamic militants from across the Arab world, some of them on the run from defeat in Afghanistan, others from Saudi Arabia and Pakistan, still others escaping increased surveillance in Western Europe, filtered into Iraq. Whether they had assistance from neighboring states is not in question; what is most interesting is that they were able to shift the scale of conflict downward to a country in which war and occupation gave them an opening.

Called into service by their American masters, untrained and reluctant Iraqi troops and police, not to mention civilian bystanders, were caught in what increasingly came to resemble the civil war that Islamists had been unable to foment in their own countries. The Islamist network shifted the level and the object of its claims downward to join an insurgency against the newest and most fragile regime in the Middle East.

The World Social Forum

As is well known, the idea of a "social forum," which developed in reaction to the World Economic Summit in Davos, led to a sequence of global meetings and demonstrations in Porto Alegre and Mumbai. It was a clear case of upward scale shift that Ruth Reitan (2003) has traced through a process similar to what we saw above for political Islam. Here I want to focus on the obverse process: a scaling down from the global level

South Asia. Islamic texts originally written in Urdu had a major influence on the movement throughout the twentieth century. Here the major figure was Mawlana Mawdudi, who attacked the "irreligious" independent states that had emerged after World War II. For him, "all nationalism was impiety, more especially as its conception of the state was European-inspired." For Mawdudi, Islam had to be political, but he favored "Islamization from above," founding, in 1941, Jama 'at-I-Islami, which he saw as a Leninist vanguard of the Islamic revolution (p. 34). This was the program of action that Qutb eventually adopted, laying the groundwork for the future linkage between Arab and South Asian Islamism (p. 36).

As political Islamism developed in these various sites, its adherents experimented with a wide repertoire of action. From outright attacks on the rulers of their countries and on foreigners, as in Egypt, to electoral competition and then civil war, as in Algeria, to providing social services in the densely populated slums of Middle Eastern cities and organizing madrasa schools in Pakistan and elsewhere, Islamist activists adapted to the variety of structures of opportunity and constraint they found around them.

But none of these strands of what became a global movement would have spread very far without the successful example of the Iranian revolution in 1977–9. Ruhollah Khomeini, who emerged as its leader, represented the clerical strand of Iranian radicalism; but another important strand was a reinterpretation of Shi'ite doctrine inspired by Marxism and the concerns of what had come to be called the Third World. "The Ayatolla's genius lay in appropriating the aspirations of the young militants" and including in his audience "the educated middle class who otherwise would have remained aloof from a personality perceived as preposterously traditional and reactionary" (p. 37).

In its stated or implied goal of reinstating the Caliphate, political Islamism was always implicitly transnational – or at least universalistic. But in Egypt, South Asia, and Iran, propaganda and collective action were first directed against local regimes, accused of having betrayed the values of the Koran and fallen into a state of jahiliyya. It was Khomeni who first raised the scale of political Islam when, in 1964, he condemned the presence of American "advisers" to the Shah (p. 40). This led to his deportation to France and, indirectly, to his contacts with other elements in the Iranian opposition and to the shift in scale of the movement's message.

The Iranian revolution had limitations as the source of transnational Islamism as the twenty-year period that elapsed between it and the formation of the broader movement developed. First, because Iran was a

Shi'a state, the majority Sunni Muslims looked upon it with diffidence. Second, for much of its first decade, the new Islamic Republic was bogged down in a costly war with Iraq, leaving few resources for proselytizing abroad. Finally, however sympathetic they were to the cause of Palestinian nationalism, the Iranians were not Arabs and did not share a common culture with the urban masses in Cairo, Jedda, or Algiers. It would take a broader international conflict, involving the superpowers, to lay the groundwork for a truly transnational movement.

War Shifts the Scale of Contention

Ironically, it was the Soviet occupation of Afghanistan and the Afghan war, financed and organized by the United States and its Saudi and Pakistani proxies, that produced the major opportunity for the shift in scale of political Islamism. It offered thousands of Islamist militants the chance to travel outside their own countries, meet others like themselves, and theorize the concept of jihad from the varieties of forms of action familiar from their home countries to a model for transnational military struggle. In this process of scale shift, the United States was an unconscious broker of alliances among different Islamic groups and ideologies.

Of course, from the beginning, there were ties across the Muslim world. Dale F. Eickelman (1997: 31) traces them among three main sources of the movement:

Many older members of Egypt's Muslim Brotherhood have strong ties with Saudi Arabia and the Gulf states.... Likewise, Bangladesh's Jama'at-I-Islami is formally autonomous but retains close ties with the movement's world headquarters in Punjab and appears to accept... major donations from individuals and institutions in Saudi Arabia and elsewhere in the Gulf for its campaign for Islamicization. In Europe and North America, first- and (to a lesser extent) second-generation immigrant communities offer better bases for the exchange of ideas and information than those available in countries of origin.

Both relational and nonrelational paths broadened the reach of political Islamism. Early developments in electronic technology helped to spread the message. Audiocassettes, which had been important instruments in the Iranian revolution, became transnational means of communication in the 1980s. They were "less a sign of direct intergroup cooperation than the popularity of topics and speakers who have developed a following large enough to allow modest profits to the informal network of kiosk venders who

distribute them" (p. 32). There were also direct connections religious figures and scholars. Unlike Catholicism, Islam has no erarchy that can certify or decertify religious teachers or mos made it easy for self-styled imams to establish mosques throu Muslim world and in the centers of immigration in Europe. M came sites for social appropriation in which "Muslim activists ar borrow from one another through face-to-face encounters and literature of like-minded groups" (p. 32).

But scale shift is more than a horizontal diffusion process: a bridging relationships both spread the movement beyond Afghan shifted it vertically to a higher level. As the most dynamic socie Middle East, Egypt was for years at the core of the movement. The Brotherhood was the most prominent of the national Islamist mov and academics from across the Islamic world who studied in Cai contact there with adepts of the Brotherhood, returning to thei countries to help found youth movements, such as the one fou Kabul University in the late 1960s (p. 33).

Not all those who played a brokerage role were sympathetic to the they brought together. In its obsession with turning back the Soviet a in Afghanistan, the United States recruited and trained mercenaries t against the Soviet-backed regime through the intermediary of the M Brotherhood and Saudi Arabia. "In the 1980s," writes Eickelman, "A resistance became a 'joint venture' of the Muslim Brotherhood an Saudis, with tacit U.S. support" (p. 37). Once connected to one and "Afghan Arabs" who had fought in Afghanistan became a restless tra tional force, and many of their camps became training grounds for mili who moved elsewhere to coordinate new insurgencies. One camp in Pa province trained Kashmiri militants, Philippine Moros, and Palestinia lamists, many of whom offered their services and their military experti other Islamist movements in the Middle East (pp. 37–8). This was the source of the transnational movement we know today as Al Qaeda, wh coordinates and finances insurgencies around the globe. It has narrowed repertoire of contention from the wide range of collective claims maki that characterized Islamism in domestic politics to an almost unique foc on causing death and destruction.

The South Asian, Egyptian, and Iranian activists who were the inte lectual sources of the first Islamist groups probably had no inkling of t global range of the movement that would grow out of their writings. Indee

to a multitude of national, regional, and local social fora in Europe and elsewhere.

From Parallel Summits to Countersummits

The major source of the idea of a "social forum" was the practice of holding "parallel summits" around official international meetings in the 1980s and 1990s, mainly in the countries of the North.[2] As we saw in Chapter 2, there has always been a close connection between international institutions and the activities of nongovernmental groups. But as the Cold War waned and the practice of holding official international summits grew geometrically, NGOs and social movements began to turn their attention to the decisions made at these meetings through holding parallel summits. Mario Pianta (2001) sees the first example of such parallel summits at official meetings at the UN Conference on the Human Environment at Stockholm in 1972, and then at the first World Conference on Women in Mexico City in 1975. But it was the gathering of a group calling itself "The Other Economic Summit," formed to coincide with and criticize a meeting of the G-7 countries in 1984, that turned the routine practice of holding parallel summits in a more contentious direction.

Countersummits were distinct from "parallel summits" in that they were frequently connected to contentious forms of politics. A dramatic connection occurred in 1988 in Berlin, where an IMF–World Bank meeting produced both alternative conferences and a major demonstration in which hundreds of groups participated (Pianta 2001: 172; Gerhards and Rucht 1992). In the 1990s countersummits became almost routine accompaniments to meetings of international institutions. In some cases, these events were organized by ad hoc coalitions (see Chapter 9); in others, permanent organizations were responsible (Pianta 2001: 174). In the mid-1990s the model was extended from the great international financial institutions to meetings of the European Council, in support of the unemployed. The trend to contentious countersummits culminated in Seattle in 1999 against the ministerial meeting of the WTO (Pianta 2001: 177).

---

[2] Parallel summits we can define, with Mario Pianta (2001: 171), as events organized by national and international civil society groups, independent of the activities of states and firms, to coincide with official summits of governments and international institutions, whose agendas they critically address with alternative policy proposals through public information and analysis, political protest, and mobilization.

The turn of the century brought two trends that would eventually transform the practice of the countersummit: first, the tendency to organize countersummits independently of official ones and, second, a geographic shift from its heartland in Western Europe to the countries of the global South (Pianta 2001: 76). The two trends combined: whereas three-quarters of the parallel summits organized between 1988 and 2001 were linked to official summits in the global North, in 2003 and in the first half of 2004, half of the events Pianta and his collaborators identified were connected to no official summit, and only 37 percent of them took place in Europe or North America (Pianta, Silva, and Zola 2004).[3]

Also in the global South, two extraordinary *encuentros* were held in the jungles of Chiapas following the Zapatista rebellion of 1994. In Chiapas in 1996, "people from over 50 countries turned up in the muddy backwater of La Realidad and signed onto an 'intercontinental network of resistance'" (Reitan 2003: 16). A second encounter was held in Spain in the following year, sponsored by the European Zapatista solidarity network Ya Basta (p. 16), giving birth to People's Global Action. The term *encuentro* was already familiar from Latin American women's movements (Sternbach et al. 1992; Schultz 1998). The Brazilian activists who mounted the first World Social Forum knew it well. When they were asked to organize "another Davos," the practice converged with the northern model of the countersummit in Porto Alegre.

From Davos to the World Social Forum

Some shifts in scale take place incrementally, whereas others turn on a "hinge" that can be clearly identified. In the case of the global justice movement, the hinge was the countersummit organized by a small group of organizations against the 1999 meeting of the World Economic Forum (WEF) in Davos (Houtart and Polet 2001: 78).[4] The most important proposal made at that meeting came from a Frenchman, Christophe Aguiton, who had worked on the European March against Unemployment and was one of the founding members of ATTAC (p. 81). Aguiton proposed coordinating a number of existing local and regional organizations to "help

---

[3] Figures for 2004 were kindly provided by Professor Mario Pianta.

[4] The founding organizations were the Coalitions against the Multilateral Agreement on Investment, the Structural Adjustment Participatory Review International Network, the World Forum of Alternatives, and ATTAC. For a fresh and early account, see Houtart and Polet 2001.

us to understand what has happened in each of our countries. . . . We think that it is through joint action that we can stabilize the long-term network coordination that we are looking for" (p. 96).

Coordination was followed by brokerage. When the WEF organizers refused the suggestion by two Brazilian businessmen, Oded Grajew and Francisco Whitaker, to open the forum to social issues, they contacted Bernard Cassen, one of the founders of ATTAC, who helped to create an organizing committee for a countersummit and suggested holding it in Brazil. With the support of the Brazilian trade-union confederation, the CUT, and the MST (Movement of Landless Farm Workers), the result was the first Porto Alegre World Social Forum (Reiten 2003: 22–3).

The Porto Alegre event represented a major upward shift in scale and a fusion of the northern model of the countersummit with the Latin American model of the *encuentro*. The spatial shift was both deliberate and opportune. In Porto Alegre, the left-wing Worker's Party (PT) was in power in a country that was both southern and large. This gave the new "global" coalition – until then, largely European – an important southern base, a domestic constituency (at least half the participants at the 2001 forum were Brazilians), and evidence from the municipality of Porto Alegre that the left can come to power and of what it can accomplish when it does.

From 2001 through 2003, the forum attracted increasing numbers of participants and observers, before shifting its venue to Mumbai in January 2004 and moving back to Brazil in 2005.[5] Each successive event brought not only an expansion in the variety of groups and institutions participating, but an expansion of its agenda and a greater degree of institutionalization. Growing out of a single event that was organized around criticism of the global pretensions of the Davos elite, the social forum was created to embrace a broad spectrum of claims and demands, condensed in the slogan "Resistance to neoliberalism, war, and militarism, and for peace and social justice." By the 2002 forum, a permanent coordinating committee had been formed and the agenda expanded to include calls for global social justice and solidarity, democracy and transparency, electoral and participatory democracy, and the struggle against dictatorship (Marcon and Pianta 2004).

---

[5] Sources on this global series of events are legion. For reports on the Porto Alegre summits go to www.forumsocialmundial.br. For coverage of the Mumbai Forum, go to www.India.indymedia.org. Extensive coverage can also be found at www.Ipsnews.net, www.Opendemocracy.net, and www.Alternet.org.

The Social Forum Shifts Downward

The success of the World Social Forum generated a process of downward scale shift to Western Europe, where the model for the social forum had originated. As we saw in Chapter 4, Europeans have a rich tradition of framing claims transnationally, even if most of their protests are domestically organized. And because Western Europe was the main source of countersummits in the years before the WSF was invented, downward scale shift was easier than it would be in the United States.

Downward scale shift is the transfer of collective action from a higher to a lower level independent of the agencies of the higher-level coordination. Just as upward scale shift leads to the identification of new targets and to the making of new claims, downward scale shift allows lower-level activists to take on local targets and make local claims in new and different ways. In the process, a loosening of the message coming from the "higher" form may occur, and the model itself can disperse into a number of different claims and forms of organization. This is what happened as thousands of activists who attended the World Social Forum took the model home. Table 7.1 records the geographic distribution of the term "social forum" from an internet search carried out in late 2004.[6]

While we have no systematic data on the diffusion downward of the social forum model to most regions of the world, it is already clear that it has taken root unevenly. For example, it is much less widely diffused in the United States than we might expect, given the excitement following the Chiapas rebellion and the Seattle protest.[7] In contrast, soon after the first Porto Alegre meeting, Western Europeans began to hold regular meetings at regional, national, and local levels that they identified as "social fora."[8]

---

[6] I am grateful to Angela Kim for the original internet research and coding that produced the data in Table 7.1.

[7] Ruth Reitan writes that there was an ultimately unsuccessful attempt to organize a forum in Washington in 2002 by the Mobilization for Global Justice group. The same occurred in New York City and Philadelphia, and also in Pittsburgh, where Dennis Brutus, a South African activist who had been involved in the WSF, was teaching at the time. In Boston, a social forum met for the first time in 2004. From a personal communication to the author.

[8] As an Italian group recorded it: "The appointment [for a European social forum] was set at Porto Alegre . . . where it was decided to organize a social forum for each continent. These regional forums will attempt to open up new spaces for democratic debate within the movement, to adapt the themes dealt with in Brazil to local realities, but also to revisit themes of regional importance with a global optic." Go to www.Lunaria.org/tertium/fse/default.html, visited on October 12, 2004. For the official website of the European Forum go to www.fse-esf.org.

Table 7.1. *Social Fora Appearing in an Internet Search, by World Region, 1999–2004*

Region	1999[a]–2001	2002	2003	2004	Total
Africa	1	3	10	13	27
Asia	1	0	2	2	5
Antipodes/Oceania	0	2	4	2	8
Central/Eastern Europe[b]	0	4	3	1	8
Latin America and Caribbean	3	11	27	15	56
Middle East	0	1	0	2	3
North America	0	7	5	5	17
Western Europe	2	15	22	9	48
Total N	7	43	73	49	172
Cumulative N	7	50	123	172	

[a] The Manila Social Forum was founded in November 1999 and the Bologna Social Forum was founded in June 2000.
[b] Turkey is coded together with Southeastern Europe.
Source: The search was carried out by searching for "social forum" in the English language in November 2004.

European Social Fora assembled in 2002 in Florence, in 2003 in Paris, and in 2004 in London.

It was following a resolution at the 2002 WSF in Porto Alegre that the first European Social Forum was held in Florence at the Medicean Fortezza da Basso, with an attendance of roughly 10,000.[9] Building on the rich associational foundation of European contentious politics, and mainly in regions with a strong associational tradition, a network of fora spread across the Italian peninsula. Why in Italy? The Italian left had been in a shambles since the collapse of the Soviet Union and the disintegration of the Italian Communist Party that followed it. Given the declining opportunities for domestic activism, progressive activists were more than ready for an international outlet. They found it first in the Zapatista rebellion of 1994, when several hundred Italians appeared in Chiapas in support of the rebels. *Ya Basta* thenceforth became an important symbol in Italian politics and its stalwarts a ready audience for new forms of transnational politics.

This growing international vocation crystallized around the formation of the Genoa Social Forum, which coordinated the massive transnational protest against the G-8 meeting in the summer of 2001. When a young protester, Carlo Giuliani, was shot and killed by the Genoa police, outrage

[9] For an account from the official website of the European Forum go to www.fse-esf.org.

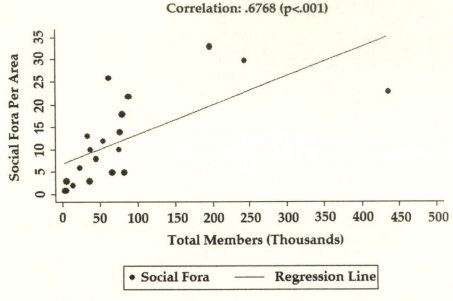

Figure 7.2 Social Fora, 2004, and PCI Members, 1984, Italy; by Geographic Region. *Source:* Internet search and Portito comunista italiano, *Dati sulle organizazzioni del partito* (Rome, 1984).

joined internationalism to produce interest in the idea of introducing the social forum all over the country. But although this international vocation of Italians activists was new, it was not detached from either domestic problems or from inherited political subcultures. On the one hand, Italian delegates to the Porto Alegre fora seemed more interested in debating Italy's internal politics than global problems; on the other, the creation of these new and "global" social forums closely shadowed the regional distribution of traditional left-wing party organizations. Figure 7.2 demonstrates this "local" in the "global" in the correlation between the location of social fora found in a computer search and the number of regional membership lists of the now largely defunct Italian Communist Party in the 1980s.[10]

[10] I am grateful to Angela Kim the carrying out the website search and correlational analysis at the regional level of the relationship between social fora and Communist Party membership. The latter data were kindly provided by Stephen Hellman. More disaggregated analysis would have been preferable than the regional level, but many social fora are organized at the regional level.

Collective Identities: Embedded and Detached

This takes us to the construction of transnational identity. Following Melucci (1988), many students of social movements have seen them as arenas in which new collective identities are fashioned. The general point is correct for some activists in some movements in some contexts, but it is scarcely universal. Embedded identities are difficult to dislodge and the "detached" identities connected to social movements are more superficial and easily reversible (Tilly 2002). Even in integral movements like political Islamism, the identity-building process took time and is still incomplete, given that many activists never leave their own country, identify with local causes, and have only weak ties to the international movement (Sageman 2004).[11]

If this is true for a movement as integral as political Islamism, in the global justice movement identities are, if anything, more diffuse and less easily embedded. This makes identity construction a key task for movement organizers. Donatella della Porta and her collaborators see the social forum as an expression of deliberative democracy (della Porta 2005a, b; della Porta et al. 2006). Over and over, their Italian respondents focused on the culture of debate, discussion, and the toleration of diversity within their ranks. In this most contentious of political cultures, the social forum model has produced a cascade of debate, discussion, and self-reflection about the creation of "tolerant" collective identities (della Porta 2005b). As della Porta (2005a: 75) writes sympathetically, "internal differences are the driving force in the search for forms of participation that respect individual 'subjectivity,' avoiding exclusive commitments and vertical control; consensus rules are privileged *vis-à-vis* majority rules; direct participation is emphasized against representative mechanisms, leaders are considered as 'speakers' or 'facilitators.'"

Of course, local and regional social fora do more than negotiate identity. They work to highlight local conflicts that make local-global connections and urge member organizations to develop concrete proposals for action. Between the annual WSF meetings, many organized preparatory workshops to help members connect to other groups and move from analysis to plans for action.[12] The promise of the downward shift of models like the social forum is that it can help activists frame their claims in global terms,

---

[11] I am grateful to Barak Mendelson for these observations.
[12] I am grateful to Jackie Smith for sharing these observations with me.

connect them to others like themselves across borders, and begin the work of constructing a global movement. That task has been facilitated by recent advances in electronic communication, but even here transnational activism may not converge into a unified global movement.

The Internet as a Vehicle of Diffusion and Scale Shift

There has always been scale shift in the dynamics of collective action. But especially when diffusion crosses both borders and levels, there are delays, distortions, and obstacles in the process. This situation may well be changing: With the expansion and greater availability of electronic communication, shifting the scale of contention has become both easier and more rapid. Scholars (W. L. Bennett 2003; Rheingold 2002; Wellman and Gulia 1999) have seen the internet helping to create "virtual communities" across space. But there are as many forms of electronic communication and uses for the internet as there are for other forms of communication (e.g., see Samuels 2004: chs. 1 and 2); as a result the novelty of the internet may soon wear off and its competition with commercial messages may be lost.[13] Also, because every technological innovation has costs as well as benefits, the internet provides a mixed blessing to movement organizers. But the internet is more than a form of communication; it is at the core of a new movement form.

The Internet as Movement Form

Most studies of the impact of the internet on social movements have focused on this new phenomenon as a form of communication, one that facilitates the rapid diffusion of information about contentious episodes among chains of activists.[14] There is little doubt that the internet is having the same facilitative and diffusing effect that print and the vernacular had during earlier centuries of movement activity (Anderson 1991; Tarrow 1998: ch. 3). But some experts think the importance of the internet goes well

---

[13] The failure of the Institute for Global Communication (IGC) in San Francisco was an early example of the inability of a movement-linked internet provider to compete with commercial providers.

[14] Judith Hellman (1999) pointed to the diffusion – and the refraction – of the image of the Chiapas rebellion through the lenses of North American activists who formed an image of a "virtual" Chiapas but also helped to protect the rebellion from repression at the hands of the Mexican army by publicizing it widely in the United States.

beyond communication, to constitute a social network remarkably similar to the reticular structure of social movements (W. L. Bennett 2003; Myers 2002; Wellman and Giulia 1999). It can also become a *tool* of collective action, for activists and others who use their skills and artistic talents to disrupt the communications processes of their opponents (Samuels 2004).

Because many social movements lack consistent, hierarchical organizational structures, these theorists argue, it is only a short step to regarding the internet itself as a form of organization (W. L. Bennett 2003). The group website, with very little need for formal organization behind it, can be used as a node for organizing protest campaigns. In a way, the internet carries to its logical conclusion a trend identified since the 1960s, as decentralized networks of activists began to take the place of the cumbersome, expensive-to-maintain bureaucratic organizations of the past.

If the internet has become a basic organizing tool on the familiar territory of liberal democratic states, its potential must be great in organizing transnational contention, where activists at great distances from one another have little opportunity to develop face-to-face ties (for examples, see Danitz and Stroebel 2001, Samuels 2004: ch. 4). As W. Lance Bennett (2003: 1) writes, "at the most general level, it may seem obvious that current networks of global protest could not exist without various uses of the Internet." Mark Lichbach and Paul Almeida (2001: 1) observe that "anti-globalization protests involve a globalized rainbow protest coalition, that is one with many different social movement organizations protesting in many cities, that is put together via the World Wide Web."

But the internet does not appear to have replaced interpersonal networking. Dieter Rucht reports from a German study of participants in the anti–Iraq war demonstration of February 15 that only 11 percent had learned of the demonstration via a website and another 6 percent via e-mail lists. "Friends, acquaintances and neighbors" were by far the most important category, with 31 percent.[15] Moreover, while the internet has had a profound effect on new entrants in the global activist ranks, it seems to have had less effect on long-standing movement organizations (W. L. Bennett 2003: 5–6).

The internet can also diffuse the character of the message. Internet-based information is rapid and telescopic, but internet-based movement networks

---

[15] Quoted with thanks from Dieter Rucht's unpublished survey of antiwar protesters on February 15, 2003, part of an eight-country study in progress under the direction of Stefaan Walgrave and Rucht. For an early report, see Verhulst and Walgrave 2003.

may lack the capacity "to attain the levels of ideological definition and decision making coherence that have characterized earlier social movements based on strong coalitions centered around leading organizations" (W. L. Bennett 2003: 2). All shifting and reticular movements reduce ideological cohesion, but the internet may be extreme in its centrifugal effects. This is in part because the typical internet-based unit of contention is the campaign, rather than more-embedded struggles with recurrent allies and enemies; but it is also due to the fact that the internet offers individual activists the opportunity for do-it-yourself ideological production, when those at the summit of their "organizations" might prefer to move in another direction or end a campaign.

If this logic is correct for domestic internet-based movements, it must be even more accurate for transnational movements. To the centrifugal effects that Bennett adduces for internet-based movements must be added the lack of enduring personal ties of activists working across borders. The weakening of international global justice campaigns following September 11 may have been partly a result of this ideological diffuseness (Mittelman 2004a) and partly the result of the shift of attention to the war in Iraq. Finally, because of the technological gap between activists in North and South, the internet may actually increase the inequality within a movement that seeks global equality (Tilly 2004b: ch. 5).

Conclusions

The processes specified in this chapter and in Chapter 6 are made up of the "nuts and bolts" of a more complex process of internationalization that includes other mechanisms, some of which we have not examined here, and depends on the particular conditions of each episode. I do not claim to have either explained transnational activism or predicted its outcomes. My aim has been to delineate processes that connect initial episodes of contention with responses and replications elsewhere and at different levels of the international system.

But we can go further, if only in a speculative mode. To recapitulate, let us review what I hope to have shown in this part of the book.

First, transnational movements do not automatically emerge like Venus on her seashell from macroprocesses like globalization or from the growth of global consciousness. They are built up through agent-specific processes like the horizontal diffusion of a form of contention, or through a shift in scale from the local or national level to the international level and back again.

Shifting the Scale of Contention

Focusing first on diffusion, I disaggregated that process into three variants: relational diffusion, which depends on attribution of similarity between initiators and adopters; nonrelational diffusion, which depends on impersonal means of transition; and mediated diffusion, which works through brokerage.

Turning to scale shift, I focused on the mechanisms of coordination, the brokerage and theorization that permit the aggregation of a variety of claimants and claims, and on the corresponding shift in claims, targets, and – more tentatively – identities, as contention moves from one level to another. Whereas diffusion is a traditional process that moves horizontally between one initiator and one adopter and has done so since long before the idea of globalization gained ground, scale shift would need to be the first process in the work of building a global social movement.

Both diffusion and scale shift vary in their nature and impact as the result of differences in their contexts and in the presence or absence of adjacent processes and mechanisms. Whereas the creation of a global Islamist movement was facilitated by the universalistic claim of an Islamic *umma*, the global justice movement had to adapt to broad geographic diversity and deep cultural differences, attempting to build unity out of the reduction of a many-headed opponent to a manageable target. Changes in the international environment have had similarly opposing effects: the outrage of September 11, 2001, launched a global hunt for Islamic terrorists and created a second-generation Islamist network, while partially displacing the global justice movement's focus on global neoliberalism into a struggle against American hegemony (Fisher 2004).

These contrasts and complexities lead to a reflection on the nature and impact of scale shift. A domestic movement that shifts in scale to the international level does not, as a result, automatically become a global movement and cease its local existence. A far more common pattern is for the *transposition* of part of activists' activities, rather than their transformation into rootless cosmopolitans. Even as they access global frames and international opportunities for scale shift, most activists remain rooted in and constrained by domestic political realities.

If this observation is correct, it may disappoint advocates of a global civil society or a world polity. But it has two positive implications for the growth of transnational politics: first, transposition allows a domestic movement to embrace transnational commitments without abandoning its domestic claims and those whose needs they try to represent; and, second, it allows a movement to spread through the impersonal ties of the media and the internet or through the weak ties of a brokerage chain, rather than depending on the more intense but narrower ties typical of relational diffusion.

Diffusion and scale shift involve partial commitments, verbal compromises, and organizational drift from one issue to another as priorities and agendas change – in other words, they involve politics. If what results is less than "globalization from below," it nevertheless is creating outlets for the daily claims of ordinary people responding to deeply felt grievances. But like globalization itself, these claims do not automatically give rise to transnational movements. Major efforts are required for the externalization of domestic claims, and even greater efforts are needed to form transnational coalitions that can transform them into effective forces for change. These two processes are the subjects of the next two chapters.

PART FOUR

The Local in the Global

8

Externalizing Contention

Twenty-six years after democracy fell in their country, a group of Chilean exiles informed Spanish magistrate Balthazar Garzón that General Augusto Pinochet was visiting London. Garzón immediately issued a extradition request to the British government to interrogate Pinochet for human rights crimes against Spanish citizens during the years when he was Chile's ruler (Lutz and Sikkink 2001b: 12). The decision electrified supporters of human rights around the world and was a beacon in their hope for the development of a law of universal jurisdiction (Lutz and Sikkink 2001a; also see Davis 2003).

Although British Home Secretary Jack Straw ultimately allowed Pinochet to return home, the events in Madrid and London set off what Ellen Lutz and Kathryn Sikkink (2001a and b) call "a justice cascade." In Argentina, an infamous torturer, Carlos Guillermo Suarez Mason, who had escaped prosecution for years, was arrested for the theft of children of Argentina's disappeared (2001b: 20–1). In Mexico, authorities arrested retired Argentine navy captain Miguel Cavallo as the plane on which he was traveling to Buenos Aires stopped to refuel in Cancun. In Italy, magistrates advanced a criminal case that had been languishing for years against Suarez Mason, Omar Santiago Riveros, and five other Argentine officers for the murder of eight Argentines of Italian descent (p. 23). Rome was also where another Argentine former officer, Jorge Olivera, was arrested in August 2000 while celebrating his wedding anniversary (p. 23). And in Chile, the cascade came full circle when, in 2004, Pinochet was indicted and a government commission called for reparations for the survivors of his reign of terror.[1]

[1] Larry Rohter, "A Torture Report Compels Chile to Reassess Its Past," November 28, 2004, at http://www.nytimes.com/2004/11/28/international/americas/28chile.

The reasons for the "justice cascade" following the Pinochet indictment were many. First, Chile has an active domestic human rights network which had been collecting information on the crimes of his regime since the mid-1970s. Second, Chileans elected a center-left government in 1999, which the British government was reluctant to offend. Third, in Spain, where thousands of Chileans had found refuge from the dictatorship, the prosecution was extremely popular.

But international opportunities seldom come together as fortuitously as they did in the Pinochet case. As one expert who followed the case pointed out, "Pinochet was the 'poster child' of the human rights movement."[2] Negative examples abound: in their claim to control the oil revenues being exploited from their lands by Shell, the Ogoni movement met stiff resistance from the Nigerian military government. Their campaign cost the life of their leader, Ken Saro-Wiwa, at the hands of the military government (Bob 2005: 115). Rubber tappers attempting to hold off the incursions of cattle ranchers demonstrated to convince the Brazilian government and its international allies of their rights, but at the cost of the life of union leader Chico Mendes (Keck 1995). Indigenous groups attempting to stop the inundation of tribal lands to construct the Narmada dam complex in India attracted the attention of international allies and deterred the World Bank from supporting the project, but ultimately lost the battle (Khagram 2002).

All of these groups worked hard to externalize their claims; most transformed them into universalistic terms that would appeal to international allies (see, especially, Bob 2005: ch. 2); and all of them – at least at first – gained international attention and intervention. How were their claims externalized? And do different kinds of claims makers externalize their claims in different ways? Finally, how does externalization relate to internal outcomes? We will see that a group can mount a shrewd and dramatic international information campaign but still fail on domestic ground.

In this chapter, I examine these questions, drawing evidence from three cases of claim externalization: human rights in Latin America, gender equality in Western Europe, and labor transnationalism in North America. Each illustrates a different pathway of externalization: the first, through information transmission and monitoring; the second, through institutional

[2] I am grateful to Reed Brody of Human Rights Watch for these reflections and for the quotation.

access; and the third, through a combination of direct action and international ties.

Externalizing Claims

Domestic actors, frustrated at their inability to gain redress from their own governments, have long sought the support of external allies. When Giuseppe Garibaldi sailed to Sicily at the head of a ragtag army of red-shirts to liberate the island from the Bourbons and to begin the process of Italian unification, he depended on the covert support of the British fleet (Mack Smith 1954). The independence movement in Greece profited from the support of British private citizens, like Lord Byron, and ultimately of the British government. And it was the United Nations that recognized the right of Jewish settlers to a national home on part of the former British mandate territory of Palestine. Externalization of contention is nothing new.

Launching the Boomerang

But until the 1980s episodes like these were the preserve of historians and advocates. It took a more deliberately transnational approach to understand the externalization of domestic contention. In the late 1990s, as the post–Cold War world began to produce dense networks of nongovernmental groups, Margaret Keck and Kathryn Sikkink (1998) theorized these relationships in a model they called "the boomerang effect." As Sikkink (2005b: 154) later described it in *Activists beyond Borders*, she and Keck "developed one type of alternative to the two-level game that we called 'the boomerang effect,' where non state actors, faced with repression and blockage at home, seek out state and non state allies in the international arena, and in some cases are able to bring pressure to bear from above on their government to carry out domestic political change." Later, Thomas Risse and Sikkink (1999) extended the boomerang into a "spiral model." Figure 8.1 reproduces Keck and Sikkink's original boomerang model.

In one sense, all Keck and Sikkink were doing was to project internationally the insight of E. E. Schattschneider (1960) that the losers in any conflict have an interest in shifting venues to bring in new allies and activate friendy audiences. But they went further in specifying that externalization depends on the workings of networks of domestic activists, their international allies,

145

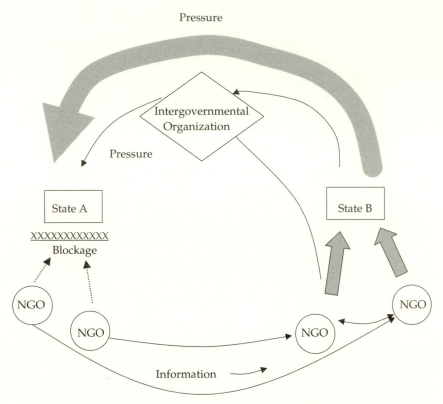

Pressure

Intergovernmental Organization

Pressure

State A

XXXXXXXXXXXX
Blockage

State B

NGO

NGO

NGO

NGO

Information

Figure 8.1 The Boomerang Model. *Source:* Adapted from *Activists beyond Borders: Advocacy Networks in International Politics*, by Margaret E. Keck and Kathryn Sikkink, p. 13. Copyright © 1998 by Cornell University. Used by permission of the publisher, Cornell University Press.

and parts of foreign states and international institutions. Their work took the study of transnational contention to a new level of empirical specificity and theoretical sophistication.

But Keck and Sikkink applied the model to essentially *bilateral* – not multilateral – relations across borders. And they looked only at cases in which domestic actors were "blocked" from expressing their claims domestically by their own states (Sikkink 2005b). The forms of pressure they examined revolved around what they called "informational politics." Their book left unspecified two other pathways of externalization: the use of institutionalized access and direct action. In this chapter I examine all three and their different implications for successful externalization.

Beyond the Boomerang

Externalization works through a sequence of phases that can differ, first, in its relationship to domestic contexts; second, in the framing of contention; and, third, through different forms of collective action.

Domestic Contexts   Keck and Sikkink (1998: 12–13) focused on what they called the "blockage" of domestic claims as the condition that leads to the desire for transnational intervention. But blockage is sometimes outright *repression* and sometimes a simple *lack of responsiveness* to domestic claims. The effects of the two are bound to be different and lead to different pathways of externalization. For example, in her recent work, Sikkink (2005b: 159) has recognized that "feminist groups and groups of indigenous peoples have often found the international arena more receptive to their demands than are domestic political institutions." That is not an example of repression but of the absence of a domestic response.

Framing   No domestic claim is inherently interesting outside a country's borders unless it framed to appeal to a broader audience (Bob 2005). This does not necessarily require outright "frame transformation": often the symbols and issues that appeal to a domestic audience can be extended without much frame transformation to an international one. But many campaigners for external support reframe domestic claims to gain international attention. The reframing of campaigns for labor or indigenous rights as human rights is a good example.

Collective Action Forms   In order to gain the attention of potential allies, weak social actors in repressive regimes have to overcome high barriers. What can they do to overcome them? In Figure 8.1, Keck and Sikkink (1998: 14) specified their actions as "information," but in their narratives they go further. In addition to providing information, domestic actors who seek international support can use institutional access or engage in attention-getting direct action. Collective action can work through three mechanisms: information diffusion, institutional access, and direct action.

These variations in domestic conditions, in framing strategies, and in forms of collective action describe three different pathways of externalization. Figure 8.2 offers a composite model of these pathways. In this chapter, I offer a differentiated and dynamic account of externalization, which varies according to the closed or open nature of domestic structures, in how the issue is framed for international consumption, and in the forms of action

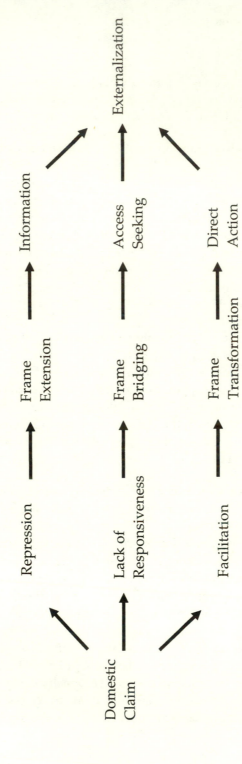

Figure 8.2 A Composite Model of Externalization

148

Table 8.1. *Three Forms of Externalization*

Object of Claim	Domestic Context	Framing Strategy	Central Mechanism	Desired Outcome
Human rights redress	Repression, facilitation	Frame extension	Information transmittal	International monitoring
Gender equality at work	Nonresponsiveness, facilitation	Frame bridging	Institutional access	ECJ rulings
Labor transnationalism	Repression, nonresponsiveness	Frame transformation	Contentious politics	Enforcement of labor rights

that link domestic claimants to their external targets. Like Keck and Sikkink, I begin with the *informational pathway*, drawing on research on human rights in Latin America. I turn next to *institutional access*, examining the issue of gender equality in the European Court of Justice. I close by examining *direct action*, drawing on research on labor transnationalism in North America. Table 8.1 summarizes the arguments that follow.

Monitoring Mistreatment

In addition to Chile, in the 1970s and 1980s military dictators held power in Argentina, Brazil, and Uruguay. Paraguay had been authoritarian for decades. Even Mexico, formally an electoral democracy, engaged in "dirty war" practices, for example, the massacre of hundreds of unarmed civilians in October 1968 (Sikkink 1993: 428–31). Where opportunities for direct action were limited and costly, information politics became the main – and often the only – form of externalization available to victims and their advocates.

But these cases were not all of a piece. For example, the Catholic Church, which was conservative in Argentina, was a major conduit for information in Chile (Brysk 1994: 44–5). In Mexico, even as dissent was squelched and opponents were "disappeared," electoral competition and interest group politics flourished (Cook 1996: 16–18). Foreign responses were uneven and unreliable: while quiet American pressure was a spur to democratization in Mexico, in Chile Washington policy makers saw a specter of communism and supported the Pinochet regime.

The international human rights regime that had begun to develop in the years after World War II was, at first, largely hortatory. "To become effective, the means had to be found to translate the human rights ideals of the declaration and treaties of the postwar period into widely shared understandings and practices" (Sikkink 1993: 414). From the 1960s on, the Organization of American States (OAS) and the UN set out formal procedures to investigate human rights abuses, while international NGOs developed strategies to expose repressive states' practices (p. 414). An international human rights network grew up, consisting of "parts of IGOs at both the international and regional levels, international NGOs on human rights, domestic NGOs on human rights, and private foundations" (pp. 415–16).[3] In this context Latin Americans responded to the abuses they began to suffer with the collapse of democracy.

Their situation was not completely bleak. With more than one hundred years of constitutional democracy behind them, Latin Americans had at least a theoretical culture of human rights to facilitate mobilization (Hawkins 2002: 50). As Patrick Ball (2000: 54) writes, during the first wave of human rights activism, "activists in countries with indigenous rights traditions, *based primarily in liberal constitutions*, were more likely to find the language of international human rights to be compelling relative to activists in countries without such traditions" (emphasis added).

Not only constitutional traditions but domestic institutions helped Latin American human rights activists find external allies. Chile again offers an example. After the 1973 coup, the Catholic Church offered a "shield of legitimacy" behind which the early human rights organizations coordinated assistance for victims of persecution (Loveman 1998: 493). For fear of risking a confrontation with the church and alienating the international community, "in its first year in power the military junta did not wish to risk an open attack on the 'humanitarian work'" of religious-based human rights groups (p. 494). Scholarly institutions like FLACSO were also bases for opposition survival and communication (Hawkins 2002: 55–62).

But these groups were trying to operate in ruthless regimes in which open dissent was greeted with imprisonment, torture, and murder. How could they externalize their claims? The existence of an international human rights regime offered two answers. First, advocates could frame domestic opposition in terms that would attract the attention of Western human rights groups and neutralize the hostility of political enemies – like the

---

[3] In particular, Scandinavian governments and publics, which have been stalwart defenders of human rights, deserve more attention than they have received in a literature that focuses heavily on the checkered record of the United States. See Ingebritsen 2005 for some evidence.

150

U.S. government – that supported authoritarianism; second, they could turn to information politics, rather than to direct action that would invite repression (Hawkins 2002: 62–7). The combination of severe repression in societies with constitutional traditions and transnational ties made the strategy of information collection and monitoring a viable weapon for domestic actors trying to externalize human rights claims.

The Institutional Access Pathway

If Latin American human rights advocates were led to rely on information politics by the repressive conditions of their countries, other advocates find external institutional channels available through which to press their claims. Campaigns against genocide, the repression of indigenous peoples and ecological damage, and in favor of indigenous rights have all been mounted against or within international institutions or through transgovernmental arrangements (O'Brien et al. 2000; Slaughter 2004). In this section I focus on campaigns on behalf of gender equality in the European Union, which has the most highly developed mechanisms for institutional access in the world and the least resistance to claims for external redress.

Multilevel Governance and Unequal Access

Access to EU institutions is not the only form of recourse that activists have in the democratic states of Western Europe: both information politics and direct action are vital parts of Europeanization, and European women's groups have used both. But the structure and logic of European decision making make institutional access a more effective pathway for many domestic claims. The European Union's central institutions are the highest level of a system of what Liesbet Hooghe and Gary Marks (2002: xi) call "multilevel governance," by which they mean "the dispersion of authoritative decision making across multiple territorial levels." This diversity of levels gives claimants the possibility of "shopping" for arenas where their claims are most likely to receive a positive reception and of combining appeals to different levels of the European system (Marks and Steenbergen 2004). Where domestic institutions are unresponsive, as in the area of gender inequality in pay, access to the European Court of Justice (ECJ) has proved a useful venue for claim externalization.

The ECJ was originally conceived of as an agent to prevent member states defecting from agreed-upon policies and to apply current agreements to future contingencies (Hooghe and Marks 2002: 26). But over the years, and with the help of the European Commission, the court has transformed the European legal order in a supranational direction (Alter 1998; Stone Sweet and Caporaso 1998; Weiler 1991). Individuals do not have direct access to ECJ, and what access they do have takes place through preliminary rulings (Article 177, now Article 234). National courts make references to the ECJ, and when that court decides the case, it is sent back to the national court for application. National courts have increasingly accepted the court's judgments as binding on their own governments (Caporaso and Jupille 2001).[4]

The implications of this expansion in judicial review were not immediately obvious to nonstate actors, most of whom continued to use the tried-and-true methods of lobbying to reach decision makers in Brussels (Wessels 2004: 202–3). But lobbying is a highly unequal mechanism, benefiting larger and more-powerful economic sectors and actors the most (pp. 203–9). While internationally oriented business groups were able to lobby effectively in European institutions, weak and divided constituencies – like women and immigrants – had far less access (Helfferisch and Kolb 2001; Guiraudon 2001). For women, the ECJ was a logical alternative, but given the indirect way in which the court works, advocates for womens' rights had to find domestic courts that would agree to refer their cases to short-circuit the resistance of domestic elites to their claims. This they did first in Belgium and then in the United Kingdom.

Reversing Gender Inequality

When the Treaty of Rome was signed, women were but a "distant presence" (Cichowski 2001: 113). Yet today, the EU possesses a broad array of equal protection regulations. How did this occur? Certainly not through contentious politics: women's issues were almost entirely absent from the evidence on European protests through the late 1990s (Imig and Tarrow 2001). It was by using a little-noticed provision in the Treaty of Rome (Article 119 EEC; now Article 141), which had been inserted to satisfy French fears of unfair business competition, that the principle of equal pay for equal work became part of the treaty (Hoskyns 1996: ch. 3). In the

[4] In a recent paper, Caporaso and Jupille (2003) found a growing number of references to "Europe," to "judicial review," and to other Euro-judicial expressions in British court cases from 1970 to 2002.

years that followed, the commission implemented and expanded the reach of this provision. But it was through the ECJ that "women [could] not only demand the right to equal pay but also received protection as pregnant workers" (Cichowski 2001: 114). From 1970 to the late 1990s, 177 cases involving gender equality laws came to the court (p. 122). In a large proportion of them, national governments, often grudgingly, acceded to the court's preliminary rulings (p. 130, and Figure 6.2).

The process began with the activation of the EU legal system by a Belgian stewardess and her lawyer in 1976. Having reached the age of forty, Gabrielle Defrenne, a Belgian national working as a stewardess for Sabena airlines, was told to take another job or lose her position with the airline (Hoskyns 1996: 68–71, 90–3). "After working through the national judicial system unsuccessfully, Ms. Defrenne brought her case to the European Court of Justice" (Caporaso 2001: 3). The ECJ ruled in her favor on the grounds of equal protection, since a male steward in her position was not required to change jobs.

The implications of the Defrenne decisions rippled across the EU – not least in the British government, which was unalterably opposed to ECJ law becoming binding in the United Kingdom. Equal pay and anti-sex discrimination acts had been passed by the Labour government in the early 1970s, but they were largely toothless and contained numerous exceptions. The Thatcher government worked to undermine even that legislation's limited aims (Alter and Vargas 2000: 455), by launching a blocking strategy in the Council of Ministers to "anticipate and seal off pathways that might lead to the erosion of national sovereignty by supranational authority" (Caporaso 2001: 3).

But this was not to be. The Defrenne case was the foundation for a long line of equal pay cases by the ECJ, many of which came from the United Kingdom and a majority of which adjusted women's pay scales upward. In this effort the British Equal Opportunity Commission combined with the trade unions, with an external assist from the European Commission, to develop the cases that led the court to hold that British practices undermined the European treaties (Alter and Vargas 2000: 458–9). For example, the commission organized joint seminars with the British unions to advise claimants how to use European law to best advantage (p. 459). Rather than a case of domestic blockage being countermanded by international networking, in the gender equality cases an interlocking network of domestic and international allies formed an "insider/outsider coalition" (Sikkink 2005b).

The key decision came in 1982 when the court found the United Kingdom to be in violation of the Equal Pay Directive. To this decision, the British government offered stiff resistance (Caporaso and Jupille 2001: 38), but the ultimate results were dramatic, both in terms of the government's compliance with the court's decisions (Cichowski 2001: 130), and in compromising the long-held principle of the sovereignty of Parliament (Caporaso and Jupille 2001: 40–1). Through resistance to a government that was not responsive to their demands and by using a frame provided by an EU-wide set of legal norms and facilitated by a quasi-governmental commission, friendly lower courts, and supranational allies, gender equality campaigners used institutional access to externalize their claims.

Direct Action in Mexico

The fundamental collective action problem of workers facing powerful external opponents is caused by the disjunction between the mobility of capital and the localization of labor (Silver 2003; Tilly 1995a). Not only are their opponents both powerful and hard to reach, but when challenged by people whose cheap labor or lack of unionization they can no longer exploit, they can move on to other venues. That basic gap is lengthened by several structural features of the current wave of globalization: sharply lowered costs of transportation; the internationalization of finance; a dominant ideology of neoliberalism; and the segmentation of production, which makes it possible for multilateral companies to subcontract important stages of their production process to firms for which they bear no legal responsibility (Anner 2004).

To these advantages of capital, add the structural disadvantages of labor. Lacking the cultural capital and the legal and financial resources of management, organized labor has grown dependent on rights and alliances at the national level. As convinced a student of the role of states in structuring contention as Charles Tilly thinks that the chances for national labor movements to fight globalization through national states are slim. In his article "Globalization Threatens Labor's Rights" (1995a), Tilly argues that the rise of global capital is leading to a decline of the state's power to protect the interests of domestic labor. "If workers are to enjoy collective rights in the new world order," he concludes, "they will have to invent new strategies at the scale of international capital" (1995a: 5, 22; also see Gentile 2003).

But *can* workers "invent new strategies at the scale of international capital"? On the one hand, the capacity of capital to move to where labor is cheapest is apparently unstoppable, and weak governments anxious for the benefits of foreign capital are often happy to serve their interests by repressing labor on their behalf. But on the other hand, for domestic political reasons, states may defend the rights of labor even at the cost of losing some sectors of industry and emphasizing others. Workers have never depended only on their rights as workers. Even in the heyday of union organization, many of the rights they enjoyed were acquired as citizens (Gentile 2003; Murillo and Schrank 2003). Even when states are busily eroding labor rights, citizen rights – and the political alliances that result from them – can act as a defense for workers. In the former corporatist systems of Latin America, states continue to defend workers' rights because of the historically validated alliances between labor-friendly parties and trade unions (Anner 2004; Murillo and Schrank 2003).

There are differences between the cases we just examined and labor transnationalism, and they make the strategies of information and institutional access less attractive to labor than they were to the human rights and women's movements. With respect to the *information pathway*, when workers have tried to use information and monitoring, these mechanisms have not had either the appeal or the capacity to compel acquiescence (Anner 2003a and b; Caraway 2001; Seidman 2003; H. Williams 2003). With respect to the *institutional pathway*, workers have no firm external channels equivalent to European women's access to the European Court of Justice. Procedures like the NAFTA labor side agreement are slow, expensive to mount, and often ignored or deflected by home-country governments or firms (H. Williams 2003).

For these reasons, workers threatened by the forces of globalization are increasingly turning to domestic direct action, often with the assistance of external allies and sometimes making use of international institutions. Direct action revolves around traditional instruments like the strike, but it also includes innovations like community-based protest events that are difficult for authorities to repress without drawing public criticism (Gentile 2002). Workers can also borrow resources from international allies to complement their capacity for contentious politics. A coalition that was formed on the U.S.-Mexican border to defend the rights of *maquiladora* workers illustrates labor's attempts to link domestic direct action to transnational alliances and institutions.

The Coalition for Justice in the Maquiladora[5]

The Mexican borderlands abutting the United States offer close to a laboratory case of the influences of globalization and their costs for workers, the environment, and human rights: a cheap and plentiful labor force in close contact with the largest consumer market in the world, "a solid industrial infrastructure, favorable tax policies, a business-friendly political climate, and relatively lax regulatory regimes" (H. Williams 1999: 139) – not to mention a Mexican government without the capacity or perhaps even the will to enforce its environmental and human rights commitments.

In the *maquiladora* industries along the border, employment in clothing, automobile parts, and electronic components grew more than 10 percent a year since 1986, but contrary to the claims of NAFTA boosters on both sides of the border, workers' incomes did not. Heather Williams reported that, as of 1999, the average wage rate had declined by a staggering 65 percent since 1981. The communities where the *maquiladora* factories are lodged face other problems related to rapid growth and indifferent regulations. In addition to long hours and backbreaking work, there are "clusters of rare cancers among residents in certain impoverished areas of Matamoros or Brownsville or Calexico, foul-smelling discharges in waterways, factories that closed up overnight and left workers without pay, fires and chemical spills that injured workers, and bosses who demanded sexual favors from employees in exchange for continued employment" (p. 143).

Faced by these abuses, in the late 1980s labor and human rights advocates from the three future NAFTA countries founded the Coalition for Justice in the Maquiladoras (CJM), which began a ten-year struggle against unscrupulous labor and environmental practices by industries on the border. At the outset, "most of the member groups were U.S. based," writes Williams, and "issues were often framed in such a manner as to attract the English-speaking press" (p. 142). It was only at a second stage that these efforts were combined with domestic direct action.

Using information from organizers working on the Mexican side of the border, CJM activists at first tried to use a monitoring strategy, using "codes of conduct" modeled on the divestment campaign in the struggle against apartheid in South Africa (p. 144). But over time, it became clear that

---

[5] This section rests heavily on the work of Heather Williams on the Coalition for Justice in the Maquiladoras. See in particular Williams 1999 and 2003.

monitoring alone would not work against determined foreign-run corporations in cahoots with local officials; more direct actions from within the border communities would be necessary (pp. 146–50). On the Mexican side, organizers began to meet with workers on a daily basis. Problems were frequently played out through wildcat worker actions or addressed by a coordinated set of transborder actions. North of the border, CJM "developed rapid-response networks of individuals who can be contacted to write letters, make phone calls, or send faxes to company executives and government officials." CJM, according to Williams, also "called for assistance from union locals and internationals, especially where there is some contractual connection between the union and the corporate parent of the target factory in Mexico" (p. 149).

How successful could this strategy be? Heather Williams's research shows a certain amount of success for cross-border collaboration. In the thirteen conflicts of the thirty she studied in which there were low levels of cross-border collaboration, all were unsuccessful; of the eighteen cases with moderate or high levels of collaboration, sixteen were successful and only two were failures (p. 151). Cross-border mobilization was at least successful in gaining immediate redress for *maquiladora* workers.

How much of this success can be attributed to direct action and how much to the intervention of their cross-border allies it is impossible to say. What is certain is what came next: as the CJM became more institutionalized and the NAFTA came into force, direct action gave way to the use of its institutional mechanisms. By the late 1990s, labor-based conflicts had moved to the district and federal courts in Mexico and the United States and to the National Administrative Offices (NAOs) created under the NAFTA labor side agreement (p. 150).

But with the institutionalization of the process, there was a decline in cross-border collaboration and in direct action. Part of the problem was goal displacement: as the locus of decision making moved upward, the principal actors – the workers at the point of production – were displaced by legal representatives and public officials with little knowledge of the issues and different concerns than those of the workers (Williams 2003). But another part of the problem was that the decline of disruptive protest made it easier for decision makers to ignore workers' claims. What seems certain is that without the willingness of workers on the Mexican side of the border to defend their rights and signal their claims to external allies, little would have improved; once direct action declined, institutional access alone was insufficient to advance their claims.

The need for domestic mobilization to buttress institutional access is not limited to the direct action pathway. Domestic mobilization played an important supportive role in both the Latin American and Western European cases I have surveyed. Even in authoritarian Argentina, where openings for direct action were limited, the famous "Mothers of the Plaza" engaged in symbolic protests that kept hope alive and signaled to others that they were not alone in opposing the military regime (Brysk 1994). In Western Europe, continued mobilization was essential to avoid the "containment" of justice (Conant 2002).

Conclusions

Keck and Sikkink's "boomerang model" showed that externalization is an important process through which weak domestic actors seek access to more-powerful nongovernmental or governmental allies (1998; also see Sikkink 2005a). But the process of externalization must be specified differently for different kinds of contentious politics. Information politics, as we saw, relies on external allies who are prepared to diffuse information about abuses to sympathetic governments and public opinion abroad, which then "boomerangs" into pressure on repressive states. Institutional access depends on the authority of international agencies to receive domestic claims and turn them into binding rules. Labor transnationalism has had some modest successes using both information and international institutions, but in the absence of more-robust tactics, neither external monitoring nor institutional access offers hope for weak social actors to make successful claims outside their borders.

Three predictive hypotheses emerge from this chapter and seem to me to provide a prudent course for activists and their supporters:

- *Information monitoring* is likely to produce successful outcomes in sectors in which bodily harm is the subject of the information, in societies in which there are institutional allies or independent sources of information, and in countries with constitutional traditions. When it is employed where there are no such traditions or where divisible goods, but not human lives, are at stake – as in industrial relations – it is less likely to succeed (Seidman 2003).
- *Access to external institutions* is most likely to succeed in sectors with recognizable legal parameters, as in gender equality in the EU, in societies with strong associational traditions, and where external institutions have

a stake in the correction of abuses. The European Union, with its robust political traditions and its supranational institutions, is the most positive example we have. But as Williams's findings about the *maquiladora* showed, a strategy of institutional access is likely to lead to dependence, co-optation and, in the absence of direct action to back it up, to failure (Williams 1999).

- *Direct action* appears to be the foundational mechanism for workers. This was clearest in the cross-border activism that empowered workers rights in the *maquiladora* in its early stages, but even in the human rights field, where the strongest case has been made for information monitoring, sustainable change will only be achieved when national governments are continually pushed to live up to their claims and when the pressure "from below" and "from above" continues (Risse and Sikkink 1999: 33).

To some extent, the differences in these three pathways reflect differences between North and South. People in the South reach out to NGOs, try to access universal values to legitimate their claims, and do so in largely bilateral, vertical ways that do not capitalize on the commonalities of their claims with others like themselves. It is striking that most of the "boomerang" cases that Keck and Sikkink's important work highlighted did not involve horizontal transnational coalitions among actors with similar claims. This may be slowly changing, as we could see in the successful southern resistance to northern trade imperialism at the Cancun summit in 2003, but the boomerang appears to fly best when it is "thrown" upward.

Europeans have learned to use institutional routines to "go over the bosses' heads" to the European Union, accessing specific institutions that have been designed to facilitate access and availing themselves of the partial "fusion of sovereignty" that marks European political culture. They too make largely vertical and parochial claims, but EU institutional routines, as well as common claims, encourage them to form coalitions with others like themselves. In recent years there have been increasing coalitions among actors with similar claims across borders within Western Europe, as we will see in the case of environmental coalitions in Chapter 9.

North American transnationalism seems to present a third pattern. Here the framework for multilateral coalition building exists through NAFTA and through other arrangements, and is often exploited, but the power differentials among the partners are so great that bilateralism often trumps multilateralism. The enormous power of the United States vis-à-vis its neighbors gives it the capacity to use internationalism when it suits its interests and to ignore it when it does not.[6] This often leaves Canadian and Mexican civil society groups like brides at a wedding whose prospective groom is too confident of his own power to show up at the altar.

This is in some ways puzzling, for the United States is the heartland of pluralistic politics. Why have Americans, for example, been slow to join in the "downward scale shift" of the social forum model, as we saw in Chapter 7? The paradox is more apparent than real when we realize that the openness of U.S. institutions may limit attempts of Americans to see the need for externalization, even when the pathways for it are are available.[7] The failure of the nuclear freeze movement of the 1980s to forge working links with the contemporary European peace movement is a good example of the deceptive attractions of domestic openness (Tarrow and McAdam 2005).

What happens when domestic activists do "go external"? The "boomerang" and its two alternative pathways tell us half the story. Some approaches seem to imply that the growth of universal norms insures that goals that can be successfully attached to those norms will be realized; others – more "realist" – argue that political power will trump even the most normatively universal claims. But there is another side to externalization: before we can tackle the kinds of claims that gain purchase internationally, we need to examine what happens after externalization. We need to turn to coalition formation.

[6] These reflections were suggested in comments on an earlier version of this chapter by David S. Meyer.

[7] This comment was suggested by Jackie Smith in response to an earlier version of this chapter.

9

Building Transnational Coalitions

Refusing the Trojan Pig[1]

Early in 1999, write Arunas Juska and Bob Edwards (2004: 187), Tom Garrett of the Animal Welfare Institute (AWI) noticed two seemingly unrelated items in the press: "First, Polish farmers were revolting against low prices with a sustained nonviolent direct action campaign that had spread to Warsaw. Second, the world's largest pork products producer, Smithfield Foods, had just announced with much fanfare, its plans to purchase the Polish pork conglomerate Animex and bring its American-style success story to Poland." What resulted when Garrett put the two stories together was a classical coalition – but across borders.

The two partners – AWI and a Polish farmer's organization, Samoobrona – were far apart in their origins and their goals: one was a left-of-center American public interest group passionate about animal welfare; the other a populist-nationalist farm organization whose leader, Andszej Lepper, was ready to use demagogic language and disruptive tactics on behalf of his supporters and was headed for Polish national politics. While AWI describes itself as "a nonprofit charitable organization founded in 1951 to reduce the sum total of pain and fear inflicted on animals by humans,"[2] Samoobrona emerged in the economic chaos of the early 1990s to

---

[1] This title, and the narrative it introduces, both come from the splendid article by Arunas Juska and Bob Edwards in Joe Bandy and Jackie Smith, eds., *Coalitions across Borders* (2004). I am grateful to the authors for detailed comments on a draft of this section.

[2] http://www.awionline.org/. Like many such organizations in the United States AWI posts action alerts, asks its "constituents" to write to officials about uncovered abuses and pending legislation, and publishes books and a periodic newsletter.

represent farmers hard hit by the "shock treatment" reforms of Leszek Balcerovic (p. 188).

These were very different organizations. Yet with a Polish-born American veterinarian acting as a bridge and a temporary convergence of interests, AWI and Samoobrona cooperated in two Polish electoral campaigns and reversed Smithfield's Polish ambitions (p. 199). AWI agreed to campaign for Lepper in these campaigns if Samoobrona would include in its platform an anti-Smithfield, humane-farming plank. In pro-American Poland, "American participation provided legitimacy to Lepper's claims about corporate farming while Lepper, in addition to his populist platform, also pushed the AWI agenda."[3] Garrett also hit upon the idea of sponsoring what he called a "Trojan Pig Tour" in September 1999 that covered five American states in which industrialized hog production had had devastating effects on local communities.

A concrete result of the trip was an AWI-made video warning Polish farmers of the fate that awaited them if Smithfield were allowed to penetrate the Polish hog economy. Distributed by Samoobrona in the midst of the parliamentary elections, and following years of agricultural depression, the video struck a chord with both the Polish public and key government officials. When Poland's State Farm Property Agent saw it, he declared, "I have seen in your video how pigs are raised humanely on family farms in Iowa. I would like to initiate this kind of husbandry in Poland" (p. 200). When the Ministry of Agriculture announced its unwillingness to support Smithfield's plans, the firm conceded defeat – at least temporarily (p. 200). Due in large part to this "insider-outsider" coalition between farmers and animal rights advocates (Sikkink 2005b), the Trojan Pig stayed outside the gates of Polish farming.

Juska and Edwards's account of the Samboobrona-AWI alliance shows that in a closely knit international economy with easy communication across space and time, actors with different but complementary aims can forge collaborative arrangements. In her analyses of international nongovernmental organizations, Jackie Smith (2004b: 278) found the coalition form increasing vis-à-vis more traditional federal forms of organization: between 1973 and 2000, the proportion of coalitions in the population of the transnational nongovernmental organizations she studied increased from 25 percent of the total to 60 percent at the turn of the century. Many of these coalitions

---

[3] From a personal communication to the author from Arunas Juska, who witnessed these campaigns.

are short-term instrumental arrangements in which none of the principals expect a permanent alliance to result. But many others are longer-term collaborations, some of which become institutionalized and have major policy impacts.

I chose the "Polish pig" coalition to introduce this chapter because it combines a number of features that are more generally important in the formation of transnational coalitions. First, the story shows how information flow across borders can externalize a local conflict when domestic mobilization combines with transnational contacts. But, second, it suggests that externalization is not enough: Forging and maintaining transnational coalitions require hard coalition work. Third, it suggests how cycles of domestic contention impact on transnational collaboration, often giving rise to – but then dissipating – temporary coalitions of interest (D. Meyer and Corrigall-Brown 2004).

Are all transnational coalitions so quickly consumed by changes in opportunity and risk? Surely not: groups like the International Campaign to Ban Landmines (ICBL) not only worked together for more than a decade but succeeded in producing an international landmines convention (Cameron, Lawson, and Tomlin 1998). The Climate Action Network (CAN) has coordinated efforts to slow global warming since the late-1980s and helped forge the Kyoto Protocol (Newell 2000). But maintaining coalitions across borders is difficult, and many transnational alliances have not outlasted the issue that brought them together. To understand why, I first offer a definition of coalitions and a typology of coalitions. Next I illustrate that typology through four examples of unequal duration and degrees of commitment. Finally, I offer several hypotheses about coalitional dynamics, arguing that combinations of threat and opportunity produce transnational coalitions, but only those with a modicum of institutionalization and capacity to socialize participants will endure.

Networks, Coalitions, and Movements

In recent years, the term "network" has become popular among both advocates and scholars of transnational politics (Keck and Sikkink 1998; Risse, Ropp, and Sikkink 1999; Castells 1996). But networks are a much looser and therefore less meaningful term than either coalitions or movements (J. Smith and Bandy 2004: 2–4; J. Fox 2002: 352). The term has both a structural and a purposive meaning. At one extreme, networks consist of simple "nodes" whose occupants may be entirely unaware of one another – for example, people who read the same newspaper or visit the same website. At the opposite end of the scale of purposiveness, networks are the structure within which groups and individuals join together for specific purposes – as did the "Polish pig" coalition. Between these poles are institutionalized links that exist for other purposes but can be appropriated for contentious collective action, as, for example, the black churches did in the American civil rights movement (McAdam, Tarrow, and Tilly 2001: ch. 2). The concept of networks is useful for mapping where the potential for coalition formation will be found, but if networks can be either purposive, structural, or both, we need a more precise term to help us to understand when purposive connections will form, under what circumstances they endure, and when they cohere into sustained social movements. This takes us to the concept of "coalitions."

Coalitions I define, with Margaret Levi and Gillian Murphy (2004: 5), as "Collaborative, means-oriented arrangements that permit distinct organizational entities to pool resources in order to effect change." The factors that produce a desire among distinct groups of actors to combine their efforts are many, but they usually combine threats and opportunities: the wish to take advantage of pooling resources (Staggenborg 1986); the need to combine against common threats (McCammon and Campbell 2002); the urge to produce solidarity among members of neighboring categories (Van Dyke 2003); and, in some cases, the attempt to approximate the logic of "minimum winning coalitions" (Levi and Murphy 2004: 30; Gupta 2003). The most important incentive to cooperate is when groups can define their goals primarily in terms of the joint political influence that they will gain from cooperation (Hathaway and Meyer 1997: 64).

But coalitions also have costs. Research on domestic coalitions shows that organizations that form them have to expend resources to maintain them. Purist members may be alienated and break away to form new organizations. Competition between coalition members can displace cooperation. And changing circumstances can erase the original motive to collaborate. Moreover, some coalition members will pay higher costs than others, and some will inevitably gain more from the collaboration than their partners, thus creating internal tensions. Going transnational may change the balance of costs and benefits, but the dynamics of transnational coalitions are not inherently different than those of domestic ones (D. Meyer and Corrigall-Brown 2004).

All social movements are made up of coalitions, but not all coalitions produce social movements. The combination that refused the Polish pig

together has dissipated (Bob 2005). I will examine such a case in American labor-NGO cooperation in Mexico.

...ent coalitions are also short-term in duration but are based on a higher ...e of involvement and have potential for future collaboration when ...solder alliances among people who recognize their shared identities ...e process of collective action. I examine such a case in the "Battle of ...tle" and in the similar demonstrations that followed it.

...ederated coalitions combine a low degree of involvement of their member ...anizations, whose major commitment remains to their own organiza-...ns' goals, with long-term collaboration. I use the example of Europe's ...vironmental groups to examine such highly institutionalized arrange-...nts and their limitations.

Conversely, *campaign coalitions* combine high intensity of involvement ...ith long-term cooperation. I examine such a case in the remarkable unity ...nd duration of the international landmines campaign.

Short-Term Coalitions

The lowest potential for sustained collective action comes from the combination of short-term cooperation with a low intensity of involvement. *Instrumental coalitions* lack a foundation of collective identity to carry them beyond the issues or conflicts that bring them together. More robust are *event-based coalitions* that form to mount international protest events, but here the problem is a different one: their dependence on the opportunities offered by international institutions puts them at the mercy of changes in international politics. The first type can be seen in the cooperation of American activists with Mexican workers and their unions; the second, by the series of "global justice" events that followed the "Battle of Seattle."

Insiders and Outsiders in Mexico[5]

At a Korean-owned apparel firm in the state of Puebla in Mexico, a labor struggle broke out in 2000. Kukdong International had set up shop to produce sweatshirts with college logos for the American apparel giants Nike

[5] I base this description largely on the report of Jeff Hermanson of the American Center for International Labor Solidarity in Washington, D.C. My thanks to Hermanson for allowing me to cite his unpublished paper, presented to the Cornell University workshop on Transnational Labor Mobilization, March 2004.

was a coalition, but we would scarcely call it a social movement. Movements are "sustained interactions between challengers and authorities on matters of policy and/or culture" (D. Meyer and Corrigall-Brown 2004: 6) that are built upon, or arrive at a sense of their inherent worth, their common identity, their strength, and the rightness of their cause through common action (Tilly 2004b). Coalitions frequently form around short-term threats and opportunities, but when the occasion for collaboration passes, many disperse or subside into "paper coalitions" (D. Meyer and Corrigall-Brown 2004: 14). Only when opportunities and threats persist and coalitions develop strong underlying identities do they become sustained social movements (della Porta and Diani 1999).

Levi and Murphy propose five sets of factors that are likely to have significant bearing on when coalitions will form and endure:[4]

- *Framing.* Can coalition members frame the issue around which they form so as to define a common interest and compatible set of tactics?
- *Trust.* Do their representatives see one another as trustworthy?
- *Credible commitments.* Can each one make their commitments credible to the other prospective members of the coalition?
- *Management of difference.* Can they resolve tensions due to differences in goals, strategies, culture, ideology, and organizational structure?
- *Selective incentives.* Can they insure that their organizations will benefit from their cooperation?

When these mechanisms cannot be sustained, or when they are diverted by changes in opportunities and risks, coalitions dissipate or subside into purely formal arrangements.

Transnational Coalition Building

Each of these problems is multiplied in the formation of transnational coalitions. First, consider the *framing of transnational campaigns*. The ecologists and trade unionists who combined at the "Battle of Seattle" had to work to overcome their differences, but they had the advantage of coming from the same political culture and operating within a similar structure of opportunities and threats. What if the ecologists had been Americans and the workers had come from the Global South, where the priority of

[4] I am most grateful to Margaret Levi and Gillian Murphy for allowing me to quote from their as-yet-unpublished paper and adopt their categories of analysis.

development outpaces the goal of protecting the environment? Cooperation between "teamsters and turtles" might not even have emerged.

Now think about Levi and Murphy's second factor – the *establishment of trust*. Trust is more difficult to establish and maintain across borders than among people who know each other. For example, despite their common aims, American Freeze campaigners in the 1980s were distrusted by the nuclear disarmament movement in Western Europe and vice versa (Tarrow and McAdam 2005). The same is true in transnational labor cooperation, in which – not without reason – southern activists often suspect North American unions of thinly disguised protectionism (Anner 2001).

As for *credible commitments*, while all the members of a transnational coalition may agree to keep their commitments, their ability to do so will depend on their resources and on the changes in their domestic environments. For example, American climate change advocates were serious about implementing the Kyoto Protocol, but once the Bush administration went back on its predecessor's commitment to the signing, working internationally took a back seat to their attempts to implement Kyoto locally (Vasi 2004).

Resolving tensions is perhaps the most difficult aspect of forming and managing transnational coalitions. Levi and Murphy (2004: 25) correctly point out that in a coalition, "there must be procedures in place . . . that permit all representatives to express their voices in ways that could influence the outcome." But procedures that are agreed to by coalition leaders may be opaque to or disregarded by participants. For example, familiar procedures to coalition members from the United States and Western Europe may be unfamiliar or even illegitimate to members from democratizing states (Wood 2004a). Even finding procedures that can insure unity is often a bone of contention in internal coalitional debates (Cullen 2004). And the ideology of activists often works against designing procedures for unifying their activities.

A Typology of Transnational Coalitions

Nevertheless, under particular circumstances and with specific kinds of aims, transnational coalitions do take shape and some of them endure. We can begin to understand the conditions under which they do so if we first distinguish among different kinds of coalitions. "The coalition," according to D. Meyer and Corrigall-Brown (2004: 13), "is a generic form that can include a broad variety of negotiated arrangements of two or more

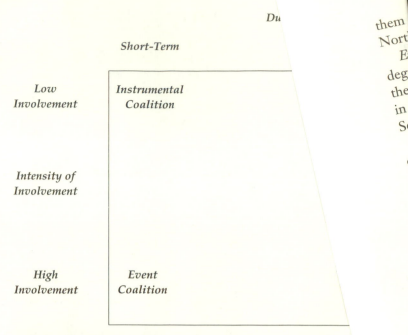

Figure 9.1 A Typology of Forms of Transnational Coalitions

organizations coordinating goals, demands, strategies of [...] events." The extent of cooperation varies over at least two di[...] degree of cooperation and its duration. Cooperation can rang[...] ing a group's name to a manifesto or website to coordination[...] negotiation of division of labor, pooling resources, all the wa[...] ing a permanent umbrella organization. In terms of duration, "[...] maintain a formal affiliation only for the support of a discrete [...] the way to making permanent arrangements for cooperation. In [...] case, "the coalition often becomes a distinct organization in its ow[...] with independent staff, membership, and fundraising" (pp. 8–9).[...] two dimensions produce a descriptive typology of coalitions, as sh[...] Figure 9.1.

The simplest type, which we saw in the case of the Polish-Am[...] collaboration, is what I call *instrumental coalitions* – the combinatio[...] short-term cooperation with a low level of involvement. Here groups c[...] together around an occasional conjuncture of interest or program, but [...] ther drift apart or maintain purely formal ties after the issue that broug[...]

and Reebok. In this conflict, a coalition of Mexican workers and American college students linked up with Mexican labor organizations, global union federations, and NGOs and "solidarity organizations" (Hermanson 2004). It was a classical case of what Kathryn Sikkink calls an "insider/outsider coalition" (Sikkink 2005b).[6]

In the 1990s Mexico was moving by fits and starts toward liberalization, leading workers in factories like the Kukdong one to attempt to defend their rights in an industrial relations system that had been controlled by state-dominated and often corrupt trade unions. In this stirring of local militancy, they were encouraged by the ruling PRI's declining electoral fortunes, by the appearance of new independent national unions, and by the efforts of worker support groups. One such group in Puebla was the CAT (Centro de Apoyo al Trabajador, or Worker Support Center), which was supported by the Labor Solidarity Center of the American AFL-CIO.

In Puebla, there was a homegrown rural radical tradition, but the Kukdong workers faced a conservative PRI government and a corrupt cor-poratist union, the FROC-CROC, which had signed a sweetheart contract with the firm (Hermanson 2004: 3–5). FROC-CROC had done much of the labor recruiting for the company when it came to Puebla in 1999, among young women from a depressed sugarcane growing region. In return, it expected to collect union dues and run a closed shop. It was only after the young workers came to work in the factory that they discovered that they were to be "represented" by FROC-CROC. Needless to say, when they had complaints to lodge against management, the union's representatives were nowhere to be found (p. 6).

The complaints did not take long to surface. CAT activists made contact with the workers, pointing out to them that because they were produc-ing sweatshirts for American college campuses, their work was covered by the codes of conduct of U.S. universities. CAT put them in touch with an American group called United Students against Sweatshops (USAS), which had grown out of a campaign in the United States against GUESS in the late 1990s (p. 6). USAS, in turn, had pressured a number of American univer-sities to set up and fund a "Worker's Rights Commission," an independent nonprofit organization to investigate conditions at factories that produce apparel for the U.S. college market (p. 7).

---

[6] By this term, Sikkink (2005b: 164–5) means "coalitions that emerge when activists operate in open domestic and international opportunity structures." For another version of the "insider/outsider coalition," see Korzeniewicz and Smith 2001.

In November 2000, learning of the Kukdong case, a USAS delegation flew to Mexico to meet with some of the workers and with CAT activists. Soon after, a boycott of the factory's cafeteria broke out. When the leaders of the boycott, with the company union looking on, were promptly fired, this led to a wildcat strike by almost all the workers (p. 7). When the case was publicized in the American press, Nike and Reebok, both of which had signed codes of conduct, urged Kukdong to settle the dispute. With the corrupt local union edged out and the workers emboldened by its domestic and international support, the company – with a new name – rehired the workers and recognized their independent union.[7]

The Kukdong campaign shows that with substantial coalitional work, even weak domestic actors can gain access to foreign support and sometimes gain their objectives, at least in the short run. Their success was not due to their transnational efforts alone. As we saw in Chapter 8, mobilization on the ground was the necessary springboard of the campaign, but coalition formation was a distinct process that gave it "legs." Spurring the workers on was an external labor activist group, CAT, supported by the AFL-CIO's Labor Solidarity Center. Offering moral support was the Union Nacional de Trabajadores (UNT), an independent labor federation run by dissident unionists from the "official" labor confederation. USAS convinced the Kukdong workers that they had support from the consumers of their products in the United States, and the Worker's Rights Commission supported these claims. There was even a Korean NGO, the Korea House of International Solidarity (KHIS), which played a critical role by "mediating and bridging the 'culture gap' between the Korean management and Mexican workers" (p. 18). Though "instrumental" and short-term, the coalition was a success for the workers.

The Battle of Seattle and Other Events

The coalition that opposed the WTO Ministerial in Seattle in 1999 was formed by activists from the West Coast of the United States and Canada

---

[7] In 2004 the renamed company, MEXMODE, and the independent union negotiated a second contract that resulted in a wage increase of 14 percent in all job categories, including a 50 percent increase for night shift workers; improvements in workplace health and safety have been part of both contracts. For more information, see the website of the Maquiladora Health and Safety Support Network, April 12, 2004, at http://mhssn.igc.org/news.htm.

only for the occasion of that event (Levi and Murphy 2004; Lichbach 2003).[8]
It reveals a combination of a labor–NGO–social movement convergence
of interests and a high intensity of involvement. Although it had relatively
little international participation, its capacity to block the Ministerial and its
triggering of a police riot gave it remarkable resonance around the world.

Since the mid-1990s, "event coalitions" have been formed around summits of the G-8, the IMF, the World Bank, the European Union and, of
course, against the American-led war in Iraq.[9] The latter developed to its
highest form the long-distance coordination of protest events that was first
experimented with during the Seattle Ministerial: organizing simultaneous
or sequential events in cities around the world against the same target. In
his web-based study, Mark Lichbach (2003) found that the "Battle of Seattle" was actually not local; it was accompanied by solidary protests in more
than fifty cities around the world.

Levi and Murphy's work shows that, in Seattle itself, there were actually
two coalitions: the first a broad-based global justice coalition designed to
bring people to the city, organize a wide range of protest and educational
events around the Ministerial, and manage relations with outside groups
and authorities. But when control was lost over minorities of protesters
and the Seattle police responded with violence and arrested hundreds of
protesters, a second, partially overlapping coalition was organized that was
able to switch gears from opposing global injustice to defending civil rights
(Levi and Murphy 2004: figs. 1 and 2).

Event-based coalitions frequently dissipate, giving rise to recriminations
among organizers about "who did what" or who failed to carry out agreed-
upon tasks. Especially when faced by the truncheons of police and the hostility of the media, protesters may get discouraged and move off into less
risky endeavors. And yet, even in the face of these disincentives, transnational protest cooperation increased in the course of the 1990s and in some
ways persisted through the turn of the century (Podobnik 2004). Part of
the reason was the recurring threats and opportunities offered by states
and international actors; another part was the institutionalization of some

---

[8] In the event, the coalition reformed in a somewhat different shape and size to oppose the
brutality of the Seattle police and the arrest of many of the movement's activists (Levi and
Murphy 2004: 8 and diagram 2).

[9] For empirical research on European- and American-based protests against the EU, the G-8,
and the World Bank, as well as the Iraq war, see Bédoyan, Van Aelst, and Walgrave 2004;
della Porta 2005b; Fisher 2003; and Verhulst and Walgrave 2003.

coalitions that were first formed around short-term events; and part was the formation of both federations and campaign coalitions.

Enduring Coalitions

When activists and advocates are determined and well organized, when they collaborate with groups of states and international institutions, and when political opportunities and resources come together, a more durable fusion of international and domestic efforts can result. We see this in the slow, halting, but ultimately successful approval of the Kyoto Protocol by a majority of the world's states; in the trade sector in the defeat of the Multilateral Agreement on Investment (MAI) through worldwide NGO mobilization in cooperation with a few friendly states; and even in the security field, where transnational mobilization comes up against the determined resistance of both military forces and diplomatic routines.

In Levi and Murphy's lexicon, enduring coalitions are long-term combinations of organizations that develop a high degree of institutionalization. Here too, we can recognize two distinct subtypes: *federations* of national organizations coordinated or franchised by international coordinating bodies that take on broad mandates, and *campaign coalitions* that form around single but long-term issues and develop a high degree of involvement. The first type is illustrated by the collaboration of European environmental organizations; the second, by the international landmines coalition.

European Environmental Federations

If there is anywhere that we would expect to find a supranational logic of coalition formation, it would be in Western Europe, where environmental groups profit from favorable public opinion, a body of European Union environmental law, an EU Directorate-General dedicated to their claims, and generous subsidies to Brussels-level environmental groups from the European Commission. The European Environmental Bureau (EEB) coordinates the Brussels-based efforts of a number of transnational and domestic environmental organizations. Informal working groups deal with specific problems, like transportation or nuclear power. "Umbrella organizations can also mobilize the efforts of environmental groups and focus their efforts so that they speak with greater force and authority to policy makers" (Dalton 1994: 172).

172

But there is a disjunction between European environmental umbrella groups, like those that are connected through the EEB, and their national chapters. First, while the former engage heavily in the politics of expertise favored by the European Commission, the latter use a combination of routine and contentious politics at home (Marks and McAdam 1999). Moreover, Brussels-level umbrella groups do not always enjoy the support of their member organizations who are more engaged in national politics and protests (Rootes 2003; 2005). The environment is inherently global, but even in tightly integrated Western Europe, and in the presence of long-term formal coalitions, environmental groups appear to persist in "acting local."

Two sets of related factors converge to explain the disjunction between national organizations and transnational coalitions in the European environmental network. First, although the problems of the environment are often lumped into a single frame, there is no single environmental issue. Even the constituent organizations of the EEB specialize on distinct sectors. And although some issues, like wind-carried industrial pollution, are logically subject to international resolution, many others are national or NIMBY issues that can only be resolved at the local or national levels.

Second, federated organizations often lack the flexibility to adapt quickly to changing circumstances. Each national organization is autonomous, and their European coordinating bodies depend on dues from their national sections and on subsidies from the European Commission. European umbrella groups convene national sections regularly to discuss common interests but with no single campaign focus to direct their energies, the umbrella groups depend on their relation to a single international institution. And when it comes right down to it, their grass-roots membership is local, at least two levels removed from the efforts of their representatives in Brussels.

The International Landmine Campaign[10]

As in many areas of transnational activism, it was interstate policies that provided the opponents of antipersonnel landmines with the basic opportunity structure around which to mobilize in the 1990s. Efforts to limit the use of

[10] I am grateful to Elizabeth Bernstein for help in understanding the dynamics of the landmine campaign in which she has played a central role. This section is based mainly on information she provided, as well as on the contributions in Cameron, Lawson, and Tomlin 1998; Hubert 2000; and Price 1998.

landmines surfaced in 1980 in a UN conference to ban weapons with indiscriminate effects (the CCW), but left enough gaps in landmine controls to produce increasing carnage on the battlefield. After the wars in Afghanistan, Angola, Mozambique, and Cambodia left thousands maimed and killed, an NGO coalition of humanitarian and public health groups emerged to try to replace the CCW with a more robust international agreement (Price 1998; J. Williams and Goose 1998).

NGOs working in postwar Cambodia in the 1980s were especially significant in launching this coalition, because they represented international religious, humanitarian, and demining groups.[11] But groups in France, Canada, and the United States were also influential as the campaign got underway. These groups might have made scant headway had it not been for the convergence of their efforts with international institutions like the International Committee of the Red Cross and the UN, and with three medium-sized states, Canada, France, and Norway, which gave the movement legitimacy, provided sites for its meetings, and formed the core of a bloc of interested governments (Maslen 1998; Lawson et al. 1998).

At first, progress in convincing states to sign a convention to ban landmines was slow and uneven, and the most important state, the United States, never did sign it (Wareman 1998). But after the core states took ownership of the campaign and landmine activist Jody Williams won the Nobel Peace Prize in 1997, the pace of adhesion picked up rapidly. Ultimately, with the lead taken by Canada and its foreign minister, Lloyd Axworthy, 112 countries signed the convention against antipersonnel mines in Ottawa in 1998 (Cameron, Lawson, and Tomlin 1998: 26–7).

The story of the successful landmines convention has sometimes been written as the result of the determination of states, like Canada, to see the issue through (Warmington and Tuttle 1998); sometimes as the triumph of a coalition of nonstate actors working in the name of universal norms against bodily harm (Price 1998); or as the slow and methodical work of international organizations like the Red Cross (Maslen 1998), or as the result of the use of innovative procedures and rare opportunities (J. Williams and Goose 1998). But, in fact, it is only possible to explain the success of the Landmines Convention as the result of a coalition of these actors, often in combinations that escaped territorial lines. (For example, while the

---

[11] They were the religious-based Coalition for Peace and Reconciliation; the humanitarian group Handicap International; and the British de-mining group, Mines Advisory Group. See Hubert 2000: ch. 2.

United States ultimately failed to sign the convention, American-based NGOs and congressmen were crucial to its early stages.)

Campaign coalitions can be found throughout the world and in many sectors of transnational activism. The loose coalition among environmental, consumer, and public health organizations that launched the antigenetic seed campaign in Western Europe was such a coalition (Kettnaker 2001). As in the coalition to ban landmines, it combined a narrow focal point with a high level of involvement, giving it the flexibility and common identity to persist. Unlike federations, which are tied to formal relations at specific levels of the international system, campaign coalitions use different venues to influence the outcome they seek; they can choose the closest or most promising target of opportunity; and they can combine contentious and routine institutional action.[12]

When Coalitions Endure

Of course, not all coalitions are built to endure. Both in the case of the Kukdong organizing drive and in the global justice demonstrations, we saw that successful coalitions are often short-lived. Some advocates have even argued that endurance is not the point of these events (Klein 2004). But many activists are disappointed when the enthusiasm and solidarity generated by an exciting international event or collaboration subside, so it is worthwhile asking under what circumstances short-term coalitions give rise to more-enduring collaborations. Three broad processes appear to describe the transition from short term to enduring coalitions: opportunity spirals, institutionalization, and socialization.

Seizing and Making Opportunities

"Groups join coalition efforts when they see their efforts on a particular set of issues and efforts as urgent and potentially efficacious," write David S. Meyer and Catherine Corrigall-Brown (2004), but coalitions form around threats and opportunities, and when these shift, the bases for cooperation may disappear as well. For example, looking at the aftermath of the anti–Iraq war movement in the United States, Meyer and Corrigall-Brown found that the factors that had produced cooperation quickly subsided when that

---

[12] I am grateful to Javier Lezaun for pointing this out from his research on the GM controversy in the European Union.

war began. As the Bush administration's tenuous legitimacy as the result of his questionable election gave way to his strength as a "war president," the unity of the February 15, 2003, demonstrations also eroded. "Although the dynamics of coming together and growing apart are mediated by personal relationships and political skill," write Meyer and Corrigall-Brown, "the critical factor is the relationship of the movement as a whole to external political circumstances, or the structure of political opportunities" (p. 25).

But just as opportunities can evaporate and the costs of coalition escalate, opportunities can be transformed as coalition members respond to them and make new opportunities, triggering *opportunity spirals*. These operate through sequences of environmental change, interpretation of that change, action, and counteraction, repeated as one action alters another actor's environment (McAdam, Tarrow, and Tilly 2001: ch. 8). For example, Levi and Murphy's account of the Seattle coalition shows how, as the focal point of the conflict changed, the center of coalitional gravity shifted as well, marginalizing some formerly central elements in the coalition and increasing the centrality of others (Levi and Murphy, 2004: 6–9; also see D. Meyer and Corrigall-Brown 2004: 29). An important part of coalition work is seeing new opportunities and using them to build an enduring basis for solidarity.

One advantage of campaign coalitions over federations is that they have the flexibility to shift their activity from one institutional venue to another. While the European Environmental Bureau is locked into working in Brussels, the campaign against genetically modified food could work at the domestic level on both individual governments that were considering how to respond to the import of genetically modified seeds, and in the EU when the European Parliament was considering labeling requirements for GM products (Kettnaker 2001). The same flexibility was true of the campaign to control global warming; when the Kyoto process was in full swing, activities focused on the national level, but after the defection of the United States from the process, activity picked up at the local level (Vasi 2004).

Institutionalization and Its Paradoxes

Admirers of international protest events sometimes see their decentralization, tactical flexibility, and autonomy as major virtues (Graeber 2002; Klein 2004). They are, but there are costs to these well-known virtues. First, it is difficult for short-lived, broad-based event coalitions to develop concrete programs. Second, the tactical creativity of international protest demonstrations can easily turn to violence as activists – frustrated by failure and enraged by the excesses of the police – turn to extreme tactics in the absence of leaders to convince them to "cool it." Third is the danger of vanguard democracy: when no institutionalized rules exist to choose leaders, regulate debate, and canvass opinions, the most militant, in Stephanie Ross's (2002: 282) words, "are able to act as vanguards by default."

In contrast to the excitement and spontaneity of decentralized international events, *institutionalization* can seem like a tired, bureaucratic solution. But in his important study of American challenging groups, William Gamson (1975) found an association between centralization and success. Although decentralization captures the energy and creativity of people who encounter others like themselves in collective efforts (Graeber 2002), Gamson's research showed that some degree of institutionalization is needed to transform these encounters into enduring coalitions. In their analysis of the nuclear freeze campaign, Will Hathaway and David S. Meyer (1997: 63) observed that "coalitions can survive over a long period of time by establishing a means of ensuring *cooperative differentiation*: maintaining a public face of solidarity towards their opponents while differentiating themselves in their relations with constituents."

In principle, transnational federations should be able to sustain a strategy of cooperative differentiation more easily than domestic ones, because the constituencies they appeal to are nationally distinct and can more easily be appealed to on different grounds. But transnational federations have other obstacles to overcome if they are to endure. Especially when coalition members try to bridge North and South, there are vast differences in resources to overcome. In her study of People's Global Action, for example, Lesley Wood (2004a) found that different northern and southern organizational traditions impede cooperation.

A striking aspect of some of the event coalitions that have emerged during the past decade has been their capacity to produce new institutional forms. We have seen in Chapter 7 how the World Social Forum both developed into an annual event and served as a model for local and regional forums. An even more striking example of institutionalization growing out of an event comes from Mexico, following the Chiapas rebellion. After that rebellion, the EZLN organized the two major *encuentros* to bring together its international sympathizers (Olesen 2002; Wood 2004a). One such long-term connection did result – a coalition called "Global People's Action" – which went on to organize global days of action on many other occasions (Wood 2004a).

Socialization through Collective Action

Transnational protest events are often seen as set-piece demonstrations that challenge policy makers, bring out the police, make for good media copy, and then disappear. But participation in such events can be transformative for those who participate in them. The experience of marching side by side with others from different countries and areas of interest can help to create broader identities and issue definitions. For example, following the European Social Forum in Florence in 2002, Donatella della Porta (2005b: 188–90) found among many participants enthusiasm for what one respondent called "bringing together 'many situations ... that in previous years, especially the last ten, did not come together enough.'" A second participant remarked, "one person maybe has a photo of Stalin, and another a photo of Jesus over his bed, all in all it doesn't matter too much, if both believe that Nestlé has to be boycotted, because with ideologies, extreme objectives, dogmatism, you can't ever get anywhere." As a third respondent pointed out, it is in the network that one "gets to know people, forms relationships, becomes a community."

Part of what della Porta was observing was the enthusiasm common to any emergent movement – a *statu nascenti*, in the words of her compatriot, Francesco Alberoni (1984). But another part of what she observed at the European Social Forum, *socialization*, was genuinely new: the combination of discovery and solidarity that is experienced when people with very different backgrounds, languages, and goals encounter one another around a broad global theme. Event coalitions may trigger opportunity spirals; they can produce new institutionalized forms of cooperation; and they can socialize participants from the local level into rooted cosmopolitans.

Conclusions

What can we conclude from the comparison of short-term instrumental and event-based coalitions and enduring federations and campaign coalitions? The most general point that emerges about instrumental coalitions is that, while they can succeed in the short run, they are unlikely to produce the bases for continued collaboration or issue broadening. The same is true of event coalitions: if they are carried away by the joys of decentralization and spontaneity, they will be difficult to transform into enduring cooperation against more concrete targets. Yet highly institutionalized transnational federations like those we saw in the European environmental sector face the problem of welding a general program onto inevitably varied responses to local political opportunities and threats. A correlate of this spatial dilemma is temporal: the shape and substance of coalitions need to change as political opportunities and threats evolve; federations – like all forms of institutionalized collective action – are slow to adapt or to change the venue of their actions

This is why campaign coalitions, which are less exciting than short-term event coalitions and have narrower ambitions and more-concrete issue foci than federations, may be the wave of the transnational future. Their focus on a specific policy issue, their minimal institutionalization, their capacity to shift venues in response to changing opportunities and threats, and their ability to make short-term tactical alliances according to the current focus of interest make them among the most fruitful strategies for transnational collaboration.

In this chapter and the preceding one, I examined two sets of processes through which domestic claims are externalized and then processed through international collective action. The message of the two chapters can be combined: externalization is only the first step in permitting domestic actors to shift their claims to venues in which they can attract support from influential allies; coalition formation is the process through which such alliances are forged. In the final section of this book I consider the results of the processes I have outlined: the domestic impacts of transnational activism in Chapter 10, and the prospects for a fusion between domestic and international contention in Chapter 11.

PART FIVE

Transnational Impacts at Home and Abroad

10

Transnational Impacts on
Domestic Activism

Cape Town, South Africa, and Greensboro, North Carolina, would seem to have little in common, especially in relation to transnational contention. Settled from Virginia in the early eighteenth century, Greensboro is a small southern city of 239,000 whose main claim to fame is that it was the site of a revolutionary war battle and of a famous lunch counter sit-in in the 1960s. Once the major producer of denim in the United States, its major industry now struggles to survive against foreign competition. Cape Town, on the other hand, is a throbbing metropolis of 2.7 million people that was first settled by white people when the British navy turned it into a coaling station on the route to India.

Although both cities are racially divided, their ethnic compositions are very different: with 25 percent African Americans and a rapidly growing Latino population, Greensboro is typical of small cities in the American South; shaped by the exclusionary policies of the apartheid regime, Cape Town is only 2.6 percent African and almost half coloured and Asian.[1] But the two cities do have something in common, improbable as it sounds: a "Truth and Reconciliation Commission."

Truth and Reconciliation in Cape Town

When Nelson Mandela led a new ANC-dominated government to power in 1994, he took over a country that was roughly 80 percent African, 10 percent coloured and Asian, and 10 percent White (Gibson 2004: 32). The gaps in

---

[1] Greensboro's figures are from http://www.ci.greensboro.nc.us/databook/GCDBDemog 2002.pdf; Capetown's statistics are from http://www.capetown.gov.za/home/20030609_1_demographics.asp.

income and circumstances among the various races were dramatic enough (pp. 32–7); what worried the new leadership was the reservoir of racial bitterness that might well up after apartheid ended.[2] Would there be a call for retributive justice from the African population for three hundred years of abuse, followed by a wave of white flight? Or could some mechanism be found to deal out transitional justice without hardening the racial split forever? The solution that was decided upon was the creation of a "Truth and Reconciliation Commission."

Truth commissions were not invented in South Africa: since the early 1980s and the transitions to democracy in Latin America, efforts had been made to identify disappeared people, root out perpetrators, and punish those found guilty of abuses (Avruch and Vejerano 2002; Hayner 1994, 2002; Van Antwerpen 2005). But most of those commissions had dodged the issue of "reconciliation"; in South Africa, this goal was placed at the center of the commission's tasks. The driving force in its creation was its deputy chair, Alex Boraine (2001), a liberal member of South Africa's parliament, who helped convinced Mandela and Bishop Desmond Tutu, its future chair, to seek reconciliation instead of retribution. Created by a law with the deceptively bland title of "The Promotion of National Unity and Reconciliation Act," the commission's understated mandate was to help deal with "what happened under apartheid."[3]

The result was a four-year quasi-judicial process that meted out little punishment – except for public humiliation – and made a great effort at racial reconciliation.[4] For three years, South Africans of every color were riveted to the sometimes devastating, always fascinating, and occasionally uplifting hearings of the TRC. An infinite number of reports and publications accompanied and followed its proceedings, but most interesting from our point of view was its international reception and its diffusion to places as far away as Greensboro, North Carolina.

---

[2] James Gibson found that in his survey 17.2 percent of the African population reported having been forced to move residence, 15.8 percent had been assaulted by the police, 41.4 percent were denied access to education, and 43.7 percent had been unable to associate with other races (Gibson 2004: 41).

[3] The act can be found at http://www.doj.gov.za/trc/legal/act9534.htm, visited on May 10, 2004. It was divided into three major committees: human rights violations, reparations, and rehabilitations and amnesty. Transcripts of hearings can be found at http://www.doj.gov.za/trc/trccom.htm, visited on May 10, 2004.

[4] Inevitably, controversy bubbled up over whether reconciliation without punishment was a possible, or even a desirable outcome. For strong but balanced accounts, see Gibson 2004 and Posel and Simpson 2002.

Truth and Reconciliation in Greensboro

On November 3, 1979, a group of radical labor organizers were mounting an antiracist rally in a black housing project in Greensboro, North Carolina, when they were attacked by a caravan of Ku Klux Klan and Nazi Party members and supporters. When the smoke cleared, five activists lay dead and several others were wounded (Bermanzohn 2003, 2004; Waller 2002). Although a former FBI informant was a member of the Klan and the bureau had infiltrated the Nazi Party, the authorities had apparently done nothing to prevent the killing.

The case produced two criminal trials, but in each one, white juries acquitted the Klan and Nazi gunmen. In a civil trial that followed, "a jury with one black member held the Greensboro police, the Klan, and the Nazis liable for one wrongful death," and the city paid one victim's family a $350,000 judgment (Bermanzohn 2004: 2). For years, as local officials preferred to move on, families and friends of the murdered militants sought satisfaction, but without success.[5] But finally, in 2001, with South Africa still in the news, a group of activists led by a former mayor formed the Greensboro Truth and Community Reconciliation Project to provide opportunities for the community to come to a better understanding of the events of 1979 and their aftermath.[6]

Toward a Model of Domestic Impacts

What does this improbable link between South Africa's national effort at reconciliation after centuries of racial injustice and an American community's attempts to deal with the memory of a local racial crime and cover-up suggest about the domestic impact of transnational activism? Four mechanisms stand out.

---

[5] The city's website devotes only one paragraph to the case: "In the 1970s Greensboro peacefully integrated its school system and the plan was cited around the nation for its success, but the decade ended on a negative note with the Klan-Nazi confrontation with CWP members and bystanders. Five people were killed and televised footage was shown across the nation. Although six Klansmen were tried for the murders, they were acquitted, an action that many people did not understand." Go to http://www.greensboro-nc.gov/newfronts/, visited on May 10, 2004, for the city's presentation.

[6] The group's initial news release called for "the appointment of a Truth Commission made up of persons of unimpeachable character and high repute to undertake an in-depth examination into the events surrounding the November 3, 1979 tragedy. . . . the essential purpose of the project is to help lead Greensboro into becoming a more just, understanding and compassionate community" (Greensboro Justice Fund 2004: 1).

The first is that new forms of activism do not simply appear in different places automatically. That transfer involves *diffusion* of forms of activity that can be adapted to a variety of national and social situations. But the spread of even precise information about an innovation does not guarantee its adoption; at least three other mechanisms are important in the domestication of an innovation: the existence of *brokerage* between its originators and its adopters; the presence of successful *mobilization* on the part of sympathetic or enthusiastic activists; and its *certification* by authoritative actors, or at least the failure of attempts to decertify it.

The Greensboro case exhibits all four of these mechanisms. It was inspired by a practice whose reputation had grown over twenty years of international experience. Brokerage was exercised through advice that the Greensboro committee received from experts with direct experience in South Africa. A local mobilizing coalition combined public officials with the activists who had pressed for exposure of the true story without success for years. And certification was gained from the support of local elites and Christian, Jewish, and Muslim clerics.[7] Figure 10.1 plots the sequence of these transnational and domestic mechanisms as they combined in the Greensboro case.

In this chapter, I turn to the impact of transnational activism on domestic activism and the responses to it. I use a number of cases, past and present, successful and unsuccessful, to illustrate how these mechanisms operate: diffusion can seen in the widespread adoption of human rights norms around the world; I examine brokerage in the role of intermediaries who assisted in the spread of the truth and reconciliation model; mobilization can be seen in the adoption of European Court of Justice decisions in Western Europe; and both certification and decertification are examined in the influence of transnational arms control networks in the Soviet Union.

Even officially sanctioned norms adapt differently in different settings. Activism that diffuses from one country to another triggers different responses and is influenced by domestic structures and practices (Risse-Kappen 1995). If this is true for activist practices, it is equally true for the response to them. As international protest events escalated in the late 1990s and dogged the meetings of international institutions, a set of countermeasures were designed to discourage their repetition. What amounts

---

[7] The sitting mayor used classical "spilled-milk" and "stirring up hornets' nests" arguments against the initiative. For the mayor's response to the proposal for a commission, go to http://discover.npr.org/features/feature.jhtml?wfId=1192894, visited on May 10, 2004.

Non-Local
Collective Action

Diffusion
and
Brokerage

Mobilization
and
Certification

Local
Adaptation

Figure 10.1 The Domestic Impact of Transnational Activism

to a new practice of protest policing diffused around the world, taking root in places as varied as Quebec City, Göteborg, Miami, and Genoa. But even police practice is conditioned by domestic structures, as we will see in the case of the Genoa G-8 protests and their aftermath.

The Diffusion and Reception of Human Rights

From the late 1940s on, NGOs, Western governments, and international institutions developed a universal concept of human rights that implicitly challenged traditional notions of sovereignty. Although the values that bound these actors together were "embedded in international human rights law, especially in the 1948 Universal Declaration of Human Rights," the UN Charter's mandate was weak (Keck and Sikkink 1998: 80, 86). Only in the 1970s, with the expansion of human rights NGOs, the growth in foundation grants, and the policies of both the UN Center for Human Rights and the Carter administration, were attempts made to put teeth into these norms (pp. 89–102). But it was the assaults on human rights by authoritarian governments that gave the international human rights movement its major impetus.

Between 1973 and 1983, according to Jackie Smith's (2004b: 268) calculations, the number of transnational human rights groups doubled, from forty-one in the earlier year to eighty-nine in the latter year. The number doubled again in the next decade, and had grown by another 25 percent by 2000. "Human rights," Smith concludes, "remains the major issue around which the largest number of TSMO's . . . organize, and a consistent quarter of all [transnational] groups work principally on this issue" (p. 269).

The rapid spread of human rights advocacy supports the claim of world polity institutionalists that we live in an era of universalization.[8] These scholars stress "the universalistic . . . level of cultural and organizational formation that operates as a constitutive and directive environment for states, business enterprises, groups, and individuals" (Boli and Thomas 1999: 3). At some level of abstraction, they are of course correct. But if there is a human rights regime today, its reception has been less than universal. Human rights have varying meanings in particular settings and come up against local norms and practices that contest it in the name of both rival universalisms and norms that are frankly parochial.

---

[8] On world polity institutionalism, see J. Meyer, Boli, and Thomas 1987; J. Meyer et al. 1987; and the contributions to Boli and Thomas 1999, especially Boli and Thomas's introduction.

commissions had been formed in at least twenty-five countries. Many had extensive "relationships with international actors and organizations based in other countries that assist[ed] with a national process in multiple ways" (ICTJ 2004: 26).

Brokerage at first developed informally, as individuals experienced with truth commissions in their own countries were invited to consult in countries undergoing similar transitions.[12] In addition to offering technical advice to newly formed commissions or would-be commissions, these agents could provide them with "comparative information, legal and policy analysis, documentation, and strategic research." The ICTJ brings together advocates, academics, legal scholars, and policy makers with expertise in the transitional justice field from different countries and publicizes both successful and unsuccessful cases of transitional justice.[13] In 2004 the center's model for setting up truth commissions was certified by the United Nations.

We do not know to what extent external brokerage actually influences how local activists in countries seek transitional justice or whether it simply provides them with legitimation for what they have decided to do on their own. For purposes of impact, it matters less than the fact that they provide support for practices that local activists might not undertake without international legitimation. But what works in one country may not adapt easily to others (D. Cohen 2003). The ICTJ's most successful efforts seem to be those in which – as in Greensboro – domestic groups are already effectively mobilizing. This takes us to the third major mechanism in producing domestic impacts for transnational activism, the mobilization of domestic actors.

Mobilization after Intervention in Europe

In Chapter 9, we saw that, in the absence of domestic mobilization, even powerful foreign groups cannot force the pace of domestic change. In

---

[12] Paul van Zyl, who had administered the South African TRC, reports that both he and Alex Boraine were at one point deluged with individual requests for consultation. Following a proposal by Priscilla Hayner, then at the Ford Foundation, van Zyl and Boraine set up the ICTJ with a major grant from Ford's Human Rights section. Interview with Paul Van Zyl, October 21, 2004.

[13] Go to http://www.ictj.org, visited on May 10, 2004, for basic information on the work of the ICTJ. For a dismal example of a process that was "intended to fail," see D. Cohen 2003 on the trials before the Ad Hoc Human Rights Court in Indonesia.

Consider universal rights for women, a problem that has been recognized periodically through the UN Conferences on Women and addressed by an extraordinary growth in nongovernmental organizations. According to Smith's (2004b: 268) calculations, the number of international NGOs working for women's rights grew by over 300 percent between 1973 and 2000.[9] But these NGOs are dominated by Western, liberal values that are by no means shared by all groups with an interest in women's lives. It is enough to follow debates at the United Nations to see that the "universalism" of women's rights discourse is less than universally accepted. For example, in order to gain consensus on a universal AIDS declaration, the UN had to satisfy both the Vatican and miscellaneous Muslim groups, which worked closely together to prevent the liberal universalism of mainstream women's rights NGOs from gaining sway (Bush 2004: ch. 4).

Diffusion makes possible the spread of forms of collective action from one part of the world and some population groups to others. But the international acceptance of human rights norms is not enough on its own to domesticate these forms of activism everywhere. For example, in his research on the internationally sponsored human rights campaign against the corrupt and autocratic rule of Daniel arap Moi in Kenya, Hans Peter Schmitz (2001) found a textbook case of how foreign states and international human rights groups can help to set a repressive reality on the road to reform. Once begun, the human rights process "spiraled" (Risse and Sikkink 1999). Through an erratic process of moral suasion and material pressure, a reluctant government was prodded to make concessions to international human rights groups, concessions that could then be built upon to advance the spiral toward democratization.

Not least among the campaign's successes was to assist in the revival of the domestic opposition, especially in the form of civil society groups but, increasingly, in the form of a social movement organization, the National Convention for Constitutional Reform Executive Committee (NCEC). Throughout the late 1980s and into the 1990s, those groups and their external allies were the major forces seeking constitutional change in Kenya. But as the issue terrain shifted from human rights to democratization, the fact that democratization was externally driven took its toll. In particular,

---

[9] Actual interest in women's rights in the NGO community may be even higher, because many groups that are not classified as "women's rights groups" have a strong interest in women – for example, groups working under the rubrics of human rights, development, and religion (Bush 2004: ch. 2).

as political organization revived, the opposition was unable to counter the ethnicization of politics and the accusation that it was the tool of foreign actors. The very factor that had allowed the opposition to struggle to its feet in the 1980s – its international ties – became a ball and chain (Schmitz 2001: 171).

Even within the same society, human rights norms have unequal purchase. As American officials were wagging their fingers in condemnation of the Chinese government's human rights practices, its representatives were encouraging the abuse of prisoners in Afghanistan, Iraq, and Guantanamo. Neither norms nor practices, to paraphrase Thomas Risse-Kappen (1994), "float freely." They depend on aspects of domestic structure and political culture but also on other mechanisms of transmission and adaptation. Three such mechanisms help them to have domestic impacts – brokerage, mobilization, and certification.

Brokerage

I have defined brokerage as *the linking of two or more previously unconnected social actors by a unit that mediates their relations with one another and/or with yet other sites*. It acts as a transnational hinge that communicates and adapts an external practice to new sites and situations. We saw it in Chapter 6 in the transmission of the strategy of nonviolence from India to the American civil rights movement and, most recently, to Serbia and Georgia. The agent of brokerage can be a private "missionary" who carries the innovation to a new site and attempts to adapt it there – an international NGO, a foundation, an international institution, or some combination of these agents. The International Center for Transitional Justice (ICTJ) demonstrates how a neutral, professional agent can facilitate domestic actors seeking justice for past abuses in both democratizing and democratic states (Van Antwerpen 2005).

Brokering Transitional Justice[10]

Long before South Africa established its Truth and Reconciliation Commission, unofficial and official bodies were looking into historical and recent

[10] I am grateful to Louis Bickford, Priscilla Hayner, and Paul van Zyl of the International Center for Transitional Justice and to Larry Cox of the Ford Foundation for their advice in preparing this section.

190

Table 10.1. *Estimated Number of Regular and "Historical" Truth Commissions, by World Region, 1974–2002*

Region	Number of Truth Commission
Africa	12
Asia	4
Europe, North America, and Australia[a]	6
Latin America	11

[a] Truth Commissions listed for the United States, Canada, and Australia are "historic
Sources: Compiled from Hayner 2002: appendix 1; National Reconciliation Pro in Ghana, at http://www.nrcghana.org/corporateprofiles.php (March 9, 2004); January 19, 2001; UNTAET (UN Transitional Administration in East Timor) Office, Fact Sheet 9, December 2001; "Commissioners Sworn in to Lead Recon tion Body," January 21, 2002, http://www.un.org/peace/etimor/DB/db210102.htm News Service, February 11, 2002, September 4, 2001, July 7, 2001; InterPress vice January 4, 2001; Agence France Presse, April 8, 2001; BBC Monitoring Eu Political, February 22, 2002; Presidential Truth Commission on Suspicious at http://truthfinder.go.kr/eng/index. htm (February 25, 2002); EFE August 14 www.usip.org/library/truth.html.

human rights abuses under a variety of regimes, usually – but no countries undergoing transitions to democracy. The largest numb efforts took place in Latin America as authoritarianism ebbed tions to democracy were undertaken (Hayner 1994, 2002). But forts were made in many other parts of the world, even where – Saxon settler societies – democracy was well established and addressed were "historical." Table 10.1 summarizes the num commissions established in different parts of the world betwe 1970s and 2001, estimated from Priscilla Hayner's work and oth

The early Latin American transitional justice campaigns cal groups responding to domestic outrage and suffering, as documented case of Argentina's "Mothers of the Plaza" (Bry as we saw in Chile in Chapter 8, international actors soon su actions, assessed their successes and weaknesses, and commu practices" to groups in other countries (Sikkink 2005b). would eventually include foundations, NGOs from nearby UN, certain governments, particularly from Scandinavia, an NGOs like the Center for the Study of Violence and Re Johannesburg. By the time the South African TRC was es

[11] Data through 2001 are aggregated from Hayner 2002, appendixes 1 a

Western Europe, Lisa Conant's (2002) work shows that, in the absence of direct action from the parties concerned or their allies, even authoritative institutions, like the European Court of Justice, have a limited reach into domestic politics. The European Court of Justice is a powerful supranational tribunal with an accepted right to intervene over the heads of national governments. But ECJ rulings apply only to the plaintiffs in cases that the court agrees to adjudicate; it takes continued mobilization for these cases to be generally implemented. As Karen Alter and Jeannette Vargas (2000: 464) write: "By following through, activists have translated legal victories into social policy changes with real impacts on the conduct of employers and the government."

Conant (2002) puts this argument succinctly in her polemic with legalists who think decisions of the European Court of Justice are sufficient for their holdings to be implemented. Using information on the outcomes of four key ECJ decisions, Conant finds that it was only in areas like telecommunications and electricity reform, in which powerful interests followed up on the court's decisions, that these decisions had an impact beyond the original cases. Conant sees a three-stage process needed for ECJ decisions to take root domestically: first, the court must identify or create rights in response to petitioners' claims; second, domestic actors must mobilize to support or resist the broader application of these rights and obligations; and, third, member states and EU institutions must accommodate these decisions by adjusting their law and policy (p. 9). As she concludes, "judicial influence over major processes of reform relies on a much broader mobilization of pressure for policy change" (p. 3).

Where social actors are weak and unmobilized, as in the cases of public-sector employees and EU immigrants seeking the right to social benefits, justice is "contained." But public employees and migrants, who have weak weapons, both domestically and in Brussels (Guiraudon 2001), work for employers who have hired them precisely to avoid paying out social benefits. In these areas, social rights were not implemented by national governments because no domestic political process followed the court's decisions. As Conant wryly concludes, "equal access to social benefits was available in courtrooms," "while a substantial degree of national discrimination persists in the realm of policy and practice" (pp. 203, 207).

These examples of "contained justice" in the European Union do not prove that supranational intervention or transnational ties are bound to fail. As we saw in Chapter 8, when they were aggressively followed up by British feminists and unions, the ECJs gender equality decisions narrowed the gaps in wages and benefits between men and women. What the ECJ cases show is that even authoritative external intervention must be accompanied by aggressive domestic mobilization And if this is the case in the presence of the most highly developed international institutions in the world, it is certainly truer elsewhere. This takes us to the issue of certification.

Certification

By certification, I mean *the validation of actors, their performances, and their claims by authorities*. Certification operates as a powerful selective mechanism in contentious politics because a certifying site always recognizes a limited range of identities, performances, and claims. Consider the claim of nationhood: although the United Nations has evaluated thousands of claims to nationhood since 1945, it has accepted only a hundred-odd of them. In 1986 the UN acted as a certifying agent for the Philippine opposition to President Marcos, but it has refused to recognize hundreds of other insurgent groups that threaten the sovereignty of one or another of its member states (McAdam, Tarrow, and Tilly 2001: 158).

UN certification is an important mechanism in the validation of *non*state actors too. The United Nations has played an important role in certifying national minorities as "indigenous" by admitting them to membership in its Working Group on Indigenous Populations (WGIP). Since 1982, that group has met annually in Geneva, partly in response to the wave of indigenous protest that emerged in the 1960s and 1970s in many parts of the world, especially in the Americas (Yashar 2005). The mandate of the working group is, first, to monitor the current circumstances of indigenous peoples and, second, to elaborate "formal standards regarding the rights of indigenous peoples and the responsibilities of states" (Dietz 2000: 40–1).

How does UN certification of a group as "indigenous" impact on its domestic position? Kelly Dietz's research suggests that "the institutionalized recognition of a political category at the level of international organizations is an indicator that – for better or worse – it has acquired some degree of status as an 'international problem' rather than a domestic matter of the state" (p. 76). Groups that are certified as "indigenous" by the UN can use that recognition as leverage to gain political influence or seek independence at home. This is why UN certification of groups as indigenous is often strongly opposed by their governments and the UN has had to be careful to categorize some groups as "minorities," as opposed to "indigenous" (pp. 79–80).

The certification of transnational activism on domestic soil is more difficult, first, because transnational activists are often foreign, and therefore suspect and, second, because their actions can threaten domestic values and power asymmetries. These obstacles not only inhibit the domestication of the goals of transnational activists; they can produce a backlash as political opportunities shift, as the changes in the success and failure of transnational arms control show in the former Soviet Union and its successor state, Russia.

Certification and Decertification in Moscow[14]

If we set out to find a country where we would expect to find little sympathy for transnational activism, it would have been the Soviet Union. Obsessed since the 1930s about "capitalist encirclement," the USSR had plenty to worry about after the Cold War began, as the United States and its allies drew a net of bases and missile emplacements around its borders (Snyder 1993: 115–16). In a highly centralized political system dominated by a strong party-state apparatus, we would expect societal forces tainted by contact with foreign actors to have little influence on policy (Evangelista 1995: 3). Yet Soviet scientists with transnational ties to their Western counterparts appear to have had just such an influence as long as the Soviet Union survived.

Scientists are a prime example of the "rooted cosmopolitans" I described in Chapter 3. They owe their training, their resources, and their primary opportunities to their roles in one society, but their membership in international professional societies and their devotion to the universal values of science provide them with perspectives and professional ties that bring them close to colleagues abroad. Even across the hardened lines of the Cold War, scientists enjoyed a common language and membership in an epistemic community (P. Haas 1992), influencing even sensitive security areas like arms control.

As post-Stalinist totalitarian pretensions gave way to authoritarian pluralism, Soviet security policy was influenced by scientists who had been participating since the 1970s in closely monitored but nevertheless fruitful arms-control exchanges with their Western counterparts.[15]

---

[14] I base this account on the original research of my colleague, Matthew Evangelista (1995, 1999), whom I thank for his advice.

[15] This view was put forward by international relations and peace movement scholars in the 1990s (see D. Meyer 1990–1; Risse-Kappen 1994).

Based on his close examination of Central Committee archives, Matthew Evangelista came to two main conclusions about these scientists' transnational networks: first, he found that "the transnational allies of domestic political actors provide resources to influence internal debates over foreign policy" (1995: 5); second, he showed how the centralized nature of the Soviet policy-making system, though it provided relatively little access to transnational actors, made it possible for their ideas to be effectively implemented once they gained a hearing (p. 1).

Soviet scientists who participated in international meetings with their counterparts from the West were carefully vetted, sometimes by the Politburo itself. But once they gained official approval in this centralized bureaucratic system, they could use their access to decision makers to press for the policies they favored, and these had resulted from their interactions with Western scientists (pp. 5, 13). As Evangelista writes, "The intercession of prominent Soviet scientists . . . working with their American colleagues and sympathetic aides to Gorbachev and Schevardnadze, helped convince the Soviet leadership to sign two major arms accords without insisting on any U.S. commitments regarding the ABM treaty or SDI" (p. 19). He concludes that "the hierarchical, centralized nature of the Soviet system meant that once the top leadership was on board, implementation of the project with all of the necessary resources was almost guaranteed" (p. 24).

But the converse also turned out to be true as the centralized Soviet Union gave way to a more pluralistic system. As Gorbachev's reforms took hold and the Soviet structure crumbled, once-carefully controlled military leaders gained political influence, and it was no longer easy for transnationally connected scientific activists to gain a hearing (pp. 25–8). Post-Gorbachev Russia was not yet a democratic system. It was not even a system with structured competition between elites. But as more windows were opened up to the outside world and the USSR's internal power structure diversified, military sectors became more influential, and "new voices were heard in Soviet discussions about strategic defenses" (p. 25). But post-Soviet Russia is not the only place where the forces of order have gained influence in the 1990s.

The Militarization of Protest Policing

Challenges by activists and advocates are not the only forms of collective action that diffuse into the domestic practices of receiving societies. Especially in this age of internationalization, intergovernmental agreements and international agencies diffuse models of response to transnational collective actions, especially when these appear to threaten governments in similar ways. Yet until recently, few scholars paid attention to the diffusion and domestic impacts of social control mechanisms across space and time. "New forms of disruption may require new forms of social control" (McCarthy, McPhail, and Crist 1999: 71–2), and the diffusion of new forms of policing in response to transnational protest events trigger equally widely diffused social control mechanisms.

The Diffusion of "Public Order Management Systems"

The strategy of protest policing that was developed in the United States in the 1960s diffused across the advanced industrial world in response to the wave of student and other contention of that period. The new American system spread through binational and then multinational contacts between American and foreign police officials (Slaughter 2004). For example, the new South African regime "shopped" for models of policing through ties with community policing factions in the American police arena. But the most important broker in the international diffusion of new forms of public order management in the 1970s was the International Association of Chiefs of Police (McCarthy, McPhail, and Crist 1999: 90).

This management system was adopted by police academies and implemented by police forces all across the industrialized world. With some local variations, the new strategy was based on three main rules of police behavior:

- Negotiate the marching routes, the tactics, and the objects of protest with protest leaders.
- Maintain continual contact with them through a single police command center that controls the actions of all the units in the field.
- Keep troublemakers away from peaceful demonstrators, never attack the latter when the former get violent, and never break off contact with demonstration leaders. (della Porta and Reiter 1998, 2004)

Between the early 1970s and the late 1990s, this model served police forces and protesters equally well. Negotiation and contact with protest leaders limited the potential for conflict between them and the police. Isolation of troublemakers made it less likely that violence would spread or that police would use violent tactics against nonviolent demonstrators. Agreement on demonstration routes would make it less likely that the life of the

197

general public would be disrupted. In the long run, the resulting Public Order Management System civilized the relations between authorities and protesters and helped to add organized protests to the accepted repertoire of political participation. But that was before the wave of international protests against the worlds' great financial institutions broke out in the 1990s.

From Public Order to Police Riot

The near takeover of the WTO Ministerial at Seattle in the 1990s frightened police forces around the world. At the Genoa anti–G-8 protests in July 2001, a young protester named Carlo Giuliano was shot by a panicked *carabiniere* riding in a jeep that had become isolated and was surrounded by protesters. The Giuliano shooting came as a shock not only because it took place during an international summit; it also broke a long-term truce between Italian protesters and the police. In the three decades since Italy's mass protest wave of the 1960s and early 1970s, the interactions between Italian demonstrators and the police were – if not harmonious – at least civil. This was the result of the implementation of the same innovations in police practice that were adopted by most of the major governments of the West. This is particularly remarkable given the fact that Italy faced a ruthless wave of both left-wing and right-wing terrorism well into the 1980s. Genoa brought an end to the informal truce between protesters and the police.

Every one of the rules of the "public order management system" adopted in the 1970s was broken in Genoa. The police failed to maintain contact with protest leaders; they did not separate the violent fringe of "black bloc" anarchists from the rest; when the former threw rocks at them, the police turned their guns, tear gas, batons, and jeeps on the peaceful protesters. An attack on a school where protesters were lodged was the culmination of this strategy. Their faces masked, the police erupted into the school, swinging truncheons to left and right before transporting anyone they could catch to a police barracks. The activists were beaten, made to stand spread-eagled for hours, and were kept incommunicado for up to three days. When these "dangerous anarchists" were finally hauled before the magistrates to be booked, all but one was immediately freed for improper arrest. Indictments since then verified not only that the police were disorganized and unprepared; many of them behaved toward the protesters as enemies of the state (della Porta and Reiter 2004).

What explained this abandonment of a police practice that had maintained relative calm on the streets of Italy for over two decades? Three reasons come to mind: First, as in Seattle, there was a radical fringe in Genoa that was bent on destruction. Second, the Italian police had studied the anti-WTO protests and might have decided that the Seattle police had been too lenient; from the first day of the Genoa Summit, they went on the offensive. Third, and probably most important, the new right-wing Berlusconi government was bent on demonstrating its international legitimacy and its domestic law-and-order credentials to its sister states in the G-8.

If Italy's had been an isolated case, the police riot in Genoa could be explained by such largely domestic factors. But the Italian police were attempting to implement a new transnational strategy of protest policing, one that substitutes force for negotiation, truncheons for the provision of porta-potties, and isolating protesters in "cages" for agreed-upon parade routes. From summits at Göteborg and Prague to Davos, New York, and Miami, police forces have been adopting harsher and more-punitive strategies toward protesters at international summits. And given the similarity of the tactics used and the growing collaboration of police forces arrayed in "the war on terror," it is hard not to believe we are seeing a common domestic policy impact of transnational activism.

Conclusions

The arguments of this chapter can be easily summarized. In it I argued that the domestic impacts of transnational activism depend on a combination of mechanisms that channel its reception into domestic politics. Four main mechanisms were proposed: diffusion, brokerage, mobilization, and certification. The observations in the chapter came from so many sectors of transnational activism that generalization is hazardous, but it will be useful to summarize them before moving to the fusion of domestic and transnational contention.

While forms of collective action like the strike or the demonstration proved to be modular as industrialization spread, the human rights norms that were propagated more recently have been less than universally accepted – even on the part of Western governments that have been loudest in their defense (Sikkink 2005a). Transnational brokers provide domestic activists with access to resources, information, and legitimacy. For transnational activism to take hold, domestic mobilization must continue after the onset of external intervention. Finally, even in highly centralized systems like the former Soviet Union, certification by powerholders can produce high-level access for a transnational movement, but identification of a campaign with foreign intervention can decertify its proponents.

So much for a summary: what are the implications of this chapter's arguments? In the past decade, advocates of transnational activist networks have highlighted many successful instances of successful intervention on behalf of actors too weak to advance their own claims. In an internationalized world, we are likely to see more and more of such intervention, so it is important to look at it without illusions. Transnational intervention fails more often than it succeeds. First, heavy-handed or culturally insensitive transnational agents can delegitimize their partners and produce a backlash against foreign intervention (Bob 2002; Snyder and Vinjamuri 2004). Domestic failure is often an outcome of the very success of transnational intervention, when domestic activists come to depend upon it (Schmitz 2001). Third, domestic cultures of dissent may be resistant to even the most logical applications of international practice (Mendelson and Gerber 2004).

I have focused on domestic politics in this chapter because that is the framework in which most people live and where the changes in transnational activism will ultimately be felt. But this focus on domestic politics is rather one-sided; it leaves unexamined the broader international impact of the new transnational activism. It also leaves unexamined the major challenge to transnational activism of the early twenty-first century: how will the rise of muscular unilateralism on the part of the world's only superpower affect internationalism and thus the future of transnational activism? In the conclusion, I turn to the major changes in the international system as I see them and to the three big questions I pose in the Introduction to this book.

11

Transnational Activism and Internationalization

As summer ended in 2001, a range of Washington-based organizations were planning a demonstration against a meeting of the World Bank and the International Monetary Fund (Gillham and Edwards 2003: 91). Made up of a coalition of national and international advocacy groups, church and community organizations, and trade unions and environmental campaigners, they had organized themselves into a coalition, Mobilization for Global Justice (MGJ). Their goal was to mount "the latest in a series of high-profile, mass demonstrations since the Battle of Seattle had nearly brought the meetings of the World Trade Organization to a halt in 1999" (p. 92). These two institutions had been targeted by a protest a year earlier, but in the wake of the killing of a young demonstrator in Genoa in July (see Chapter 10), the Washington police were preparing for a much bigger confrontation.

The organizers were prepared as well, with the panoply of electronic communication, face-to-face "spokescouncils," and radical puppetry that had become familiar in international demonstrations since Seattle. But they were by no means all "global justice" activists, for they varied in character and degree of militancy from advocacy "insiders" to activist "outsiders." And although their claims ranged from the most global to the very local – remember the "global gardeners" in Chapter 4 – their plans were structured around the focal point of these international institutions. Everything seemed to conspire to promise the most vast, energetic, and potentially disruptive international protest of the year 2001.

But when four terrorist airplane-bombs crashed into the World Trade Center, the Pentagon, and the Pennsylvania countryside on September 11, everything changed for the MGJ. In their careful reconstruction, Gillham and Edwards specify the various responses of the organizers. Of the roughly eighteen events and protests that were planned for the week of the World Bank – IMF meeting, ten were canceled outright and four others were revised to respond to the new situation. The most disruptive protests and theatrical events, like radical puppetry, were canceled, and several new and more conventional activities were decided upon. A number of groups that had worked to plan MGJ events dropped out or scaled back their involvement. In particular, the AFL-CIO, which had always been queasy about working alongside radical peace groups, pulled its forces from the coalition to devote its energies to disaster relief. Strains quickly appeared in the coalition, in part echoing traditional ideological differences, but in part on the basis of different appreciations of the national tragedy. Some groups wanted to cancel the demonstration, others determined to maintain it as planned, while others turned swiftly to what they already saw as the growing threat of war.

The result was that many people who had been expected to travel to Washington didn't show up. Most of the media stayed away and the broad panoply of meetings, protests, trainings, and marches that had been meticulously planned around the theme of global justice collapsed in favor of a much smaller and more-conventional protest. The disaster on September 11 was a historic hinge, not only for the United States and its relations with the rest of the world, but for a movement that had found a surprisingly warm reception in the heart of global capitalism.

Would the movement collapse, go into hibernation, or survive in a different form (Mittelman 2004a)? Some of its components shifted permanently into antiwar activities; others – stunned by the attacks on September 11 – subsided into passivity as the country prepared for war; still others soldiered on in a campaign that attempted to reframe global injustice around the target of American militarism. Like many social movements, the global justice movement's fate depended heavily on forces outside its control.

What Is Happening Here?

The derailment of the September 2001 protests underscores many of the assumptions and findings of this book: about internationalism and globalization; about the wide variety and varied sources of "rooted cosmopolitanism," about the fragility of a global movement faced by the unimpaired power of states, and about the processes of transnational contention and their significance. It also affords a convenient foundation on which to summarize the previous chapters and will help to respond to the broad questions raised at the end of Chapter 1:

- To what extent and how does the expansion of transnational activism change the actors, the connections among them, the forms of claims making, and the prevailing strategies in contentious politics?
- Does the expansion of transnational activism and the links it establishes between nonstate actors, their states, and international politics create a new political arena that fuses domestic and international contention?
- If so, how does this affect our inherited understanding of the autonomy of national politics from international politics?

Internationalism and Internationalization

The story of the failed September 2001 Washington protest allows us to summarize the main findings of this study and propose answers to some broader questions. First, the Washington event lends support to my contention that the new transnational activism recruits supporters around the focal points of international institutions, regimes, and events. Like the European Union that was the target of the "tuna war" in Chapter 4, the Davos meeting that led to the formation of the World Social Forum in Chapter 7, the work of the International Center for Transitional Justice that we encountered in Chapter 10, and much more, internationalism is a structure of threat and opportunity within which the new transnational activism has emerged.

Some observers have seen internationalism as no more than the public face of globalization; others have seen it as no more than intensified horizontal ties between states; still others only as international economic exchange. My view is that it is a triangular structure of opportunities, resources, and threats within which transnational contention is mobilized. Internationalism's horizontal axis is indeed found in a dense network of intergovernmental and transnational ties; its vertical axis consists of the extraordinary growth of international institutions, treaties, and regimes; and it provides the framework within which global economic exchange is organized. This structure provides the opportunity space within which efforts to control globalization, advance human rights, reverse environmental threats, dislodge dictatorships, and, most recently, oppose resurgent militarism are made.

For simplicity and to focus on contentious processes, I have treated internationalism as a static process, but there has been evidence of growing internationalization throughout this book. Internationalization is the broad process through which the density of both horizontal and vertical ties expands and opportunities and threats are externalized. We have seen evidence of it in the increasing number of international organizations, in the greater reach and influence of international institutions, in the growth of decision making and standards setting by transgovernmental committees and compacts, and in the extent to which nonstate actors are using international venues to advance their claims.

Processes of Transnational Contention

Within this broad process, nonstate actors are present in three sets of contentious processes. Two more "domestic" processes were described in Part Two – global framing and internalization. Two international processes that I called externalization and coalition building were described in Part Four. Linking the two are the two transitional processes I examined in Part Three – diffusion and scale shift.

In both the planning of the protest against the World Bank and IMF meeting and its derailment after September 11, many of the processes we have seen at work in this book were present. That event will help us to summarize the findings of these chapters; its disappointing outcome will guard us against excessive hope for the creation of a brave new world.

- *Global framing.* In Washington, even palpably domestic issues, like the plight of the homeless, were included under the global umbrella of a protest against these international institutions; but more important was the framing of domestic inequality as the result of global processes. Global justice protesters have helped even conservative Americans see the costs of rampant outsourcing of goods and services.
- *Internalization.* The Washington protesters were also using the event to challenge domestic opponents on domestic ground; as we saw in Chapter 5, internalization of international pressures has gone further in the European Union, where farmers, fisherman, pensioners, and anti-GM protesters target their national officials as proxies for hard-to-reach international institutions. But Americans, too, use international venues to challenge domestic opponents.

- *Diffusion*. Throughout this book we have seen the transnational broker-age and theorization of forms of contentious politics, which are then adopted and adapted in places very different than their place of origin. As in the spread of the Gandhian model of nonviolence in Chapter 6, a new form of protest organization – the so-called "Seattle model" – was planned for the streets of Washington until September 11 intervened.
- *Scale shift*. Scale shift is a vertical process that diffuses collective action – and often the response to it – to higher or lower levels. We saw it in its most lethal form in the creation of a global Islamist network and its most pacific in the groups that adapted the World Social Forum model to the local level in Western Europe. In Washington, activists from the American Northeast and the West came to Washington to join a national protest event.
- *Coalition formation*. Finally, "insiders" like the AFL-CIO and the Sierra Club joined uneasily in the Washington protest with outsiders like Anti-Capitalist Convergence and the Ruckus Society in an "event coalition" like the ones we saw in Chapter 9. Transnational campaign coalitions are the surest sign that enduring networks of activists and advocates can have an impact on global governance.
- Note the process that did *not* appear in the Washington protest – *ex-ternalization*. Only one group in the Washington protest even took it upon itself to maintain ties with foreign allies, and there were almost no foreigners present at the demonstration. This may be a function of the perceived centrality of the United States, of the isolation of that country from other centers of resistance to neoliberalism, or of the parochialism of American progressivism. In any case, it underscores the difficulty of creating truly global movements, even when the target of a campaign is a clearly global institution.

If internationalization continues to expand, we can expect all of these con-tentious processes to become more prominent.

Rooted Cosmpolitanism

The new transnational activism is as multifaceted as the internationalism within which it has emerged. Although globalization and global neoliber-alism are frames around which many activists mobilize, the protests and organizations we have seen in this study are not the product of a global imaginary but of domestically rooted activists who target dictatorship, human rights abuse, HIV/AIDS, or militarism and its side products, or emerge from within religious denominations or their surrogates. Nor are the forms of their activism limited to the ones that appear in the press or on the internet. From sturdy port inspectors defending seamen's rights on shore to Greenpeace opposing oil platforms at sea; from well-dressed NGO insiders in New York and Geneva to activists on the ground in Sudan or Afghanistan; from quiet supporters of the "good" NGOs supporting peace, the environment, or human rights to the noisy protesters of Seattle or Genoa, transnational activism is a many-sided phenomenon. Its activists are the connective tissue of the global and the local, working as activators, brokers, and advocates for claims both domestic and international.

The events of September 11 revealed that transnational activism has a "dark side," one that we saw in Chapters 3 and 7. As the enthusiastic supporters of the Mobilization for Global Justice were planning to protest global neoliberalism peacefully, the "birds of passage" of political Islamism, disguised as "nested pigeons" in immigrant ghettos, were preparing to destroy the Pentagon and the World Trade Center. Although there is little in common between the liberal and progressive groups that planned the Washington demonstration and the militant adepts of political Islamism who attacked the World Trade Center, both reflect the tangled skein of transnational ties that weave our world together.

Resilient States, Fragile Movements

Notice that I did not claim that the processes I have examined are breaking down the walls of the state system. Internationalism takes a number of forms that impinge on but do not destroy the power of states: the "multilevel governance" that Liesbet Hooghe and Gary Marks (2002) uncovered in the European Union; the "complex multilateralism" described by O'Brien and his collaborators (2000); and the weaker mechanisms of NAFTA, the International Landmines Convention, and the Kyoto process. Internationalism is not an inexorable force working against the state but a loose framework of institutions, regimes, practices, and processes that include state actors and penetrate domestic politics. The lesson of the story that began this chapter and of many of the episodes described in this book is that internationalism is partial and many-faceted and intersects with the determined powers of states and the international institutions they have created. Later I turn to the question of whether it is reversible and reversing.

The 2001 Washington demonstration also underscores the fact that, in contrast to the hopes of many advocates, states are still robust in respect to transnational activism. From a sleeping giant that seemed unable to defend itself against the terrorist attacks of the 1990s, the United States responded to the September 11 outrages like a wounded tiger, transmuting itself into an aggressive military power abroad and a semipraetorian state at home. That dynamic profoundly affected the American global justice movement too, as the story of the Washington protest suggested. In response to September 11 and the war fever that it triggered, many American activists retreated from the broad terrain of global neoliberalism to the more immediate ground of electoral politics, where their lack of success in 2004 was palpable. Were they turning permanently inward? It is too soon to tell, but despite the thinly veiled attacks of the Bush administration against the UN, large majorities of Americans – even elites – still supported the organization after 9/11.

Both domestic and transnational movements depend on external threats and opportunities; but these are more volatile in international politics, where institutional routines are less established, allies and enemies change their strategies at will, and there is no single core of public authority. If we define internationalism as a triangular opportunity space made up of states, international institutions, and nonstate actors, we are bound to see states – especially powerful ones – asserting themselves periodically within this framework and movements struggling to reshape themselves around these changes, as we did in the failed Washington demonstration in September 2001.

Moreover, the world of the early twenty-first century is not neatly divided into a camp of statists and globalizers on one side opposed by a composite movement for "global justice" on the other. Such condensation makes for exciting politics and popular journalism, but it is reductionist on both counts. On the one hand, the post–Iraq war world is a lot more multilateral than it seemed when American forces stormed into Baghdad in March 2003; on the other, the "global justice" movement is a lot more fragile than its advocates hoped. Through its energy and diversity, the movement helped to dignify and generalize a wide variety of claims that might otherwise have remained local. But its geographic and sectoral dispersion and the different targets of its components made it difficult to sustain as a unified movement. To be sure, the movement put new issues on the global agenda; but states and institutions have inherited and are processing them.

Processes and Mechanisms

Some readers may have wondered why I have focused so much attention in this book on political processes and their constituent mechanisms. In response to earlier efforts of this kind (McAdam, Tarrow, and Tilly 2001), some complained at what they regarded as a description of processes in place of the crisper correlational analyses that some regard as the only true social science. I have argued that specifying the mechanisms of contentious politics, and trying to understand how these mechanisms combine in political processes, can tell us how robust those processes are likely to be and will help us to understand their outcomes.

Consider diffusion, the most widespread and easily observed transnational process we examined. Were we to adapt only the dominant "relational" model of diffusion from domestic practice, we could produce high levels of significance connecting diffusers and adopters of particular forms of contentious politics. But would we be able to understand how, say, the Zapatista solidarity network was diffused from Chiapas to North American and Western Europe partly through *non*relational means? Or the key role of international brokers in the mediated spread of nonviolent strategy from India to the United States and from there to Serbia and Georgia?

Moreover, better specification of the mechanisms of diffusion not only traces its pathways but helps to understand its reach and outcomes. Diffusion through established networks of trust is the surer and more durable pathway, but its reach is limited by its dependence on the preexisting ties of those who pass on the message. Nonrelational diffusion – for example, through the internet – has greater reach, but its impersonal nature makes its impact thinner than that of relational diffusion. Mediated diffusion depends on brokers who connect otherwise unconnected actors, and thereby gain leverage over the content of the message. Trying to understand transnational contention by observing its processes and specifying their mechanisms is not a lesser form of analysis than correlational work; it is a different kind of causal analysis.

But identifying the processes of contentious politics that form within internationalism is only the first task in understanding that complex phenomenon. Eventually, we will need to turn seriously to the methodological questions that have been ignored in this book and attempt to put together different processes with one another and with different contexts. That is a task for another time, and, probably, for other researchers. Instead, I want to try to respond to the three big questions posed at the outset: What is new in the new transnational activism? Does it involve a fusion of domestic and transnational contention? What does it say about the inherited divide between national and international politics?

What's New?

The disappointment to activists of protests like the September 2001 event in Washington, D.C., undermine hopes that a global movement of resistance will triumph in a state-centered world. But seen in the light of the changes in contentious politics over the past few decades, even this failed demonstration offers evidence that something new is happening. We can summarize these changes in three ways: in new "global" attitudes, in new forms of organization, and in the shifting campaigns and composite forms of transnational activism.

New Attitudes

We saw in Chapter 4 that while the vast majority of citizens identify primarily with their localities and their national states, younger citizens are more likely to feel attachments to the continental or global levels than their elders Moreover, even in the wake of 9/11, large numbers of people interviewed in the World Values Study believed that key policy areas – like the environment, immigration, and development – are best dealt with by international institutions (Jung 2005). While there is little evidence of either mass or elite globalism, there is growing evidence that young people communicate more easily across borders, and that activists participate around common themes across the world, as we saw in both the movement against the Iraq war in 2003 and in the rapid diffusion of the model of the World Social Forum.

This does not mean (and it is worth repeating) that transnational activism is displacing activists' domestic involvements or escaping national constraints. Consider the massive number of Italians who marched past the Coliseum in February 2003: some had their attention turned from domestic to transnational activism by the Zapatista rebellion of 1994; others by the Genoa G-8 protests of 2001; still others by the "social forums" that emerged in Europe and in Italy after Porto Alegre. When della Porta and her collaborators interviewed many of them on their way to Genoa or in Florence, they identified strongly with the struggle against globalization (della Porta et al. 2006). But the majority were deeply embedded in domestic forms of activism. Outraged by their government's abuse of peaceful protesters in Genoa, their turn to transnational activism filled a gap that had opened in Italian politics with the collapse of the the Communist Party (see Figure 7.2). The new activists represent less a migration from domestic to international arenas than a transmutation of domestic activism.

New Forms of Organization

New forms of organization are being created that bring people together in transnational campaigns and coalitions. Spokescouncils and working groups have replaced the bureaucratic organizations of the past and mediate between the need for coordination and group autonomy. Between these events, most participants melt back into their own societies, but organizers remain in touch with one another through friendship networks, e-mail contacts, and, increasingly, through on-line internet connections.

There is no doubt that the internet speeds the organization of event coalitions and eases the maintenance of between-event coalitions. It is at the core of a new type of movement organization, one that is no longer dependent on fixed, place-based activities (W. L. Bennett 2005). It has produced forms of activism indigenous to its technology – "hactivism" – which range in form from on-line comedy to entering and corrupting official websites for political purposes (Samuels 2004). It is also a tool in "cyber terrorism" and has helped to build and maintain the "dark side" of transnational activism (Sageman 2004). But it is less clear that, in the absence of trust-producing face-to-face contacts, the internet can create a social movement.

Like every other new form of communication, the internet both increases the speed of communication and creates inequalities of access. Moreover, when it comes to building a unified movement, ease of access to communication is a mixed blessing, because every activist who is capable of building a website can challenge established organizers and disperse a unified movement into a number of separate campaigns. Finally, states and countermovements have proved adept at using the internet too, responding in real time to on-line activist campaigns and using their information channels to infiltrate and oppose them.

At the other extreme of organization are the campaign coalitions we examined in Chapter 9. These are unglamorous, require constant negotiation, engage in education and lobbying and seldom protest, and usually focus on concrete and often technical objectives. Many collaborate with institutional and governmental elites, requiring compromises that can disappoint the hopes of their more ardent supporters. But some, including the landmines coalition, the European anti-GM movement, and the coalition that derailed the Cancun summit, have proved remarkably successful. Moreover, in Seattle, at Cancun, and at the World Social Forum, we see increasing cooperation between social activist "outsiders" and "insider" NGO advocates producing hybrid forms of activism and organization.

Shifting Campaigns and Composite Organizations

In other ways as well, the panoply of forms of transnational activism and activities is changing. Two kinds of connections are especially striking: the ease with which activists who enter politics in one campaign can shift smoothly to cognate campaigns, and the rise of composite movement organizations.

In the months and years after September 11, 2001, many activists from the global justice campaign moved rapidly into antiwar activities, often framing their new target as an extension of their opposition to global social injustice (Fisher 2004). Whether opposition to American militarism is part of the movement against neoliberalism or is a case of transnational "movement spillover" (D. Meyer and Whittier 1994) may be a matter of definition. What is certainly true is that there was a rapid "spillover" of activists from the global justice protests of the late 1990s to the antiwar movement at the beginning of the Iraq war.

There are costs to every movement "spillover." While "global justice" is a collective action frame so broad that it could proceed for years without evident failure, opposing a war about to be launched by a determined government can fail – as the antiwar movement failed when President Bush decided to go to war against Iraq (D. Meyer and Corrigall-Brown 2004). Moreover, gaps soon appeared between the American branch of the movement, which was forced to operate in an atmosphere of outraged patriotism, and its transnational allies, whose movement could depend on the instinctive anti-Americanism that is present – and growing – in many parts of the world (Maney, Woehrle, and Coy 2003).

Just as impressive as the flexibility of the new activists is the composite nature of their organizations. A robust trend that began in the 1990s was a shift from single-issue to multi-issue organizing by transnational movement organizations. Although most such organizations still focus on a single set of goals, Jackie Smith (2004b) found a doubling in the number of groups adopting multi-issue organizing frames. This trend is especially striking in the global South, because of the different mobilizing opportunities and constraints they face. As in Eastern Europe before 1989, dictatorship and corruption provide opportunities and threats that encourage the formation of broad-based opposition groups instead of the focused campaign coalitions more typically found in pluralistic systems. Both flexible campaigning and multifocused organizations suggest that we are seeing a change in the actors, the connections among them, their forms of claimsmaking, and the prevailing strategies of contentious politics.

But both these trends have potential costs. Just as many American activists shifted from campaigning against the World Bank and the IMF to the antiwar movement in 2003, many more moved back into domestic politics in the election campaign of 2004. No doubt they did so for reasons related to their antiwar convictions – the outgoing president was, after all, the chief war maker. But their move also reflected the complex nature of the new internationalism: it is neither a flatly horizontal system of states, nor a suprastate structure, but a triangular opportunity space that reaches into domestic politics. We still do not know if the transposition of American activists from the international to the domestic sphere after the Iraq war will turn them permanently away from transnational activity or reflect a fusion of domestic and international contention.

The Fusion of Domestic and International Contention

Is internationalization a cumulative process, or are we seeing only outcroppings of internationalism in a sea of states? To put this question more generally, "Is there evidence from the new transnational activism that the traditional divide between domestic and transnational contention is breaking down? As in all big questions for which there is scattered and inconclusive evidence, the answer is still "maybe" and "in part." If such a fusion is occurring, it will be seen through three main channels: a breakdown in the resilience of domestic structures; changes in the repertoires of domestic contention; and a growing connection between internal contention and international conflict.

Resilience and Change in Local Contention

In trying to gain domestic purchase for international issues, grass-roots activists must embed them in domestic cleavages and frame them in ways that matter to their compatriots. In doing so, the connection to "global" movements is stretched, sometimes to the breaking point, by the very "weight" of the local in peoples' consciousness. This is what happened to the September 2001 Washington demonstration, after which many activists tried to frame their antiwar message in domestic terms (Maney, Woehrle, and Coy 2003).

But national security is the area in which state interests are most likely to trump transnational commitments (Keohane and Nye 1971). A better test of the question of whether the traditional divide between domestic and international contention is breaking down is the environment. Even here, however, the evidence is mixed. Focusing on Western Europe, Christopher Rootes (2005: 22) sees a limited transnationalization of environmental protest. Although three of the five environmental groups he studied in Britain (Friends of the Earth, Greenpeace, and the World Wildlife Federation), always transnational in inspiration and aspiration, have, in recent years, become more so, Rootes failed to discern "the development of a substantial *non-elite* audience/constituency for such views" (pp. 39–41).

In contrast, the campaign against climate change shows clear local-global connections. As Harriet Bulkeley and Michele Betsill point out in *Cities and Climate Change* (2003), local governments have a great deal of expertise in the fields of energy management, transportation, and planning that can be turned to fighting climate change. International efforts to enlist localities in the fight against global climate change began in 1991, with the creation of an International Council for Local Environmental Initiatives (ICLEI). Its mission was to build and serve a worldwide movement of local governments to achieve and monitor tangible improvements in global environmental conditions through cumulative local actions. Cities for Climate Portection (CCP) was established as the vehicle to spread this message (ICLEI 1997; Vasi 2004). Bogdan Vasi's (2004) research shows a wide diffusion of environmental activism to cities in Australia, Canada, and the United States during the 1990s.

The anti-GM campaign in Western Europe shows the clearest fusion between domestic and transnational activism. Vera Kettnaker's (2001) research shows that, as local activists were attacking experimental fields and picketing outside supermarkets at the local level, their attention shifted to the EU when the European Parliament was considering labeling requirements for GM products. In the anti-GM campaign, Europeans fused local and transnational activism.

Persistence and Change in the Classical Repertoire

Another way of specifying the question of whether transnational and domestic activism are fusing builds on Charles Tilly's concept of the "repertoire of contention" (1978, 1995b). Many American and Canadian activists
who took part in the anti-WTO protest in Seattle tried to bring that model
home. In her analysis of New York and Toronto activists who went to Seattle,
Lesley Wood sketches six attributes of the model, consisting of "black bloc"
street tactics, radical puppetry, blockade tactics, legal collectives, affinity
groups, and a spokescouncil mode of organization. In the year following
Seattle, local social movement organizations working on immigration, police brutality, housing, and student issues experimented with these tactics
in both cities (2004b: 1). Wood found that only in New York City was the
transfer successful.

What can explain these differences? Domestic structures seemed to do
the lion's share of the work of diffusion. In New York, Wood argues, the
city's larger size permitted a greater number of activist organizations and
fragmented them around a large number of issues. In Toronto, the Ontario
provincial government served as a magnet for public claims making, and
the use of commissions served to co-opt activists. The Torontonian structure of activism resisted innovation, whereas New York's was more open to
innovation.

The adoption of the social forum model of local organization in both
Western Europe and Latin America represents the most remarkable fusion of transnational and domestic repertoires. Of course, "downward scale
shift" also involves a shift in objects and claims of contention, as we saw in
Chapter 7. It is possible that these "new" forms of organization are simply
producing old local wine in new global bottles; but it is also possible that
new political identities and new forms of democratic practice will emerge
from this fusion of the local and the global (della Porta 2005a).

Internal Contention and International War

The strongest evidence for the fusion of domestic and international contention comes from the connections between international and domestic
conflict. It is well known that since the end of World War II, domestic violence has displaced international war as the major source of armed conflict
(Gurr et al. 1993), although the level of civil violence peaked in the early
1990s. More important for the "fusion" hypothesis is the growing interface

214

between domestic and international conflict. Three trends appear to be at the heart of this interface:

- The end of the Cold War removed the major constraint on states interfering in other states' internal affairs.
- The effective end of classical colonialism – from both East and West – left in its wake a large number of weak states.
- These two trends combine to open opportunities for internal minorities to assert themselves and ally with external state and nonstate sponsors.

In Chapter 7, we saw evidence of the peaceful externalization of domestic claims making. But the interface between domestic and international conflict has been extending into violence. It includes secessionist movements that ally with external lobby states or actors against their own governments (Jenne 2001, 2004); it extends to domestic violence that is coordinated with international terrorist organizations, making domestic actors subjects of the international "War on Terror" (Sageman 2004); and it is often met by coalitions of foreign states that intervene as "peacemakers" in a process that has been called, with only some exaggeration, "postmodern imperialism" (Fearon and Laitin 2003).

The collapse of the Soviet empire in East Central Europe and Central Asia produced lethal combinations of all three trends: secessionist movements assisted by external lobbies, internal terrorism linked willy-nilly to the "War on Terror," and multilateral intervention by coalitions of "peacemaking states." "During those years," writes Charles Tilly (2003: 77),

major powers (including the United States and the United Nations) responded to the weakening of central authority in the Warsaw Pact, the Soviet Union, and Yugoslavia by signaling increased support for claims of leaders to represent distinct nations currently under alien control. That signaling encouraged leaders to emphasize ethnic boundaries, compete for recognition as valid interlocutors for oppressed nations, attack their ostensible enemies, suppress their competitors for leadership, and make alliances with others who would supply them with resources to support their mobilization.

Once they had triggered ethnopolitical violence, many of these external "lobbies" drew back from the chaos that their interventions had encouraged. But as Erin Jenne (2004) shows, even weak domestic actors were determined on domestic violence to bring their external sponsors to intervene on their side in domestic disputes. And by that time, "international arms merchants, drug runners, diamond merchants, oil brokers, and others who benefited from weak central political control had moved in" (Tilly 2003: 77). In an internationalized world, one kind of local-global interface produces a chain of consequences.

Unlike classical territory-acquiring imperialism, in the context of the new internationalism interventions are mainly multilateral, humanitarian, and – at least in their intentions – short-term. This produces massive problems of coordination, responsibility, and, especially, problems of exit. As Fearon and Laitin (2003: 2–3) conclude, "the problem of *exit* from postmodern imperialist ventures is nearly intractable" and, we might add, can trigger still more violent fusions between international and domestic contention, as the United States has learned to its dismay in Iraq.

Combining these insights, it would be fair to say that the new transnational contention has its greatest impact where foreign states become involved in domestic conflicts. But we still lack the serious investment in panel studies or in time-series analyses that can tell us whether and how the new transnationalism is fusing with domestic contention. Is internationalization a cumulative process, or in these examples are we seeing only exceptional cases of internationalism in a state-centered world? We are left with the third "big" question: how does the fusion of domestic and transnational activism affect our inherited understanding of the autonomy of national politics from international politics? This question is particularly important in the light of the retreat from internationalism in the United States after September 11, 2001.

After Internationalism?

When I began to collect the materials for this study, optimists were seeing a global civil society growing out of the changes that had emerged following the fall of the Soviet empire. From the increasing density of international nongovernmental organizations; the growing global consciousness among ecological, human rights, indigenous, labor, peace, and women's organizations; and ever-more-dense intergovernmental compacts and negotiations and a treaty signings, many saw the power of states declining and global governance developing apace (Ikenberry 2003: 537; Slaughter 2004).

Not all assessments of these trends were positive. Pessimists warned of the power of these organizations and institutions and worried about the lack of representativeness of the advocacy groups that surrounded them. From the right, there was skepticism about the force for good of nongovernmental organizations and of international intervention; from the left, there was worry about the power of the IMF or the WTO, which had wrested power over domestic economies from national polities and voters. Realists resisted both optimism and pessimism, insisting, as they always had, that powerful states would continue to dominate the international arena and that – with the death of the Soviet Union – the United States would govern the world through the panoply of international institutions it had created in its image.

The world after September 11, 2001, looks very different. As Robert O. Keohane (2002a: 29) would write soon afterward, "The attacks on the United States on 11 September 2001 have incalculable consequences for domestic politics and world affairs." Advocates of global civil society were appalled by the fact that a transnational network – the Al Qaeda organization – was responsible for attacking the heart of Western society and refused to recognize it as part of the new transnationalism. Students of international institutions, who postulate that "multilateral institutions should play significant roles whenever interstate cooperation is extensive in world politics" (p. 35), were proved overly optimistic when 9/11 produced a failure of either the United Nations or the European Union to take effective action. And those who saw the United States exercising "soft power" and using multilateral negotiation had to face the fact that military aggression was emerging as that country's chosen instrument of power.

Do these policy turns and policy failures tell us, as Stanley Hoffmann (2003), among others, warned, that internationalism may be over? Or that it is, at best, no more than a thin cloak that can be whipped off to expose a hard core of naked power when national interests are threatened? Or will there be an inevitable return to internationalism as the costs of unilateralism become more clear, in both Iraq and elsewhere? Theory, as Keohane (2002a: 36) pointed out soon after, "is not tested by the immediate reactions of policymakers, much less by those of the press"; in the months following 9/11, he bravely saw international institutions regaining their authority.

As this book was completed and American-led "coalition" forces and their Iraqi puppets were reeling from insurgency from within and international revulsion from without, the verdict was still out on whether September 11 and the Iraqi adventure that it justified have put the seal on five decades of internationalization. But those who believe in internationalism and shrink from the orgy of national chauvinism that followed September 11 must take a longer view. And this for several reasons.

First, there are general gains to be made from internationalism. G. John Ikenberry (2003: 534) argues that while the circumstances of the first few years of the new century gave the American government both the

217

opportunity and the incentive to act unilaterally, "the circumstances that led the United States to engage in multilateral cooperation in the past are still present." In fact, even in the current situation of world politics, Ikenberry sees incentives for a return to multilateralism (pp. 534–44).

One of these incentives was predicted by Ernst Haas (1958) four decades ago – the need for cooperation spawned by the functional needs of a globalizing economy. Another is the tissue of transgovernmental arrangements and international institutions that already cover the globe, producing concrete interests in collaboration (Slaughter 2004). A third is the presence of norms of collaboration that have grown up around these contacts and interests. For example, the now-hegemonic American legal-institutional political tradition has diffused a rule-of-law orientation that produces international order. These potential sources of multilateralism, Ikenberry (2003: 534, 544) concludes, "still exist and continue to shape and restrain the Bush administration, unilateral inclinations notwithstanding."

As we reflect in 2005 on the lies and half truths that led to the Iraq adventure, on the systematic abuse of prisoners by American agents in Saddam Hussein's torture chambers, and on the doctrine of preemptive strike that lies behind both of these, Ikenberry's speculations may seem optimistic. But as long as we are in the realm of speculation, why not go one step further? If the world of today is as interdependent as Keohane (2002b) has argued, and if, as I have argued, the structure of internationalism is triangular, there may be processes both within and outside America's borders that could tame the unilateralism that followed September 11.

We have seen some of these processes at work in the outpouring of dissent against the Iraq war and in the global rejection of American aggression in public opinion polls around the world. We have also seen them in the refusal of many states – under pressure of their citizens – to fall in line with the Bushite designs for a *pax Americana* across the Middle East. Like this author, Ikenberry (2003: 544) sees a new internationalism that involves "like-minded coalitions of governments and civil society . . ., the inclusion of NGOs in the governance structures of UN agencies, and various forms of multi-stakeholder, public-private, public policy networks."

Will the transnational movement against the Iraq war with which I began this book be remembered as the end of a period of internationalism that reached its apogee in the late 1990s? Or will it be seen as the beginning of a move toward a more sustained integration between international and domestic politics? If this book's findings are sustained, I would offer three speculations.

First, as we have seen throughout, transnational activism will be episodic and contradictory, and it will have its most visible impact on domestic politics.

Second, international institutions, regimes, and treaties will continue to reflect state relations and state power, but transnational activists will increasingly find in them a "coral reef" where they both lobby and protest, encounter others like themselves, identify friendly states, and, from time to time, put together successful global-national coalitions.

Finally, as the story that introduced this chapter illustrates, transnational activism does not resemble a swelling tide of history but is more like a series of waves that lap on an international beach, retreating repeatedly into domestic seas but leaving incremental changes on the shore.

Glossary

ABM	antiballistic missile
ACT UP	AIDS Coalition to Unleash Power
AFL-CIO	American Federation of Labor – Congress of Industrial Organizations
AIDS	Acquired Immune Deficiency Syndrome
ANC	African National Congress
ATTAC	Association for the Taxation of Financial Transactions for the Aid of Citizens (Association pour la taxation des transactions pour l'aide aux citoyens)
AWI	Animal Welfare Institute
BSE	bovine spongiform encephalopathy
CAN	Climate Action Network
CAP	Common Agricultural Policy
CAT	Worker Support Center (Centro de Apoyo al Trabajador)
CCP	Cities for Climate Protection
CCW	Convention on Conventional Weapons
CIA	Central Intelligence Agency
CJM	Coalition for Justice in the Maquiladoras
CORE	Congress of Racial Equality
CUT	United Workers' Central (Central Unica dos Trabalhadores)
CWP	Communist Workers Party
ECJ	European Court of Justice
EEB	European Environmental Bureau
EU	European Union
EZLN	Zapatista Army of National Liberation (Ejército Zapatista de Liberación Nacional)

FLASCO	Latin American Faculty of Social Sciences (Facultad Latinoamericana de Ciencias Sociales)
FOC	Flag of Convenience
G-7	Group of Seven
G-8	Group of Eight
GM	genetic modification
GSP	Generalized System of Preferences
HIV	Human Immunodeficiency Virus
ICBL	International Convention to Ban Landmines
ICLEI	International Council for Local Environmental Initiatives
ICTJ	International Center for Transitional Justice
IGC	Institute for Global Communication
IGO	intergovernmental organization
ILO	International Labor Organization
IMF	International Monetary Fund
ITF	International Transport Workers' Federation
KHIS	Korean House of International Solidarity
MAI	Multilateral Agreement on Investment
MGJ	Mobilization for Global Justice
MOWM	March on Washington Movement
MST	Movement of Landless Farm Workers (Movimento dos trabahadores sem terra)
NAFTA	North American Free Trade Agreement
NAO	National Administrative Office
NATO	North Atlantic Treaty Organization
NCEC	National Convention for Constitutional Reform Executive Committee
NGO	nongovernmental organization
NYPD	New York Police Department
OAS	Organization of American States
OSCE	Organization for Security and Co-operation in Europe
PRI	Institutional Revolutionary Party (Partido Revolucionario Institucional)
PT	Workers' Party (Partido dos trabalhadores)
SDI	Strategic Defense Initiative
TOES	The Other Economic Summit
TRC	Truth and Reconciliation Commission
TSMO	transnational social movement organization

Glossary

UNT	National Union of Workers (Union Nacional de Trabajadores)
USAS	United Students against Sweatshops
WEF	World Economic Forum
WGIP	Working Group on Indigenous Populations
WSF	World Social Forum
WTO	World Trade Organization
YIA	Yearbook of International Associations

Sources

Ackerman, Bruce. 1994. "Rooted Cosmopolitanism." *Ethics*, 104: 516–35.

Ackerman, Peter, and Jack DuVall. 2000. *A Force More Powerful.* New York: St. Martin's Press.

Adamson, Fiona B. 2002. "Mobilizing at the Margins of the System: The Dynamics and Security Impacts of Transnational Mobilization by Non-State Actors." Unpublished paper, Columbia University, Department of Political Science.

Al-Ali, Najde, and Khalid Koser, eds. 2002. *New Approaches to Migration? Transnational Communities and the Transformation of Home.* New York: Routledge.

Alberoni, Francesco. 1984. *Movement and Institution.* New York: Columbia University Press.

Alter, Karen. 1998. "'Who Are the Masters of the Treaty?' European Governments and the European Court of Justice." *International Organization*, 52: 121–47.

Alter, Karen, and Jeannette Vargas. 2000. "Explaining Variation in the Use of European Litigation Strategies: EC Law and UK Gender Equality Policy." *Comparative Political Studies*, 33: 452–82.

Ancelovici, Marcos. 2002. "Organizing against Globalization: The Case of ATTAC in France." *Politics and Society*, 30: 427–63.

Anderson, Benedict. 1991. *Imagined Communities: Reflections on the Origin and Spread of Nationalism.* London: Verso.

1998. *The Spectre of Comparisons: Nationalism, Southeast Asia and the World.* New York: Verso.

Andretta, Massimiliano. 2005. "Il framing del movimento contro la globalizzazione neoliberista." *Rassegna Italiana di Sociologia* 46.

Andrews, Kenneth. 2002. "Movement-Countermovement Dynamics and the Emergence of New Institutions: The Case of 'White Flight' Schools in Mississippi." *Social Forces* 80: 911–36.

2004. *Freedom Is a Constant Struggle.* Chicago: University of Chicago Press.

Anner, Mark. 2001. "The Paradox of Labor Transnationalism: Northern and Southern Trade Unions and the Campaign for Labor Standards in the WTO." Paper presented to the workshop on Transnational Contention, Cornell University.

2003a. "Between Monitoring and Organizing: International NGO and Union Strategies to End Sweatshop Practices." Paper presented to the annual meeting of the American Political Science Association, Philadelphia.

2003b. "Industrial Structure, the State, and Ideology: Shaping Labor Transnationalism in the Brazilian Auto Industry." *Social Science History*, 27: 603–34.

2004. "Between Solidarity and Fragmentation: Labor Responses to Globalization in the Americas." Ph.D. diss., Cornell University, Department of Government.

Appiah, Kwame Anthony. 1996. "Cosmopolitan Patriots." In Joshua Cohen, ed., *For Love of Country*. Boston: Beacon Press.

Aquarone, Alberto. 1959. *Due cosituenti settecentesche: Note sulla convenzione di Filadelfia e sull'Assemblea nazionale francese*. Pisa: Nistri-Lischi.

Arquilla, John, and David Ronfeldt, eds. 2001. *Networks and Netwars: The Future of Terror, Crime and Militancy*. Santa Monica, CA: Rand Corporation.

Arrighi, Giovanni, and Beverly Silver. 1999. *Chaos and Governance in the Modern World System*. Minneapolis: University of Minnesota Press.

Auyero, Javier. 2001. "Global Riots." *International Sociology*, 16: 33–53.

2003. "Relational Riot: Austerity and Corruption Protest in the Neoliberal Era." *Social Movement Studies*, 2: 117–45.

Auyero, Javier, and Timothy Moran. 2004. "The Dynamics of Collective Violence. Dissecting Food Riots in Contemporary Argentina." Unpublished manuscript.

Avruch, Kevin, and Beatriz Vejerano. 2002. "Truth and Reconciliation Commissions: A Review Essay and Annotated Bibliography." *Online Journal of Peace and Conflict Resolution*, Spring. http://www.trinstitute.org/ojpck/4_2 recon.htm.

Ayres, Jeffrey M. 2002. "Transnational Political Processes and Contention against the Global Economy." In Jackie Smith and Hank Johnston, eds., *Globalization and Resistance: Transnational Dimensions of Social Movements*. Lanham, MD: Rowman and Littlefield.

Bailyn, Bernard. 1967. *The Ideological Origins of the American Revolution*. Cambridge, MA: Harvard University Press.

Ball, Patrick. 2000. "State Terror, Constitutional Traditions, and National Human Rights Movements: A Cross-National Quantitative Comparison." In John A. Guidry, Michael D. Kennedy, and Mayer N. Zald, eds., *Globalizations and Social Movements: Culture, Power, and the Transnational Public Sphere*. Ann Arbor: University of Michigan Press.

Bandy, Joe, and Jackie Smith, eds. 2004. *Coalitions across Borders: Transnational Protest and the Neoliberal Order*. Lanham, MD: Rowman and Littlefield.

Bédoyan, Isabelle, Peter Van Aelst, and Stefaan Walgrave 2004. "Limitations and Possibilities of Transnational Mobilization: The Case of the EU Summit Protesters in Brussels, 2001." *Mobilization*, 9: 39–54.

Bennett, Andrew. 2003. "Beyond Hempel and Back to Hume: Causal Mechanisms and Causal Explanation." Paper presented to the annual meeting of the American Political Science Association, Philadelphia.

Sources

Bennett, W. Lance. 2003. "Communicating Global Activism." *Information, Communication & Society*, 6: 143–68.

2005. "Social Movements beyond Borders: Understanding Two Eras of Transnational Activists." In Donatella della Porta and Sidney Tarrow, eds., *Transnational Protest and Global Activism*. Lanham, MD: Rowman and Littlefield.

Bennett, W. Lance, Victor Pickard, Taso Lagos, Carl L. Schroeder, Courtney-Evans Caswell, and David Iozzi. 2004. "Managing the Public Sphere: Journalistic Construction of the Great Globalization Debate." *Journal of Communication*, 54: 437–55.

Berman, Eli, and David D. Laitin. 2005. "Hard Targets: Theory and Evidence on Suicide Attacks." http://dss.ucsd.edu/~elib/RatMartyrs.pdf.

Bermanzohn, Sally. 2003. *Through Survivors' Eyes: From the Sixties to the Greensboro Massacre*. Nashville: Vanderbilt University Press.

2004. "A Survivor's Story, a Scholar's Words." *Chronicle of Higher Education*, 50: 5B.

Bernstein, Thomas P., and Xiaobo Lü. 2003. *Taxation without Representation in Contemporary Rural China*. Cambridge: Cambridge University Press.

Béroud, Sophie, René Mouriaux, and Michel Vakaloulis. 1998. *Le mouvement social en France: Essai de sociologie politique*. Paris: SNEDIT.

Bloemraad, Irene. 2005. "The Limits of de Tocqueville: How Government Facilitates Organisational Capacity in Newcomer Communities." *Journal of Ethnic and Migration Studies*.

Bloom, Mia. 2004. *Devising a Theory of Suicide Terror*. ISERP Workshop on Contentious Politics. New York: Columbia University Press.

Bob, Clifford. 2002. "Merchants of Morality." *Foreign Policy*: 36–45.

2005. *The Marketing of Rebellion: Insurgents, Media and Transnational Support*. Cambridge: Cambridge University Press.

Boli, John, and George Thomas, eds. 1999. *Constructing World Culture: International Nongovernmental Organizations since 1875*. Stanford: Stanford University Press.

Bondurant, Joan. 1958. *Conquest of Violence: The Gandhian Philosophy of Conflict*. Princeton: Princeton University Press.

Boraine, Alex. 2001. *A Country Unmasked*. Oxford: Oxford University Press.

Brysk, Alison. 1994. *The Politics of Human Rights in Argentina: Protest, Change, and Democratization*. Stanford: Stanford University Press.

Brzezinski, Zbigniew. 1997. *The Grand Chessboard: American Primacy and Its Geostrategic Imperatives*. New York: Basic Books.

Bulkeley, Harriet, and Michele Betsill. 2003. *Cities and Climate Change: Urban Sustainability and Social Policy*. London: Routledge.

Bush, Evelyn L. 2004. "Transnational Religion and Secular Institutions: Structure, Framing and Influence in Human Rights." Ph.D. diss., Cornell University, Department of Sociology.

Bush, Evelyn L., and Pete Simi. 2001. "European Farmers and Their Protests." In Doug Imig and Sidney Tarrow, eds., *Contentious Europeans: Protest and Politics in an Emerging Polity*. Lanham, MD: Rowman and Littlefield.

Buss, Doris, and Didi Herman. 2003. *Globalizing Family Values: The Christian Right in International Politics*. Minneapolis: University of Minnesota Press.

Calhoun, Craig. 2002. "The Class Consciousness of Frequent Travelers: Towards a Critique of Actually Existing Cosmopolitanism." In Steven Vertovec and Robin Cohen, eds., *Conceiving Cosmopolitanism: Theory, Context, and Practice*. Oxford: Oxford University Press.

Cameron, Maxwell A., Robert J. Lawson, and Brian W. Tomlin, eds. 1998. *To Walk without Fear: The Global Movement to Ban Landmines*. Oxford: Oxford University Press.

Caporaso, James A. 2001. "Citizenship and Equality: A Long and Winding Road." Paper presented to the annual meeting of the International Studies Association, Chicago.

Caporaso, James A., and Joseph Jupille. 2001. "The Europeanization of Gender Equality Policy and Domestic Structural Change." In Maria Green Cowles, James A. Caporaso, and Thomas Risse, eds., *Transforming Europe: Europeanization and Domestic Change*. Ithaca: Cornell University Press.

2003. "The Second Image Overruled: European Law, Domestic Institutions, and Westphalian Sovereignty." Unpublished paper, University of Washington.

Caraway, Teri L. 2001. "Solidarity across Borders: Transnational Labor Activism and Empowering Workers in Indonesia." Paper presented to the annual meeting of the American Political Science Association, San Francisco.

Carroll, William K., and Meindert Fennema. 2002. "Is There a Transnational Business Community?" *International Sociology*, 17: 393–419.

Castells, Manuel. 1996. *The Rise of the Network Society*. Oxford: Blackwell.

Chabot, Sean. 2002. "Transnational Diffusion and the African-American Reinvention of the Gandhian Repertoire." In Jackie Smith and Hank Johnston, eds., *Globalization and Resistance: Transnational Dimensions of Social Movements*. Lanham, MD: Rowman and Littlefield.

2003. "Crossing the Great Divide: The Gandhian Repertoire's Transnational Diffusion to the American Civil Rights Movement." Ph.D. diss., University of Amsterdam.

Checkel, Jeffrey. 2001. "Rational Choice, Constructivism and the Europeanization of Citizenship." In James A. Caporaso, Maria Green Cowles, and Thomas Risse, eds., *Transforming Europe: Europeanization and Domestic Change*. Ithaca: Cornell University Press.

Cichowski, Rachel A. 2001. "Judicial Rulemaking and the Institutionalization of the European Union Sex Policy." In Alec Stone Sweet, Neil Fligstein, and Wayne Sandholtz, eds., *The Institutionalization of Europe*. Oxford: Oxford University Press.

Clark, John D., ed. 2003a. *Globalizing Civic Engagement: Civil Society and Transnational Action*. London: Earthscan.

2003b. *Worlds Apart: Civil Society and the Battle for Ethical Globalization*. London: Earthscan.

Cockburn, Alexander, and Jeffrey St. Clair. 2000. *Five Days That Shook the World: Seattle and Beyond*. London: Verso.

Cohen, David. 2003. "Intended to Fail: The Trials before the Ad Hoc Human Rights Court in Jakarta." International Center for Transnational Justice, New York.

Cohen, Michael. 2003. "A Season of Hope in Argentina." *Challenge*, 46: 37–58.

Cohen, Michael, and Margarita Gutman, eds. 2003. *Argentina in Collapse? The Americas Debate*. New York: New School.

Cohen, Mitchell. 1992. "Rooted Cosmopolitanism." *Dissent*: 478–83.

Coleman, William D., and Sarah V. Wayland. 2005. "Global Civil Society and Nonterritorial Governance. Some Empirical Reflections." *Global Governance* II.

Conant, Lisa J. 2002. *Justice Contained: Law and Politics in the European Union*. Ithaca: Cornell University Press.

Cook, Maria Lorena. 1996. *Organizing Dissent: Unions, the State, and the Democratic Teachers' Movement in Mexico*. University Park: Pennsylvania State University Press.

Cox, Robert, and Harold K. Jacobson. 1973. *The Anatomy of Influence: Decision Making in International Organizations*. New Haven: Yale University Press.

Croci, Osvaldo. 1995. "Le Canada et l'Europe: De l'indifférence à la friction." *L'Europe en formation*, 298: 41–51.

Cullen, Pauline. 2004. "Obstacles to Transnational Cooperation in the European Social Policy Platform." In Joe Bandy and Jackie Smith, eds., *Coalitions across Borders: Transnational Protest and the Neoliberal Order*. Lanham, MD: Rowman and Littlefield.

Dalton, Russell. 1994. *The Green Rainbow: Environmental Groups in Western Europe*. New Haven: Yale University Press.

Dalton, Russell, and Robert Rohrschneider. 2002. "Political Action and the Political Context: A Multi-Level Model of Environmental Activism." In Dieter Fuchs, Edeltraud Roller, and Bernhard Weßels, eds., *Citizen and Democracy in East and West: Studies in Political Culture and Political Process*. Opladen: Westdeutscher Verlag.

Danitz, Tiffany, and Warren P. Strobel. 2001. "Networking Dissent: Cyber Activists Use the Internet to Promote Democracy in Burma." In John Arquilla and David Ronfeldt, eds., *The Advent of Netwar Revisited*. Santa Monica, CA: Rand Corporation.

Davis, Madeleine, ed. 2003. *The Pinochet Case: Origins, Progress and Implications*. London: Institute for Latin American Studies.

della Porta, Donatella. 2005a. "Making the Polis: Social Forums and Democracy in the Global Justice Movement." *Mobilization* 10: 73–88.

2005b. "Multiple Belongings, Flexible Identities, and the Construction of 'Another Politics': Between the European Social Forum and Local Social Fora." In Donatella della Porta and Sidney Tarrow, eds., *Transnational Protest and Global Activism*. Lanham, MD: Rowman and Littlefield.

della Porta, Donatella, Massimiliano Andretta, Lorenzo Mosca, and Herbert Reiter. 2006. *Globalization from Below: Transnational Activists and Protest Networks*. Minneapolis: University of Minnesota Press.

della Porta, Donatella, and Mario Diani. 1999. *Social Movements*. Oxford: Blackwell.

2004. "'Contro la guerra senza se ne ma': The Protests against the Iraki War." In Vincent della Sala and Sergio Fabbrini, eds., *Italian Politics Yearbook, 2003*. Providence, RI: Berghahn Books.

della Porta, Donatella, Hanspeter Kriesi, and Dieter Rucht, eds. 1999. *Social Movements in a Globalizing World*. Houndsmills: Macmillan Press.

della Porta, Donatella, and Lorernzo Mosca, eds. 2003. *Globalizzazione e movimenti sociali*. Rome: Manifestolibri.

della Porta, Donatella, and Herbert Reiter. 1998. "The Policing of Protest in Western Democracies." In Donatella della Porta and Herbert Reiter, eds., *Policing Protests: The Control of Mass Demonstrations in Western Democracies*. Minneapolis: University of Minnesota Press.

2004. "The Policing of Global Protest: The G8 at Genoa and Its Aftermath." Paper presented at the International Conference on Protest, Policing, and Globalization, Gothenburg.

della Porta, Donatella, and Sidney Tarrow, eds. 2005. *Transnational Protest and Global Activism*. Lanham, MD: Rowman and Littlefield.

Deutsch, Karl W., et al. 1957. *Political Community and the North Atlantic Area: International Organization in the Light of Historical Experience*. Princeton: Princeton University Press.

Dietz, Kelly. 2000. "Globalized Resistance: An Event History Analysis of Indigenous Activism." M.A. thesis, Cornell University, Department of Sociology.

Dollinger, Philippe. 1970. *The German Hansa*. Stanford: Stanford University Press.

Drescher, Seymour. 1987. *Capitalism and Antislavery: British Mobilization in Comparative Perspective*. New York: Oxford University Press.

Edelman, Marc. 1999. *Peasants against Globalization: Rural Social Movements in Costa Rica*. Stanford: Stanford University Press.

Edwards, Michael, and John Gaventa, eds. 2001. *Global Citizen Action*. Boulder: Lynne Rienner Publishers.

Eickelman, Dail F. 1997. "Trans-state Islam and Security." In Susanne Hoeber Rudolph and James Piscatori, eds., *Transnational Religion and Fading States*. Boulder: Westview Press.

Evangelista, Matthew. 1995. "The Paradox of State Strength: Transnational Relations, Domestic Structures, and Security Policy in Russia and the Soviet Union." *International Organization*, 49: 1–38.

1999. *Unarmed Forces: The Transnational Movement to End the Cold War*. Ithaca: Cornell University Press.

Evans, Peter. 2005. "Counter-Hegemonic Globalization: Transnational Social Movements in the Contemporary Global Political Economy." In Thomas Janoski, Alexander Hicks, and Mildred Schwartz, eds., *Handbook of Political Sociology*, ch. 32. Cambridge: Cambridge University Press.

Fearon, James D., and David D. Laitin. 2003. "Postmodern Imperialism." Stanford: Stanford University.

Ferree, Myra Marx, William A. Gamson, Jürgen Gerhards, and Dieter Rucht. 2002. *Shaping Abortion Discourse: Democracy and the Public Sphere in Germany and the United States*. Cambridge: Cambridge University Press.

Finnemore, Martha. 1999. "Rules of War and Wars of Rules: The International Red Cross and the Restraint of State Violence." In John Boli and George Thomas, eds., *Constructing World Culture: International Nongovernmental Organizations since 1875*. Stanford: Stanford University Press.

Finnemore, Martha, and Kathryn Sikkink. 1998. "International Norm Dynamics and Political Change." *International Organization*, 52: 887–917.

Fisher, Dana R. 2003. "Beyond Kyoto: The Formation of a Japanese Climate Change Regime." In Paul G. Harris, ed., *Global Warming and East Asia: The Domestic International Politics of Climate Change*. New York: Routledge.

2004. "Transnational Coalitions and Social Movement Spillover: From Globalization to Anti-war." Paper presented to the "One Year Later" Conference, Bard College.

Florini, Ann, M., ed. 2000. *The Third Force: The Rise of Transnational Civil Society*. Washington, DC: Carnegie Endowment.

2003. *The Coming Democracy: New Rules for Running a New World*. Washington, DC: Island Press.

Foner, Nancy. 2001. "Transnationalization Then and Now: New York Immigrants Today and at the Turn of the Twentieth Century." In Hector R. Cordero-Guzmán, Robert C. Smith, and Ramón Grosfoguel, eds., *Migration, Transnationalization and Race in a Changing New York*. Philadelphia: Temple University Press.

Fox, Jonathan. 2002. "Lessons from Mexico-US Civil Society Coalitions." In David Brooks and Jonathan Fox, eds., *Cross-Border Dialogues*. La Jolla: Center for US-Mexican Studies.

Fox, Jonathan, and L. David Brown. 1998. *The Struggle for Accountability: The World Bank, NGOs, and Grassroots Movements*. Cambridge, MA: MIT Press.

Fox, Jonathan, and Gaspar Rivera-Salgado, eds. 2004. *Indigenous Mexican Migrants in the United States*. La Jolla: Center for US-Mexican Studies and Center for Comparative Immigration Studies.

Fox, Richard G. 1997. "Passage from India." In Richard G. Fox and Orin Starn, eds., *Between Resistance and Revolution: Cultural Politics and Social Protest*. New Brunswick: Rutgers University Press.

Gamson, William A. 1975. *The Strategy of Social Protest*. Homewood, IL: Dorsey Press.

1992. "The Social Psychology of Collective Action." In Aldon Morris and Carol McClurg Mueller, eds., *Frontiers in Social Movement Theory*. New Haven: Yale University Press.

Gaspard, Françoise, and Farhad Khosrokhavar. 1995. *Le foulard et la République*. Paris: La Découverte.

Gentile, Antonina. 2002. *Docker Resistance in the 1990s: Transnational and Domestic Alliance Activism under Conditions of Globalization*. Paper presented to the annual meeting of the American Political Science Association, Boston.

2003. "Workers with Citizens; Workers as Citizens: Dockers Contending Neoliberal Globalisation and Post-Sept. 11 Statism." Paper presented to the annual meeting of the American Political Science Association, Philadelphia.

Gerhards, Jürgen, and Dieter Rucht. 1992. "Mesomobilization: Organizing and Framing in Two Protest Campaigns in West Germany." *American Journal of Sociology*, 98: 555–95.

Gibson, James. 2004. *Overcoming Apartheid: Can Truth Reconcile a Divided Nation?* New York: Russell Sage Foundation.

Gillham, Patrick, and Bob Edwards. 2003. "Global Justice Protesters Respond to the September 11 Terrorist Attacks: The Impact of an Intentional Disaster on Demonstrations in Washington, D.C." In Jack Monday, ed., *Impacts and Human Responses to the September 11th Disasters: What Research Tells Us*. Natural Hazards Research and Information Center. Boulder: University of Colorado.

Goldstone, Jack, and Charles Tilly. 2001. "Threat (and Opportunity): Popular Action and State Response in the Dynamics of Contentious Action." In Ronald R. Aminzade et al., eds., *Silence and Voice in the Study of Contentious Politics*. Cambridge: Cambridge University Press.

Graeber, David. 2002. "The New Anarchists." *New Left Review*, 13: 61–73.

Greensboro Justice Fund. 2004. "Greensboro Massacre Selection Panel Begins Work to Name Truth Commissioners." Greensboro, NC.

Grenier, Paola. 2004. "The New Pioneers: The People behind Global Civil Society." In Helmut Anheier, Marlies Glasius, and Mary Kaldor, eds., *Global Civil Society*. Thousand Oaks, CA: Sage Publications.

Guarnizo, Luis Eduardo, Alejandro Portes, and William Haller. 2003. "From Assimilation to Transnationalism: Determinants of Transnational Political Action among Contemporary Migrants." *American Journal of Sociology*, 108: 1211–48.

Guidry, John A., Michael D. Kennedy, and Mayer N. Zald, eds. 2000. *Globalizations and Social Movements: Culture, Power and the Transnational Social Movement*. Ann Arbor: University of Michigan Press.

Guiraudon, Virginie. 2001. "Weak Weapons of the Weak: Transnational Mobilization around Migration." In Doug Imig and Sidney Tarrow, eds., *Contentious Europeans: Protest and Politics in an Emerging Polity*. Lanham, MD: Rowman and Littlefield.

Gupta, Devashree. 2003. "Coalitions in Theory and Practice: A Critical Review of Existing Research." Unpublished paper, Cornell University, Department of Government.

Gurr, Ted Robert, with contributions by Barbara Harff, Monty G. Marshall, and James R. Scarritt. 1993. *Minorities at Risk*. Washington, DC: U.S. Institute for Peace.

Haas, Ernst. 1958. *The Uniting of Europe: Political, Social, and Economic Forces, 1950–1957*. Stanford: Stanford University Press.

Haas, Peter. 1992. "Introduction: Epistemic Communities and International Policy Coordination." *International Organization*, 46: 1–35.

Habermas, Jürgen. 1992. "Citizenship and National Identity: Some Reflections on the Future of Europe." *Praxis International*, 12: 1–19.

Hall, Stuart. 2002. "Political Belonging in a World of Multiple Identities." In Steven Vertovec and Robin Cohen, eds., *Conceiving Cosmopolitanism: Theory, Context, and Practice*. Oxford: Oxford University Press.

Hannerz, Ulf. 1990. "Cosmopolitans and Locals in World Culture." *Theory, Culture and Society*, 7: 237–51.

1996. *Transnational Connections: Culture, People, Places*. London: Routledge.

Hathaway, Will, and David S. Meyer. 1997. "Competition and Cooperation in Movement Coalitions: Lobbying for Peace in the 1980s." In Thomas R. Rochon and David S. Meyer, eds., *Coalitions and Political Movements: The Lessons of the Nuclear Freeze*. Boulder: Lynne Rienner Publishers.

Hawkins, Darren. 2002. "Human Rights Norms and Networks in Authoritarian Chile." In Sanjeev Khagram, James V. Riker, and Kathryn Sikkink, eds., *Restructuring World Politics: Transnational Social Movements, Networks, and Norms*. Minneapolis: University of Minnesota Press.

Hayner, Priscilla B. 1994. "Fifteen Truth Commissions – 1974 to 1994: A Comparative Study." *Human Rights Quarterly*, 16: 597–655.

2002. *Unspeakable Truths: Facing the Challenge of Truth Commissions*. New York: Routledge.

Held, David. 1995. *Democracy and the Global Order: From the Modern State to Cosmopolitan Governance*. Cambridge: Polity Press.

Helfferisch, Barbara, and Felix Kolb. 2001. "Multilevel Action Coordination in European Contentious Politics: The European Women's Lobby." In Doug Imig and Sidney Tarrow, eds., *Contentious Europeans: Protest and Politics in an Emerging Polity*. Lanham, MD: Rowman and Littlefield.

Hellman, Judith. 1999. "Real and Virtual Chiapas: Magic Realism and the Left." In Leo Panitch and Colin Leys, eds., *Socialist Register, 2000: Necessary and Unnecessary Utopias*. London: Merlin Press.

Hermanson, Jeff. 2004. "Global Corporations, Global Campaigns: The Struggle for Justice at Kukdong International in Mexico." Unpublished paper, American Center for International Labor Solidarity, Washington, DC.

Herring, Ronald J. 2005. "Miracle Seeds, Suicide Seeds and the Poor: NGOs, GMOs, Farmers and the State." In Mary F. Katzenstein and Raka Ray, eds., *From State to Market: Poverty and Changing Social Movement Strategies in India*. Lanham, MD: Rowman and Littlefield.

Higgins, Nicholas. 2000. "Zapatista Uprising and the Poetics of Cultural Resistance." *Alternatives: Social Transformation and Humane Governance*, 25: 359–74.

Hoffmann, Stanley. 1966. "Obstinate or Obsolete? The Fate of the Nation-State and the Case of Western Europe." *Daedalus*, 95: 862–915.

2003. "The High and the Mighty: Bush's National-Security Strategy and the New American Hubris." *American Prospect*, January 13: 28–31.

Hollinger, David. 2002. "Not Universalists, Not Pluralists: The New Cosmopolitans Find Their Own Way." In Steven Vertovec and Robin Cohen, eds., *Conceiving Cosmopolitanism: Theory, Context, and Practice*. Oxford: Oxford University Press.

Hooghe, Liesbet, and Gary Marks. 2002. *Multi-Level Governance in European Politics*. Lanham, MD: Rowman and Littlefield.

Horton, Aimee Isgrig. 1989. *The Highlander Folk School: A History of Its Major Programs, 1932–1961*. Brooklyn: Carlson Publishing.

Hoskyns, Catherine. 1996. *Integrating Gender: Women, Law and Politics in the European Union*. London: Verso.

Houtart, François, and François Polet, eds. 2001. *The Other Davos: The Globalization of Resistance to the World Economic System*. London: ZED Books.

Hubert, Don. 2000. *The Landmine Ban: A Case Study in Humanitarian Advocacy*. Providence, RI: Thomas J. Watson Jr. Institute for International Studies.

ICLEI. 1997. *Local Government Implementation of Climate Protection. Interim Report*. United Nations Conference of Parties of the Supreme Body of the Framework Convention on Climate Change, Kyoto.

ICTJ. 2004. "Truth Commissions and NGOs: The Essential Relationship." International Center for Transnational Justice, New York.

Ikenberry, G. John. 2003. "Is American Multilateralism in Decline." *Perspectives on Politics*, 1: 533–50.

Imig, Doug, and Sidney Tarrow, eds. 2001. *Contentious Europeans: Protest and Politics in an Emerging Polity*. Lanham, MD: Rowman and Littlefield.

    2001. "Mapping the Europeanization of Contention: Evidence from a Quantitative Data Analysis." In Doug Imig and Sidney Tarrow, eds., *Contentious Europeans: Protest and Politics in an Emerging Polity*. Lanham, MD: Rowman and Littlefield.

Imig, Doug, and Maria Trif. 2003. "Developing a European Sphere of Social Movements: A Transatlantic Perspective." Paper presented to the workshop on Transnational Convergence or Divergence, Paris.

Ingebritsen, Christine. 2005. *Scandinavia in World Politics*. Lanham, MD: Rowman and Little Field.

Jackson, Maurice, Eleanora Peterson, James Bull, Sverre Monsen, and Patricia Richmond. 1960. "The Failure of an Incipient Social Movement." *Pacific Sociological Review*, 3: 35–40.

Jenne, Erin. 2001. "Secessionism as a Bargaining Posture: A Data Analysis of Secessionist Minorities in the Postwar Period." Paper presented to the annual meeting of the American Political Science Association, Chicago.

    2004. "Ethnic Bargaining across Borders: A Comparison of Minority Demands in Kosovo and Vojvodina." Paper presented to the workshop on Nationalism, Secession and Inter-Ethnic Cooperation and Conflict, Cornell University.

Joll, James. 1964. *The Anarchists*. Boston: Little Brown.

Jung, Jai Kwan. 2005. "Globalization and Global Identities: An Over-Time and Cross-National Comparison from the World Values Survey in 1981–2001." Paper presented to the Midwest Political Science Association, Chicago.

Juska, Arunas, and Bob Edwards. 2004. "Resisting the Trojan Pig: The United States–Poland Coalition against Corporate Pork Production." In Joe Bandy and Jackie Smith, eds., *Coalitions across Borders: Transnational Protest and the Neoliberal Order*. Lanham, MD: Rowman and Littlefield.

Katzenstein, Peter J. 1976. "International Relations and Domestic Structures: Foreign Economic Policies of Advanced Industrial States." *International Organization*, 30: 1–45.

1984. *Corporatism and Change: Austria, Switzerland and the Politics of Industry*. Ithaca: Cornell University Press.

1985. *Small States in World Markets: Industrial Policy in Europe*. Ithaca: Cornell University Press.

ed. 1996. *The Culture of National Security: Identity and Norms in World Politics*. New York: Columbia University Press.

2005. *A World of Regions: Asia and Europe in the American Imperium*. Ithaca: Cornell University Press.

Katzenstein, Peter J., Robert Keohane, and Stephen Krasner. 1999. "International Organization and the Study of World Politics." In Peter J. Katzenstein, Robert Keohane, and Stephen Krasner, eds., *Exploration and Contestation in the Study of World Politics*. Cambridge, MA: MIT Press.

Kay, Tamara. 2005. "Labor Transnationalism and Global Governance: The Impact of NAFTA on Transnational Labor Relations in North America." *American Journal of Sociology*.

Keane, John. 2003. *Global Civil Society?* Cambridge: Cambridge University Press.

Kearney, Michael. 1995. "The Local and the Global: The Anthropology of Globalization and Transnationalism." *Annual Review of Anthropology*, 24: 547–65.

Keck, Margaret. 1995. "Social Equity and Environmental Politics in Brazil." *Comparative Politics*, 27: 409–24.

Keck, Margaret, and Kathryn Sikkink. 1998. *Activists beyond Borders: Advocacy Networks in International Politics*. Ithaca: Cornell University Press.

Keohane, Robert O. 1984. *After Hegemony: Cooperation and Discord in the World Political Economy*. Princeton: Princeton University Press.

2002a. "The Globalization of Informal Violence, Theories of World Politics, and the 'Liberalism of Fear.'" *Dialog-IO*, Spring: 29–43.

2002b. *Power and Governance in a Partially Globalized World*. New York: Routledge.

Keohane, Robert O., and Helen V. Milner, eds. 1996. *Internationalization and Domestic Politics*. Cambridge: Cambridge University Press.

Keohane, Robert O., and Joseph S. Nye, eds. 1971. *Transnational Relations and World Politics*. Cambridge, MA: Harvard University Press.

2001[1979]. *Power and Interdependence: World Politics in Transition*. Rev. ed. New York: Addison-Wesley.

Kepel, Gilles. 2002. *Jihad: The Trail of Political Islam*. Cambridge, MA: Harvard University Press.

Kettnaker, Vera. 2001. "The European Conflict over Genetically-Engineered Crops, 1995–1997." In Doug Imig and Sidney Tarrow, eds., *Contentious Europeans: Protest and Politics in an Emerging Polity*. Lanham, MD: Rowman and Littlefield.

Khagram, Sanjeev. 2002. "Restructuring the Global Politics of Development: The Case of India's Narmada Valley Dam." In Sanjeev Khagram, James V. Riker, and Kathryn Sikkink, eds., *Restructuring World Politics: Transnational Social Movements, Networks, and Norms*. Minneapolis: University of Minnesota Press.

Khagram, Sanjeev, James V. Riker, and Kathryn Sikkink, eds. 2002. *Restructuring World Politics: Transnational Social Movements, Networks, and Norms*. Minneapolis: University of Minnesota Press.

Kim, Young S. 1999. "Constructing a Global Identity: The Role of Esperanto." In John Boli and George Thomas, eds., *Constructing World Culture: International Nongovernmental Organizations since 1875*. Stanford: Stanford University Press.

King, Martin Luther, Jr. 1958. *Stride toward Freedom: The Montgomery Story*. New York: Harper.

Klandermans, Bert. 1992. "The Social Construction of Protest and Multi-Organizational Fields." In Aldon Morris and Carol Mueller, eds., *Frontiers in Social Movement Theory*. New Haven: Yale University Press.

Klandermans, Bert, Marga de Weerd, José Manuel Sabucedo, and Mario Rodriguez. 2001. "Framing Contention: Dutch and Spanish Farmers Confront the EU." In Doug Imig and Sidney Tarrow, eds., *Contentious Europeans: Protest and Politics in an Emerging Polity*. Lanham, MD: Rowman and Littlefield.

Klein, Naomi. 2004. "Reclaiming the Commons." In Tom Mertes, ed., *A Movement of Movements: Is Another World Really Possible?* London: Verso.

Kolb, Felix. 2005. "The Impact of Transnational Protest on Social Movement Organizations: Mass Media and the Making of ATTAC Germany." In Donatella della Porta and Sidney Tarrow, eds., *Transnational Protest and Global Activism*. Lanham, MD: Rowman and Littlefield.

Korzeniewicz, Roberto P., and William S. Smith. 2001. *Protest and Collaboration: Transnational Civil Society Networks and the Politics of Summitry and Free Trade in the Americas*. Buenos Aires: Programa de Estudios sobre Instituciones Económicas Internationales (PIEI) de FLASCO.

Kramer, Lloyd S. 1988. *Threshold of a New World: Intellectuals and the Exile Experience in Paris, 1830–1848*. Ithaca: Cornell University Press.

Krauss, Ellis, and T. J. Pempel, eds. 2004. *Beyond Bilateralism: U.S.-Japan Relations in the New Asia-Pacific*. Stanford: Stanford University Press.

Kriesi, Hanspeter, Ruud Koopmans, Jan Willem Duyvendak, and Marco Giugni. 1995. *New Social Movements in Western Europe: A Comparative Analysis*. Minneapolis: University of Minnesota Press.

Krueger, Alan, and Jill Maleckova. 2003. "Education, Poverty, and Terrorism: Is There a Causal Connection?" *Journal of Economic Perspectives*, 17: 119–44.

Kyle, David. 1999. "The Otavalo Trade Diaspora: Social Capital and Transnational Entrepreneurship." *Ethnic and Racial Studies*, 22: 422–46.

Lawson, Robert J., Mark Gwozdecky, Jill Sinclair, and Ralph Lysyshyn. 1998. "The Ottawa Process and the International Movement to Ban Landmines." In Maxwell A. Cameron, Robert J. Lawson, and Brian W. Tomlin, eds., *To Walk without Fear: The Global Movement to Ban Landmines*. Oxford: Oxford University Press.

Lee, Chang Kil, and David Strang. 2003. "The International Diffusion of Public Sector Downsizing." Unpublished paper, Cornell University, Department of Sociology.

Lefébure, Pierre, and Eric Lagneau. 2001. "Media Construction in the Dynamics of Europrotest." In Doug Imig and Sidney Tarrow, eds., *Contentious Europeans: Protest and Politics in an Emergng Polity*. Lanham, MD: Rowman and Littlefield.

Levi, Margaret, and Gillian Murphy. 2004. "Coalitions of Contention: The Case of the WTO Protests in Seattle." Unpublished paper, University of Washington, Department of Political Science.

Lichbach, Mark Irving. 2003. "Global Order and Local Resistance: Structure, Culture, and Rationality in the Battle of Seattle." Unpublished paper, University of Maryland, Political Science Department.

Lichbach, Mark Irving, and Paul D. Almeida. 2001. "Global Order and Local Resistance: The Neoliberal Institutional Trilemma and the Battle of Seattle." Unpublished paper, University of California, Riverside, Political Science Department.

Lillie, Nathan. 2003. "A Global Union for Global Workers: The International Transport Workers' Federation and the Representation of Seafarers on Flag of Convenience Shipping." Ph.D. diss., Cornell University, New York State School of Industrial and Labor Relations.

Lindenberg, Marc, and Coralie Bryant. 2001. *Going Global: Transforming Relief and Development NGOs*. Bloomfield, CT: Kumarian Press.

Loveman, Mara. 1998. "High-Risk Collective Action: Defending Human Rights in Chile, Uruguay, and Argentina." *American Journal of Sociology*, 104: 477–525.

Lutz, Ellen, and Kathryn Sikkink. 2001a. "International Human Rights Law and Practice in Latin America." *International Organization*, 54: 249–75.

2001b. "The Justice Crusade: The Evolution and Impact of Foreign Human Rights Trials in Latin America." *Chicago Journal of International Law*, 2: 1–34.

Mack Smith, Dennis. 1954. *Cavour and Garibaldi, 1860: A Study in Political Conflict*. Cambridge: Cambridge University Press.

Maney, Gregory, Lynne Woehrle, and Patrick Coy. 2003. "Challenging and Harnessing Hegemony: The U.S. Peace Movement after 9/11." Unpublished paper, Hofstra University, Sociology Department.

March, James G., and Jonah Olson. 1999. "The Institutional Dynamics of International Political Orders." In Peter J. Katzenstein, Robert Keohane, and Stephen Krasner, eds., *Exploration and Contestation in the Study of World Politics*. Cambridge, MA: MIT Press.

Marcon, Giulio, and Mario Pianta. 2004. "Porto Alegre-Europa: I percorsi dei movimenti globali." Unpublished paper, University of Urbino.

Marks, Gary, and Liesbet Hooghe. 2003. "National Identity and European Integration: A Multi-Level Analysis of Public Opinion." Unpublished paper, Wissenschaftszentrum Berlin für Sozialforschung.

Marks, Gary, and Doug McAdam. 1996. "Social Movements and the Changing Structure of Political Opportunity in the European Union." In Gary Marks and et al., eds., *Governance in the European Union*. Thousand Oaks, CA: Sage Publications.

1999. "On the Relationship of Political Opportunities to the Form of Collective Action: The Case of the European Union." In Donatella della Porta, Hanspeter Kriesi, and Dieter Rucht, eds., *Social Movements in a Globalizing World*. New York: St. Martin's Press.

Marks, Gary, and Marco Steenbergen, eds. 2004. *European Integration and Political Conflict*. Lanham, MD: Rowman and Littlefield.

Martin, Lisa L., and Beth Simmons. 1999. "Theories and Empirical Studies of International Institutions." In Peter J. Katzenstein, Robert Keohane, and Steven Krasner, eds., *Exploration and Contestation in the Study of World Politics*. Cambridge, MA: MIT Press.

Marx, Karl. 1967. "The Critique of Hegel's Philosophy of Law." In Loyd D. Easton and Kurt H. Guddat, eds., *Writings of the Young Marx on Philosophy and Society*. Garden City, NY: Anchor Books.

Maslen, Stuart. 1998. "The Role of the International Committee of the Red Cross." In Maxwell A. Cameron, Robert J. Lawson, and Brian W. Tomlin, eds., *To Walk without Fear: The Global Movement to Ban Landmines*. Oxford: Oxford University Press.

McAdam, Doug. 1983. "Tactical Innovation and the Pace of Insurgency." *American Sociological Review*, 48: 735–54.

1996. "Conceptual Origins, Current Problems, Future Directions." In Doug McAdam, John McCarthy, and Mayer N. Zald, eds., *Comparative Perspectives on Social Movements: Political Opportunities, Mobilizing Structures, and Cultural Framings*. Cambridge: Cambridge University Press.

1999. *Political Process and the Development of Black Insurgency, 1930–1970*. Rev. ed. Chicago: University of Chicago Press.

McAdam, Doug, John McCarthy, and Mayer N. Zald, eds. 1996. *Comparative Perspectives on Social Movements: Political Opportunities, Mobilizing Structures and Cultural Framings*. Cambridge: Cambridge University Press.

McAdam, Doug, and Dieter Rucht. 1993. "Cross-National Diffusion of Movement Ideas." *Annals of the American Academy of the Political and Social Sciences*, 528: 56–74.

McAdam, Doug, and William H. Sewell Jr. 2001. "It's about Time: Temporality in the Study of Social Movements and Revolutions." In Ronald R. Aminzade et al., eds., *Silence and Voice in the Study of Contentious Politics*. Cambridge: Cambridge University Press.

McAdam, Doug, Sidney Tarrow, and Charles Tilly. 2001. *Dynamics of Contention*. Cambridge: Cambridge University Press.

McCammon, Holly J., and Karen E. Campbell. 2002. "Allies on the Road to Victory: Coalition Formation between the Suffragists and the Woman's Christian Temperance Union." *Mobilization*, 7: 231–51.

McCarthy, John, Clark McPhail, and John Crist. 1999. "The Diffusion and Adoption of Public Order Management Systems." In Donatella della Porta, Hanspeter Kriesi, and Dieter Rucht, eds., *Social Movements in a Globalizing World*. New York: St. Martin's Press.

McCarthy, John, and Mayer N. Zald. 1977. "Resource Mobilization and Social Movements: A Partial Theory." *American Journal of Sociology*, 82: 1212–41.

McMichael, Philip. 1996. *Development and Global Change: A Global Perspective*. Thousand Oaks, CA: Pine Forge Press.

2005. "Globalization." In Thomas Janoski, Robert Alford, Alexander Hicks, and Mildred Schwartz, eds., *Handbook of Political Sociology*, ch. 29. Cambridge: Cambridge University Press.

Melucci, Alberto. 1988. "Getting Involved: Identity and Mobilization in Social Movements." In Bert Klandermans, Hanspeter Kriesi, and Sidney Tarrow, eds., *From Structure to Action: Comparing Social Movements across Cultures*. Greenwich, CT: JAI Press.

Mendelson, Sarah, and Theodore P. Gerber. 2004. "Struggling to Engage the Public: Activist Culture and the Effectiveness of NGO's in Russia." Paper presented to the PONARS Conference, University of Washington, Seattle.

Merry, Sally Engle. 2003a. "Constructing a Global Law – Violence against Women and the Human Rights System." *Law and Social Inquiry*, 28: 941–79.

2003b. "Rights Talk and the Experience of Law: Implementing Women's Human Rights to Protection from Violence." *Human Rights Quarterly*, 25: 343–81.

2004. "Global Law: Human Rights and the Meanings of Culture." Unpublished paper, Wellesley College, Department of Anthropology.

Merton, Robert K. 1957. *Social Theory and Social Structure*. Rev. and enlarged ed. Glencoe, IL: Free Press.

Meyer, David S. 1990. *A Winter of Discontent: The Nuclear Freeze and American Politics*. New York: Praeger.

1990–1. "How We Helped End the Cold War (and Let Someone Else Take All the Credit)." *Nuclear Times*, Winter: 9–14.

Meyer, David S., and Catherine Corrigall-Brown. 2004. "Coalitions and Political Context: The Movements against Wars in Iraq." Unpublished paper, University of California, Irvine, Department of Sociology.

Meyer, David S., and Nancy Whittier. 1994. "Social Movement Spillover." *Social Problems*, 41: 277–98.

Meyer, John W., John Boli, and George M. Thomas. 1987. "Ontology and Rationalization in the Western Cultural Account." In George M. Thomas, John W. Meyer, Francisco O. Ramirez, and John Boli, eds., *Institutional Structure: Constituting State, Society, and the Individual*. Beverly Hills, CA: Sage Publications.

Mittelman, James H. 2004a. "Where Have All the Protesters Gone?" *Yale Global Online*. http//yaleglobal.yale.edu/display.article?id = 4637.

2004b. *Whiter Globalization? The Vortex of Knowledge and Ideology*. London: Routledge.

Moravcsik, Andrew. 1996. *The Choice for Europe: Social Purpose and State Power*. Cambridge, MA: Harvard University Press.

Murillo, Maria Victoria, and Andrew Schrank. 2003. "With a Little Help from My Friends: Partisan Politics, Transnational Alliances, and Labor Rights in

Latin America." Unpublished paper, Columbia University and Yale University, Departments of Political Science.

Myers, Daniel J. 2002. "Social Activism through Computer Networks." In Orville Vernon Burton, ed., *Computing in the Social Sciences and Humanities*, 124–37. Urbana: University of Illinois Press.

Newell, Peter. 2000. *Climate for Change: Non-state Actors and the Global Politics of the Greenhouse*. Cambridge: Cambridge University Press.

Norris, Pippa. 2000. "Global Governance and Cosmopolitan Citizens." In Joseph S. Nye and John D. Donahue, eds., *Governance in a Globalizing World*. Washington, DC: Brookings Institute Press.

Nussbaum, Martha C. 1996. "Patriotism and Cosmopolitanism." In Joshua Cohen, ed., *For Love of Country*. Boston: Beacon Press.

O'Brien, Kevin J. 2002. "Villagers, Elections, and Citizenship." In Merle Goldman and Elizabeth Perry, eds., *Changing Meanings of Citizenship in Modern China*. Cambridge, MA: Harvard University Press.

O'Brien, Kevin J., and Lianjing Li. 2004. "Popular Contention and Its Impact on Rural China." Unpublished paper, University of California, Berkeley, Political Science Department.

O'Brien, Robert, Anne Marie Goetz, Jan Aart Scholte, and Marc Williams. 2000. *Contesting Global Governance: Multilateral Economic Institutions and Global Social Movements*. Cambridge: Cambridge University Press.

Ohmae, Kenichi. 1995. *The End of the Nation State*. London: HarperCollins.

Olesen, Thomas. 2002. "Long Distance Zapatismo: Globalization and the Construction of Solidarity." Ph.D. diss., University of Aarhus, Denmark, Department of Political Science.

———. 2005. *International Zapatismo: The Construction of Solidarity in the Age of Globalization*. London: ZED Books.

Ostergaard-Nielsen, Eva. 2001. "Transnational Political Practices and the Receiving State: Turks and Kurds in Germany and the Netherlands." *Global Networks*, 1: 261–82.

———. 2003. *Transnational Politics: Turks and Kurds in Germany*. London: Routledge.

Pape, Robert A. 2003. "The Strategic Logic of Suicide Terrorism." *American Political Science Review*, 97: 343–61.

Paulson, Justin. 2000. "Peasant Struggles and International Solidarity: The Case of Chiapas." In Leo Panitch and Colin Leys, eds., *Socialist Register, 2001*. London: Merlin Press.

Pempel, T. J., ed. 2005. *Remapping East Asia: The Construction of a Region*. Ithaca: Cornell University Press.

Pianta, Mario. 2001. "Parallel Summits of Global Civil Society: An Update." In Mary Kaldor, Helmut Anheier, and Marlies Glasius, eds., *Global Civil Society, 2003*. Oxford: Oxford University Press.

Pianta, Mario, Federico Silva, and Duccio Zola. 2004. "Global Civil Society Events: Parallel Summits, Social Fora, Global Days of Action." www.1se.ac.uk/Depts/global/Yearbook/outline2004.htm.

Pichierri, Angelo. 1998. *Città Stato: Economia e politica del modello anseatico*. Venice: Marsiglio.

Pinard, Maurice. 1971. *The Rise of a Third Party: A Study in Crisis Politics*. Englewood Cliffs, NJ: Prentice-Hall.

Piven, Frances Fox, and Richard Cloward. 1977. *Poor People's Movements: Why They Succeed, How They Fail*. New York: Vintage Books.

Podobnik, Bruce. 2004. "Resistance to Globalization: Cycles and Evolutions in the Globalization Protest Movement." Paper presented to the annual meeting of the American Sociological Association, San Francisco.

Polanyi, Karl. 1957. *The Great Transformation*. Boston: Beacon Press.

Portes, Alejandro. 1999. "Conclusion: Towards a New World – the Origins and Effects of Transnational Activities." *Ethnic and Racial Studies*, 22: 463–77.

   2000. "Globalization from Below: The Rise of Transnational Communities." In Don Kalb, Marco van der Land, Richard Staring, Bart van Steenbergen, and Nico Wilterdink, eds., *The Ends of Globalization: Bringing Society Back In*. Lanham, MD: Rowman and Littlefield.

Posel, Deborah, and Graeme Simpson, eds. 2002. *Commissioning the Past: Understanding South Africa's Truth and Reconciliation Commission*. Johannesburg: University of the Witwatersrand Press.

Price, Richard. 1998. "Reversing the Gun Sights: Transnational Civil Society Targets Land Mines." *International Organization*, 52: 613–44.

   2003. "Transnational Civil Society and Advocacy in World Politics." *World Politics*, 55: 2003.

Rabkin, Jeremy A. 2003. *Why Sovereignty Matters*. Washington, DC: AEI Press.

Reitan, Ruth. 2003. "How Civil Society Went Global: Analyzing the Process of Scale Shift from the Localized 'IMF Riot' to the World Social Forum." Unpublished paper, Central and Eastern European International Studies Association Meetings, Budapest.

Rheingold, Howard. 2002. *Smart Mobs: The Next Social Revolution*. Cambridge, MA: Perseus Publishing.

Risse, Thomas, Stephen C. Ropp, and Kathryn Sikkink, eds. 1999. *The Power of Human Rights: International Norms and Domestic Change*. Cambridge: Cambridge University Press.

Risse, Thomas, and Kathryn Sikkink. 1999. "The Socialization of International Human Rights Norms into Domestic Practices: Introduction." In Thomas Risse, Stephen C. Ropp, and Kathryn Sikkink, eds., *The Power of Human Rights: International Norms and Domestic Change*. Cambridge: Cambridge University Press.

Risse-Kappen, Thomas. 1994. "Ideas Do Not Float Freely: Transnational Coalitions, Domestic Structures, and the End of the Cold War." *International Organization*, 48: 185–214.

   1995. "Structures of Governance and Transnational Relations: What Have We Learned?" In Thomas Risse-Kappen, ed., *Bringing Transnational Relations Back In*. Cambridge: Cambridge University Press.

   1996. "Collective Identity in a Democratic Community." In Peter J. Stein, ed., *The Culture of International Security*. New York: Columbia University Press.

Rochon, Thomas R. 1988. *Mobilizing for Peace: The Antinuclear Movements in Western Europe*. Princeton: Princeton University Press.

Roederer, Christilla. 1999. "CAP Reforms and the Transformation of Domestic Politics: The Paradox of Farm Protest in France (1983–1993)." Paper presented to the Fourth European Conference of Sociology, Aarhus.
2000. "Popular Struggle and the Making of Europe's Common Agricultural Policy: Farm Protest in France, 1983–1993." Ph.D. diss., University of South Carolina, Department of Government.

Rogers, Everett M. 1983. *Diffusion of Innovations*. New York: Free Press.

Rootes, Christopher. 2003. "Conclusion: Environmental Protest Transformed?" In Christopher Rootes, ed., *Environmental Protest in Western Europe*. Oxford: Oxford University Press.
2005. "A Limited Transnationalization? The British Environmental Movement." In Donatella della Porta and Sidney Tarrow, eds., *Transnational Protest and Global Activism*. Lanham, MD: Rowman and Littlefield.

Rosenau, James. 1997. *Along the Domestic-Foreign Frontier: Exploring Governance in a Turbulent World*. Cambridge: Cambridge University Press.
2003. *Distant Proximities: Dynamics beyond Globalization*. Princeton: Princeton University Press.

Rosenau, James, and David C. Earnest. 2004. "On the Cutting Edge of Globalization, before and after 9/11." Paper presented to the annual meeting of the American Sociological Association, San Francisco.

Rosenau, James N., David C. Earnest, Yale H. Ferguson, and Ole R. Holsti. Forthcoming. *On the Cutting Edge of Globalization: An Inquiry into American Elites*. Lanham, MD: Rowman and Littlefield.

Ross, Stephanie. 2002. "Is This What 'Democracy' Looks Like? The Politics of the Anti-globalization Movement in North America." In Leo Panitch and Colin Leys, eds., *Socialist Register, 2003: Fighting Identities: Race, Religion and Ethnonationalism*. London: Merlin Press.

Rucht, Dieter. 2002. "The EU as a Target of Mobilisation: Is There a Europeanisation of Conflict?" In Richard Balme, Didier Chabanet, and Vincent Wright, eds., *L'action collective en Europe*. Paris: Presses de Sciences Po.

Ruggie, John G. 1998. *Constructing the World Polity: Essays on International Institutionalization*. London: Routledge.

Rydgren, Jens. 2004. "Explaining the Emergence of Radical Right-Wing Populist Parties: The Case of Denmark." *West European Politics*, 27: 474–502.
2005. "Is Extreme Right-Wing Populism Contagious? Explaining the Emergence of the New Party Family." *European Journal of Political Research* 44.

Sageman, Marc. 2004. *Understanding Terror Networks*. Philadelphia: University of Pennsylvania Press.

Sambanis, Nicholas. 2004. "Using Case Studies to Expand Economic Models of Civil War." *Perspectives on Politics*, 2: 259–79.

Samuels, Alexandra Whitney. 2004. "Activism and the Future of Political Participation." Ph.D. diss., Harvard University, John F. Kennedy School of Government.

Sandholtz, Wayne, and Alec Stone Sweet, eds. 1998. *European Integration and Supranational Governance*. New York: Oxford University Press.

Sbragia, Alberta M. 2001. "Italy Pays for Europe: Political Leadership, Political Choice, and Institutional Adaptation." In Maria Green Cowles, James A. Caporaso, and Thomas Risse, eds., *Transforming Europe: Europeanization and Domestic Change*. Ithaca: Cornell University Press.

Schattle, Hans. Forthcoming. *Global Citizenship*. Lanham, MD: Rowman and Littlefield.

Schattschneider, E. E. 1960. *The Semisovereign People: A Realist's View of Democracy in America*. New York: Holt, Rinehart and Winston.

Schell, Jonathan. 2003. *The Unconquerable World: Power, Nonviolence, and the Will of the People*. New York: Metropolitan Books.

Schmitz, Hans Peter. 2001. "When Networks Blind: Human Rights and Politics in Kenya." In Thomas Callaghy, Ronald Kassimir, and Robert Latham, eds., *Intervention and Transnationalism in Africa: Global-Local Networks of Power*. Cambridge: Cambridge University Press.

2004. "Transnational Mobilization and Domestic Regime Change: Kenya and Uganda in Comparative Perspective." Unpublished paper, Syracuse University, Department of Political Science.

Scholte, Jan Aart, and Albrecht Schnable, eds. 2002. *Civil Society and Global Finance*. London: Routledge.

Schultz, Markus. 1998. "Collective Action across Borders: Opportunity Structures, Network Capacities, and Communicative Praxis in the Age of Advanced Globalization." *Sociological Perspectives*, 41: 587–616.

Scott, Robert A. 2003. *The Gothic Enterprise: A Guide to Understanding the Medieval Cathedral*. Berkeley: University of California Press.

Seidman, Gay. 2003. "Monitoring Multinationals: Lessons from the Anti-Apartheid Era." *Politics and Society*, 31: 381–406.

Sharp, Gene. 1973. *The Politics of Nonviolent Action*. Boston: Porter Sargent Publishers.

1993. *From Dictatorship to Democracy: A Conceptual Framework for Liberation*. Boston: Albert Einstein Institution.

Shue, Vivienne. 1988. *The Reach of the State*. Stanford: Stanford University Press.

Sikkink, Kathryn. 1993. "Human Rights, Principles, Issue-Networks, and Sovereignty in Latin America." *International Organization*, 47: 411–41.

2005a. *Mixed Messages: U.S. Human Rights Policy and Latin America*. Ithaca: Cornell University Press.

2005b. "Patterns of Dynamic Multilevel Governance and the Insider-Outsider Coalition." In Donatella della Porta and Sidney Tarrow, eds., *Transnational Protest and Global Activism*. Lanham, MD: Rowman and Littlefield.

Sikkink, Kathryn, and Jackie Smith. 2002. "Infrastructures of Change: Transnational Organizations, 1953–93." In Sanjeev Khagram, James V. Riker, and Kathryn Sikkink, eds., *Restructuring World Politics: Transnational Social Movements, Networks, and Norms*. Minneapolis: University of Minnesota Press.

Silver, Beverly J. 2003. *Forces of Labor: Workers' Movements and Globalization since 1870*. Cambridge: Cambridge University Press.

Sklair, Leslie. 2001. *The Transnational Capitalist Class*. Oxford: Blackwell.

Skrbis, Zlatko. 1999. *Long Distance Nationalism: Diasporas, Homelands and Identities.* Brookfield: Ashgate Publishing.

Slaughter, Anne-Marie. 2004. *A New World Order.* Princeton: Princeton University Press.

Smith, Jackie. 2002a. "Globalization and Social Movements: Exploring Connections between Global Integration and Political Mobilization." Unpublished paper, SUNY, Stony Brook, Department of Sociology.

2002b. "Bridging Global Divides? Strategic Framing and Solidarity in Transnational Social Movement Organizations." *International Sociology*, 17: 505–28.

2004a. "Democratizing Globalization? Impacts and Limitations of Transnational Social Movements." Unpublished paper, SUNY, Stony Brook, Department of Sociology.

2004b. "Exploring Connections between Global Integration and Political Mobilization." *Journal of World-Systems Research*, 10: 255–85.

Smith, Jackie, and Joe Bandy. 2004. "Introduction: Cooperation and Conflict in Transnational Protest." In Joe Bandy and Jackie Smith, eds., *Coalitions across Borders: Transnational Protest and the Neoliberal Order.* Lanham, MD: Rowman and Littlefield.

Smith, Jackie, Charles Chatfield, and Ron Pagnucco, eds. 1997. *Transnational Movements in Global Politics.* Syracuse: Syracuse University Press.

Smith, Jackie, and Hank Johnston, eds. 2002. *Globalization and Resistance: Transnational Dimensions of Social Movements.* Lanham, MD: Rowman and Littlefield.

Smith, Jackie, and Dawn Wiest. 2005. "Uneven Globalization: Understanding Variable Participation in Transnational Social Movement Organizations." *Social Forces.*

Smith, Robert R. 2003. "Migrant Membership as an Instituted Process: Transnationalization, the State and the Extra-Territorial Conduct of Mexican Politics." *International Migration Review*, 37: 297–343.

Snow, David A., and Robert D. Benford. 1988. "Ideology, Frame Resonance, and Participant Mobilization." In Bert Klandermans, Hanspeter Kriesi, and Sidney Tarrow, eds., *From Structure to Action: Social Movement Participation across Cultures.* Greenwich, CT: JAI Press.

1992. "Master Frames and Cycles of Protest." In Aldon Morris and Carol McClurg Mueller, eds., *Frontiers in Social Movement Theory.* New Haven: Yale University Press.

Snow, David A., E. Burke Rochford Jr., Steven K. Worden, and Robert D. Benford. 1986. "Frame Alignment Processes, Micromobilization, and Movement Participation." *American Sociological Review*, 51: 464–81.

Snyder, Jack. 1993. "East-West Bargaining over Germany: The Search for Synergy in a Two-Level Game." In Peter Evans, Harold K. Jacobson, and Robert D. Putnam, eds., *Double-Edged Diplomacy: International Bargaining and Domestic Politics.* Berkeley: University of California Press.

Snyder, Jack, and Leslie Vinjamuri. 2004. "Tkial and Ekrors: Principle and Pragmatism in Strategies of International Justice." *International Security*, 28: 5–44.

Soule, Sarah A. 1997. "The Student Divestment Movement in the United States and Tactical Diffusion." *Social Forces*, 75: 855–82.

Soysal, Yasemin. 1994. *Limits of Citizenship: Migrants and Postnational Membership in Europe*. Chicago: University of Chicago Press.

Speranza, Gino C. [1906] 1974. "Political Representation of Italo-American Colonies in the Italian Parliament." In Francesco Cordasco and Eugene Bucchioni, eds., *The Italians: Social Backgrounds of an American Group*. Clifton, NJ: Augustus M. Kelley.

Sprinzak, Ehud. 2000. "Rational Fanatics." *Foreign Policy*, 120 (September–October): 66–73.

Staggenborg, Suzanne. 1986. "Coalition Work in the Pro-Choice Movement: Organizational and Environmental Opportunities and Obstacles." *Social Problems*, 33: 374–90.

Sternbach, Nancy Saporta, Marysa Navarro-Aranguren, Patricia Chuchryk, and Sonia E. Alvarez. 1992. "Feminisms in Latin America: From Bogota to San Bernardo." In Arthur Escobar and Sonia E. Alvarez, eds., *The Making of Social Movements in Latin America: Identity, Strategy, and Democracy*. Boulder: Westview Press.

Stiglitz, Joseph E. 2002. *Globalization and Its Discontents*. New York: W. W. Norton.

Stiles, Kendall, ed. 2000. *Global Institutions and Local Empowerment: Competing Theoretical Perspectives*. New York: St. Martin's Press.

Stone Sweet, Alec, and James A. Caporaso. 1998. "From Free Trade to Supranational Polity: The European Court and Integration." In Wayne Sandholtz and Alec Stone Sweet, eds., *European Integration and Supranational Governance*. New York: Oxford University Press.

Stone Sweet, Alec, Wayne Sandholtz, and Neil Fligstein, eds. 2001. *The Institutionalization of Europe*. New York: Oxford University Press.

Strang, David, and John Meyer. 1993. "Institutional Conditions for Diffusion." *Theory and Society*, 22: 487–511.

Tarrow, Sidney. 1967. *Peasant Communism in Southern Italy*. New Haven: Yale University Press.

　　1989. *Democracy and Disorder: Protest and Politics in Italy, 1965–1974*. New York: Oxford University Press.

　　1992. "Mentalities, Political Cultures and Collective Action Frames: Constructing Meanings through Action." In Aldon Morris and Carol McClurg Mueller, eds., *Frontiers in Social Movement Theory*. New Haven: Yale University Press.

　　1995. "Europeanisation of Conflict: Reflections from a Social Movement Perspective." *West European Politics*, 18: 225–8.

　　1998. *Power in Movement: Social Movements and Contentious Politics*. 2nd ed. Cambridge: Cambridge University Press.

　　2004. "Center-Periphery Alignments and Political Contention in Late-Modern Europe." In Christopher Ansell and Giuseppe di Palma, eds., *Restructuring Territoriality: Europe and the United States Compared*. Cambridge: Cambridge University Press.

Tarrow, Sidney, and Doug McAdam. 2005. "Scale Shift in Transnational Contention." In Donatella della Porta and Sidney Tarrow, eds., *Transnational Protest and Global Activism*. Lanham, MD: Rowman and Littlefield.

te Brake, Wayne. 1998. *Shaping History: Ordinary People in European Politics, 1500–1700*. Berkeley: University of California Press.

Thomas, George M., John W. Meyer, Francisco O. Ramirez, and John Boli. 1987. *Institutional Structure: Constituting State, Society and Individual*. Newbury Park, CA: Sage Publications.

Tilly, Charles. 1978. *From Mobilization to Revolution*. Reading, MA: Addison-Wesley.

1986. *The Contentious French*. Cambridge, MA: Harvard University Press.

1992. *Coercion, Capital, and European States, AD 990–1992*. Cambridge, MA: Blackwell.

1995a. "Globalization Threatens Labor's Rights." *International Labor and Working Class History*, 47: 1–23.

1995b. *Popular Contention in Great Britain, 1758–1834*. Cambridge, MA: Harvard University Press.

2002. *Stories, Identities and Political Change*. Lanham, MD: Rowman and Littlefield.

2003. *The Politics of Collective Violence*. Cambridge: Cambridge University Press.

2004a. *Contention and Democracy, 1650–2000*. Cambridge: Cambridge University Press.

2004b. *Social Movements, 1768–2004*. Boulder: Paradigm Publishers.

Turnbull, Peter. 2004. "Dockers *versus* the Directive: The War on Europe's Waterfront." Unpublished paper, Cardiff University.

Van Antwerpen, Jonathan. 2005. "Rooted and Uprooted Cosmopolitans: The Transnational Trajectory of 'Reconciliation' Discourse." Prepared for the Capstone Conference of the SSRC Program on Philanthropy and the Non-Profit Sector, Florence.

Van Dyke, Nella. 2003. "Crossing Movement Boundaries: Factors that Facilitate Coalition Protest by American College Students." *Social Problems*, 50: 226–50.

Vasi, Ion Bogdan. 2004. "The Adoption and Implementation of Local Governmental Actions against Climate Change." Ph.D. diss., Cornell University, Department of Sociology.

Vejvoda, Ivan. 1997. "Cogito ergo ambulo; First Steps in Belgrade." *Bulletin of the East and Central Europe Program*: 1–2. New School for Social Research, New York.

Verhulst, Joris, and Stefaan Walgrave. 2003. "Worldwide Anti-War in Iraq Protest: A Preliminary Test of the Transnational Movements Thesis." Paper presented to the Second ECPR International Conference, Marburg.

Vertovec, Steven, and Robin Cohen, eds. 2002. *Conceiving Cosmopolitanism: Theory, Context, and Practice*. Oxford: Oxford University Press.

Waldinger, Roger, and David Fitzgerald. 2004. "Transnationalism in Question." *American Journal of Sociology*, 109: 1171–95.

Waldron, Jeremy. 1992. "Minority Cultures and the Cosmopolitan Alternative." *University of Michigan Journal of Law Reform*, 25: 751–92.

2000. "What Is Cosmopolitan?" *Journal of Political Philosophy*, 7: 227–43.

Waller, Signe. 2002. *Love and Revolution: A Political Memoir: People's History of the Greensboro Massacre, Its Setting and Aftermath*. Lanham, MD: Rowman and Littlefield.

Walton, John, and Charles Ragin. 1990. "Global and National Sources of Political Protest: Third World Responses to the Debt Crisis." *American Sociological Review*, 55: 876–90.

Walton, John, and David Seddon, eds. 1994. *Free Markets and Food Riots: The Politics of Global Adjustment*. Oxford: Blackwell.

Walton, John, and Jonathan Shefner. 1994. "Latin America: Popular Protest and the State." In John Walton and David Seddon, eds., *Free Markets and Food Riots: The Politics of Global Adjustment*. Oxford: Blackwell.

Walzer, Michael. 1971. *Revolution of the Saints: A Study in the Origins of Radical Politics*. New York: Atheneum.

Wareman, Mary. 1998. "Rhetoric and Policy Realities in the United States." In Maxwell A. Cameron, Robert J. Lawson, and Brian W. Tomlin, eds., *To Walk without Fear: The Global Movement to Ban Landmines*. Oxford: Oxford University Press.

Warmington, Valerie, and Celina Tuttle. 1998. "The Canadian Campaign." In Maxwell A. Cameron, Robert J. Lawson, and Brian W. Tomlin, eds., *To Walk without Fear: The Global Movement to Ban Landmines*. Oxford: Oxford University Press.

Waterman, Peter. 2001. "Internationalists in the Americas: Agitators, Agents and Communicators." Paper presented to the Tercer Congreso Internacional de Latinoamericanistas en Europa, Barcelona.

Wayland, Sarah V. 2004. "Ethnonationalist Networks and Transnational Opportunities: The Sri Lankan Tamil Diaspora." *Review of International Studies*, 30: 405–26.

Weiler, Joseph. 1991. "The Transformation of Europe." *Yale Law Journal*, 100: 2403–83.

Wellman, Barry, and Milena Gulia. 1999. "Net Surfers Don't Ride Alone: Virtual Communities as Communities." In Barry Wellman, ed., *Networks in the Global Village*. Boulder: Westview Press.

Wessels, Bernard. 2004. "Contestation Potential of Interest Groups in the EU: Emergence, Structure, and Political Alliance." In Gary Marks and Marco Steenbergen, eds., *European Integration and Political Conflict*. Lanham, MD: Rowman and Littlefield.

Wessels, Wolfgang, and Dieter Rometsch. 1996. "Conclusion: European Union and National Institutions." In Wolfgang Wessels and Dieter Rometsch, eds., *The European Union and Member States: Towards Institutional Fusion?* Manchester: Manchester University Press.

Wilkie, James W., ed. 2001. *Statistical Abstract of Latin America* 37. Los Angeles: UCLA Latin American Center.

Williams, Heather. 1999. "Mobile Capital and Transborder Labor Rights Mobilization." *Politics and Society*, 27: 139–66.

2003. "Of Labor Tragedy and Legal Farce: The Han Young Factory Struggle in Tijuana, Mexico." *Social Science History*, 27: 525–50.

Williams, Jody, and Stephen Goose. 1998. "The International Campaign to Ban Landmines." In Maxwell A. Cameron, Robert J. Lawson, and Brian W. Tomlin, eds., *To Walk without Fear: The Global Movement to Ban Landmines*. Oxford: Oxford University Press.

Wood, Lesley. 2004a. "Bridging the Chasms: The Case of People's Global Action." In Joe Bandy and Jackie Smith, eds., *Coalitions across Borders: Transnational Protest and the Neoliberal Order*. Lanham, MD: Rowman and Littlefield.

2004b. "The Diffusion of Direct Action Tactics: From Seattle to Toronto and New York." Ph.D. diss., Columbia University, Department of Sociology.

Wood, Lesley, and Kelly Moore. 2002. "Target Practice: Community Activism in a Global Era." In Benjamin Shepard and Ronald Hayduk, eds., *From ACT UP to the WTO: Urban Protest and Community Building in the Era of Globalization*. London: Verso.

Wyman, Mark. 1993. *Round-Trip to America: The Immigrants Return to Europe, 1880–1930*. Ithaca: Cornell University Press.

Yashar, Deborah. 2005. *Contesting Citizenship in Latin America: The Rise of Indigenous Movements and the Postliberal Challenge*. Cambridge: Cambridge University Press.

Yearley, Steven. 1996. *Sociology, Environmentalism, Globalization*. London: Sage Publications.

Index

Index

Index

Great Britain: anti–Iraq war protests in, 15; BSE crisis and, 90, 96; cathedral building in, 106; immigrant communities in, 55–6; Spanish "fish wars" and, 83–5; women's rights activism and, 153–4, 193

Greenpeace, 84, 213

Greensboro, NC, 183–6

"Growth and Stability" pact (EU), 31, 88–9, 96

Guarnizo, Luis, 52

GUESS, 169

Haas, Ernst, 22, 218

Haiti, 65

Hall, Stuart, 40

Handicap International, 174

Hannerz, Ulf, 41

Hansa, 36–7

Hathaway, Will, 177

Hayner, Priscilla, 190, 191

Hegel, G. W. F., 38

Held, David, 40

Hellman, Judith, 117, 119, 136

Helvey, Robert, 111

Hengyang County (China), 120–1

higher education, access to, 36

Highlander Folk School, 108

HIV (human immunodeficiency virus), 189

Hoffmann, Stanley, 217

Hooghe, Liesbet, 9, 71, 82, 206

Houser, George, 107

human rights activism, 44, 144, 147, 149–51, 158, 186, 188–90

Hungary, 65

identity(ies), 2–3, 7; assimilation and, 55; certification and, 50; constructivism and, 22; of cosmopolitans, 41; global citizenship and, 27, 68–72, 209; in global justice movement, 135–6; of Hansa merchants, 37; of immigrants, 49; of international institutions, 27; national/supranational attachments and, 4, 70–2, 209; in political Islamism, 135; scale shift and, 121, 122, 135–6, 139. *See also* diaspora nationalism

Ikenberry, John, 217–18

Imig, Doug, 85–6, 91, 93, 152

immigrant activism, 43, 48–56, 105; "birds of passage" and, 51, 53–6, 206; contradictions in, 54–6; historical, 1–2, 49; "nesting pigeons" and, 51, 53, 54–6, 206

India, 53–4, 55, 76, 144, 190

indigenous peoples, 115, 147, 194

informational pathways: diffusion and, 116–17; externalization and, 144, 146, 149–51, 155, 156–7, 158, 163

insider/outsider actors, 29, 45, 48, 153, 169, 211

institutional access, 144, 146, 149, 151–4, 155, 157, 158–9

institutionalization, 176–7

institutions, international, 7, 10, 21; access to, 144, 146, 149, 151–4, 155, 157, 158–9; cosmopolitanism and, 39; globalization and, 6, 25–7; global thinking and, 69; identities of, 27; internalization and, 95; as targets of resistance, 6, 26–7, 95, 129–31

instrumental coalitions, 167–8, 178

interdependence, complex, 9, 20–1, 27

internalization, 12, 77–96; "affair of the head scarf" and, 77–9; composite polities and, 80–5; defined, 32, 80; European Union and, 80–8, 90–4; international institutions and, 95; MGJ protests and, 204; model of, 80; in Spanish "fish wars," 83–5

International Association of Chiefs of Police, 197

International Center for Nonviolent Conflict, 113

International Center for Transitional Justice (ICTJ), 190

International Committee of the Red Cross, 174

International Convention to Ban Landmines (ICBL), 173–5, 206; internationalism and, 26, 163

International Council for Local Environmental Initiatives (ICLEI), 213

internationalism/internationalization, 3, 15–34, 203–5; constructivism and, 20, 21–2; co-optation/conflict/cooperation, 27–8; dark side of, 43, 206, 210; defined, 8, 25; forms of contention and, 103; global framing and, 33, 62; globalization and, 16–19, 27, 203; international relations theory and, 20–2; liberal institutionalism and, 20; neorealism and, 20; as opportunity structure for activism, 7–9, 19, 20, 25, 27–8, 96, 203–4, 207; social movement theory and, 22–4; structural equivalence and, 65; vs. unilateralism, 217–19

International Labor Organization (ILO), 26

Index

London (England), 15, 55–6, 133
Los Angeles, Calif., 52
Loveman, Mara, 150
Lutz, Ellen, 143

Madrid (Spain), 15
Malatesta, Enrico, 4
Mandela, Nelson, 183–4
Maoism, 4
maquiladora industries, 26, 53, 156–8, 159
March on Washington Movement (MOWM), 108
Marcon, Giulio, 131
Marcos, Subcomandante, 114, 117, 119
Marks, Gary, 9, 71, 82, 206
Marx, Karl, 38
Marxist perspectives, 10, 104
Mawdudi, Mawlana, 124, 125
May First workers' holiday, 4
Mays, Benjamin, 107
McAdam, Doug, 23, 24–5, 88; gentle hand of, xiv
McDonald's, 31, 74
McMichael, Philip, 5, 18–19
media, 62, 72, 101, 110, 114, 115–16, 117
mediated diffusion, 101, 104, 106, 108, 116–17, 139, 208. *See also* brokers/brokerage
Melucci, Alberto, 61, 135
Mendelson, Sarah, 75
Mendes, Chico, 144
Merabishvili, Ivane, 113
Merton, Robert, 41
Mexico: communication technologies in, 50, 53; human rights activism in, 149; immigrant communities in U.S. and, 52–3; "justice cascades" and, 143; Puebla labor coalitions in, 168–70; Zapatista solidarity in, 101, 113–17, 118, 130, 136, 177. *See also* North American Free Trade Agreement
Meyer, David S., 166, 175–6, 177
Meyer, John, 22
Middle East, 65. *See also* Islamism; Israeli-Palestinian conflict
migration, transnational, 8
Milosoevic, Slobodan, 109–11
Mines Advisory Group, 174
missionaries, 3, 106, 190. *See also* brokers/brokerage
Mittelman, James, 69
Mixtec, 50, 53
mobilization, international, 4, 7, 120, 186, 192–4, 199–200

Mobilization for Global Justice (MGJ), 201–2, 204–5, 207, 213
modularity, 4, 101, 102–3
Moore, Kelly, 60, 62
Mothers of the Plaza, 158, 191
Movement of Landless Farm Workers (MST), 131
Mozambique, 174
multi-issue activism, 44–5, 73, 211–12
multilateralism, complex, 9, 206
Mumbai (India). *See* World Social Forum
Murphy, Gillian, 47, 164, 165, 166, 171, 176
Muslim Brotherhood, 124, 127

Nansen, Fridjof, 39
Narmada Dam (India), 144
National Convention for Constitutional Reform Executive Committee (NCEC), 189
National Front, 55, 78
national/supranational attachments, 4, 70–2, 209
négritude movement, 39
neoliberalism, 6, 17, 19, 31, 73, 205
neorealism, 20
"nesting pigeons," 51, 53, 54–6, 206
Netherlands, 52, 55
networks: advocacy/activist, 8, 10, 22, 24, 43; defined, 163–4; trust, 2, 101, 103–4, 105, 210
new institutional sociologists, 10
New York City, 52, 59–60, 76, 214
New Zealand, 15
Nigeria, 41, 144
Nigerian market women, 41
nongovernmental organizations (NGOs), 7, 8; growth of, 189; human rights and, 150; as insider actors, 29, 211; multi-issue frames and, 73; parallel summits and, 129; social movement theory and, 24; women's rights and, 189
nonrelational diffusion, 101, 118, 139, 208; in American Revolution, 106; of nonviolent resistance movements, 108; of political Islamism, 104, 126; in Zapatista solidarity, 115–16. *See also* communication technologies
nonstate actors, 9, 19, 20, 21–2, 23–4. *See also* ordinary people
nonviolent resistance movements, 4, 101, 106–13, 117–18, 190
Norris, Pippa, 71
North Africa, austerity protests in, 65

255

Index